'This book is an engaging investigation of the received wisdom – and received prejudices – about capitalism, neoliberalism, markets, and market activity. With subtlety and nuance, it shows that much of this received wisdom does not stand up to investigation. People of all ideological stripes will learn something from – and be challenged by – this book. It deserves to be read by all those working on the moral foundations of market society.'

Jason Brennan, *Georgetown University, Washington*

CAPITALISM FOR REALISTS

In an age of extreme political polarization and waning of reasoned debate across political divides, *Capitalism for Realists* carefully explores the inner workings of capitalism in a consciously non-partisan and balanced way. Does the modern capitalist economy alleviate poverty and exploitation, or exacerbate them? What, exactly, is 'neoliberalism,' and how well or poorly has it performed in the past 40 years? Does capitalism undermine democracy, or is it rather one of its key necessary conditions? How have altruism, cooperation, tolerance, violence, and trust fared under the influence of the modern market society? Should we analyse capitalism through the mainstream economic lens or a more critical Marxist perspective? This book offers answers to these questions.

Synthesizing decades of research across disciplines, *Capitalism for Realists* offers an overarching perspective on the modern economy by theoretically unifying many of the claims and conclusions about it offered by various traditionally rivalrous social science paradigms, such as institutional, neoclassical, and public choice economics on the one hand, and Marxist sociology on the other. The book presents and critically assesses the latest data and debates on such crucial contemporary issues as the relationship between poverty, exploitation, inequality, and capitalism, the nature of 'neoliberalism' and the successes and failures of both state-led industrial policy and the Washington consensus, capitalist peace theory, historical origins of modern capitalism, and more. What emerges is a clear picture of the merits and demerits of the modern economy too nuanced to be simplified and categorized by the prevailing political discourses.

Rich in empirical detail, this lively, accessible book will appeal to undergraduate and graduate students with interests in sociological theory, political theory, economics, and political and economic sociology.

Tibor Rutar is Assistant Professor in the Department of Sociology at the University of Maribor, Slovenia, and author of *Rational Choice and Democratic Government: A Sociological Approach* (Routledge, 2021).

Routledge Studies in Political Sociology

This series presents the latest research in political sociology. It welcomes both theoretical and empirical studies that pay close attention to the dynamics of power, popular protest and social movements, as well as work that engages in debates surrounding globalisation, democracy and political economy.

Capitalism for Realists
Virtues and Vices of the Modern Economy
Tibor Rutar

Multiculturalism and the Nation in Germany
A Study in Moral Conflict
Paul Carls

The Contentious Politics of Expertise
Expert, Activism and Grassroots Environmentalism
Riccardo Emilio Chesta

Political Legitimacy
Realism in Political Theory and Sociology
Terje Rasmussen

Comparing and Contrasting the Impact of the COVID-19 Pandemic in the European Union
Linda Hantrais, Marie-Thérèse Letablier

The Political Attitudes of Divided European Citizens
Public Opinion and Social Inequalities in Comparative and Relational Perspective
Christian Lahusen

CAPITALISM FOR REALISTS

Virtues and Vices of the Modern Economy

Tibor Rutar

Routledge
Taylor & Francis Group

LONDON AND NEW YORK

Cover image: © Getty Images

First published 2023
by Routledge
4 Park Square, Milton Park, Abingdon, Oxon OX14 4RN

and by Routledge
605 Third Avenue, New York, NY 10158

Routledge is an imprint of the Taylor & Francis Group, an informa business

British Library Cataloguing-in-Publication Data
A catalogue record for this book is available from the British Library

Library of Congress Cataloging-in-Publication Data
Names: Rutar, Tibor, 1989– author.
Title: Capitalism for realists: virtues and vices of the modern economy /
Tibor Rutar.
Description: Milton Park, Abingdon, Oxon; New York, NY:
Routledge, 2023. | Includes bibliographical references and index. |
Identifiers: LCCN 2022025887 | ISBN 9781032305912 (hardback) |
ISBN 9781032305929 (paperback) | ISBN 9781003305811 (ebook)
Subjects: LCSH: Economic history. | Capitalism. |
Economics—Sociological aspects.
Classification: LCC HC59.3 .R88 2023 |
DDC 330.9—dc23/eng/20220622
LC record available at https://lccn.loc.gov/2022025887

ISBN: 978-1-032-30591-2 (hbk)
ISBN: 978-1-032-30592-9 (pbk)
ISBN: 978-1-003-30581-1 (ebk)

DOI: 10.4324/9781003305811

Typeset in Bembo
by codeMantra

CONTENTS

FIGURES

1
CAPITALISM'S CRITICS AND DEFENDERS

A possibility of reconciliation

The youth rebels against capitalism, again

In the early 1840s, a young German man who later became an infamous world-historic figure got the opportunity to take a first-hand look at the profound social transformations wrought by capitalism and the Industrial Revolution in England. He was far from impressed.

The ensuing rapid social change was, for sure, profound. But Friedrich Engels was, unsurprisingly, most struck by the profoundly miserable and unjust condition the working masses had found themselves in amidst the Industrial Revolution. He famously reported on this social calamity in his book the *Condition of the Working Class in England*. In it, he wrote of the pains and miseries, the poverty and disease, experienced by industrial workers in cities like Manchester and Liverpool, and he warned his fellow Germans that the same fate awaits them as capitalism develops to the same extent in Germany as it already had in England. Engels' portrayal of the suffering and oppression of the English working class is vivid and is usually one of the first associations we have when thinking about Industrial Revolution-era England.

Engels got a deep, close-up look at modernity, but even a mere superficial glance at society in the first part of the 19th century probably suggested an overwhelming impression, especially to the poor and dispossessed, that capitalism, the Industrial Revolution, and modernity in general were not really all that great.

Today, however, the same superficial glance should suffice in giving precisely the opposite impression. In contemporary wealthy regions of the world where capitalism is highly developed, material standards of living are so unimaginably higher than in Engels' time that it should not take a deep analysis to appreciate them. Even in the least well-off parts of the world, conditions today can hardly be compared to what came before. But, more importantly, today we are also in

DOI: 10.4324/9781003305811-1

possession of clear, reliable, and wide-ranging statistical figures on what has been happening to the world since Engels' time – figures that are freely available to anyone who would like to go beyond surface-level appearances and anecdotes.

The figures are incredible – but, apparently, not well known.[1] Extreme world poverty stood at about 80% in the early 19th century, but then it dropped first to around 60% in mid-20th century and to less than 10% in the second decade of the 21st century.[2] Before the 20th century, child and infant mortality rates across the world were typically above 20%, 30%, or even 40%.[3] These figures were plummeting through the 20th century as the world has been economically developing. Today, the global average stands at between 3 and 5% (2017), while in the most economically developed countries, the typical figure is below 0.5–1%.[4] The middle class started growing with the close of the 19th century, and it then expanded immensely through the 20th century, first in the developed world and then in developing world as markets spread and globalization ramped up. Although capitalism most certainly was not the only cause behind these improvements (socialist states, for example, also witnessed a sharp drop in child mortality in the second part of the 20th century), it was undoubtedly a central force.

One might think that these figures alone, and especially the world-historic collapse of Communism at the end of the 20th century, would largely do away with anti-market or anti-capitalist political sentiments. Yet, one would be badly mistaken in thinking so. Anti-capitalism and socialism as a political ideology are very much alive and well today.

Proving that, the late Marxist sociologist Erik Olin Wright published an influential book with the succinctly provocative title *How to Be an Anti-capitalist in the Twenty-first Century* just a few years ago.[5] Outside of the academe, one prominent contemporary socialist manifesto is printed after another. The editor of youth-run *Current Affairs* magazine, Nathan Robinson, published his *Why You Should Be a Socialist* in 2019, while the editor of a similarly youth-run *Jacobin* magazine, Bhaskar Sunkara, came out with his *The Socialist Manifesto* that same year.[6] Socialism was also very much on display in the general public and political sphere in recent years. In the wake of the 2016 US presidential election, the democratic socialist Senator Bernie Sanders was energetically backed during the election campaign by a large swathe of young Americans as the Democrat candidate (against Hilary Clinton). He was again strongly (though insufficiently in the end) supported in the 2020 campaign. These and other developments, such as the rise to fame of democratic socialist Representatives Alexandria Ocasio-Cortez and Rashida Tlaib, prompted the American media to create a series of mini-documentaries such as *Speaking Frankly: Socialism* (CBSN) and *Why Democratic Socialism Is Gaining Popularity in The United States* (CNBC) with multiple millions of views.

If in 2010 Wright could, without raising any eyebrows, declare in his earlier book *Envisioning Real Utopias* that 'the word "socialism" lies completely outside of mainstream political life' in the US, the last decade has clearly flown in the face of any such claim.[7] Socialism of at least a certain kind is definitely back on the agenda. A whole generation of youth is, once again, being educated on anti-capitalism, socialism, and Marxism. This is perhaps most visible online where, in the past five or six years, dozens upon dozens of young, now internet-famous, public figures slowly rose through the ranks of YouTube creators and now run channels with hundreds of thousands, even millions of subscribers.[8] This 'BreadTube' as it is called by some features not only ordinary left-wing political content on daily affairs but also long-form video essays on anti-capitalist ideology, socialist history, and Marxist social theory.

That socialism is back as a political ideal can also be seen in other ways. According to *Gallup*, young adults in the US have been quite enthusiastic about socialism for the past ten years.[9] Almost half of them viewed socialism positively in 2019, 2010, and any year in between. This is in sharp contrast to the opinions of older generations, in which only one in three people view socialism positively (in 2019, this has increased for Gen Xers to 39%). Perhaps crucially, 66% of young adults had a favourable disposition towards capitalism in 2010, a share that has steadily been dropping every couple of years to only 51% in 2019. The organization *Democratic Socialists of America*, which has seen its once meagre membership numbers swell in the past few years to almost 100,000, went from a small group of mostly elderly citizens (the median age of its members was 68 in 2013) to a thriving political organization of energetic young people (in 2017, the median age dropped to 33).[10]

To some, this is surprising, inexplicable, or even bizarre. How can socialism and Marxism be back after the practical implementation of the former and the theoretical edifice of the latter have ostensibly been so thoroughly discredited in the second half of the 20th century? On the one hand, liberal democratic capitalism so convincingly defeated really existing authoritarian socialism that some have proclaimed the 1990s to have moved human history closer to its 'end.'[11] That this might be true is evinced even by the self-described communist China today, which is economically anything but socialist or communist and is actually quite capitalist (although it is also far from being a free-market society). On the other hand, Marxism as a social-science paradigm has not fared much better. As will be seen below, one of the most illustrious contemporary Marxist research programmes that tried to rigorously renew Marxism for the present – Analytical Marxism – has turned out to be a dead end. Most of what is analytical in Marxism and in accordance with modern social-science methodology was found not to be specifically Marxist, while most of the distinctively Marxist claims and theories are hard to justify on the grounds of modern social science.

To others, however, the reanimation of the socialist movement and the anti-capitalist critique of *status quo* is not only welcome but quite expected and justified. It is such because, according to the critics, capitalism has an inherent and palpably dark side to it, namely making life miserable for many, even *a large part* of the population, in any given society. As Wright describes it, 'the hallmark of capitalism is poverty in the midst of plenty.'[12] He admits that 'it is not an illusion that capitalism has transformed the material conditions of life in the world and enormously increased human productivity; many people have benefited from this.'[13] But he nevertheless insists that, 'equally, it is not an illusion that capitalism generates great harms and perpetuates eliminable forms of human suffering.'[14]

The NYU Marxist sociologist Vivek Chibber agrees. In *Understanding Capitalism*, he asks,

> How can it be that in a society with such enormous resources and wealth, a thin layer of the population at the top gets to have everything, while millions upon millions experience life as a daily grind, a struggle just to make ends meet?[15]

Or, as he puts it more succinctly, 'This system creates enormous wealth but also great misery for the majority.'[16] So, it is not only that in capitalism some small minority of people will simply be down on their luck, as would be the case in any system. Instead, as Chibber explicitly puts it, 'millions upon millions' of Americans and even 'the majority' of population suffer 'great misery' under capitalism.[17]

Wherever one falls on this spectrum between the perplexed defenders of capitalism and the indignant anti-capitalists, the purpose of the present book is to show that both camps should be taken seriously and learned from and that, equally, both sides are much too one-sided in their outlook if taken on in isolation. Most books on the topic of capitalism and economic development deal with these issues from either a left-wing – and Marxist – or a right wing – and libertarian – perspective. I take a different route. I attempt to marry the two sides and present an integrative, synthetic overview of capitalism, and a theoretical framework for understanding it in both its negative and positive aspects.

Analytical Marxism, 'an empty set'

In the late 1970s and early 1980s, a group of scientifically minded Marxists was brought together by the publication of G. A. Cohen's impressive tome *Karl Marx's Theory of History: A Defence*, a rigorous reconstruction and defence of Marx's historical materialism in the strict tradition of analytical philosophy.[18] Cohen laboriously explicated the hidden or only half worked-out assumptions underpinning Marx's theory and mounted a conceptual philosophical defence both of these assumptions and the ostensibly logical conclusions flowing from them when mixed together. Jon Elster, Erik Wright, Adam Przeworski, and others were impressed with Cohen's feat and, although substantively critical of it, were inspired by it to undertake their own reconstructions, reparations, and updates of various middle-range Marxist theories and claims with an explicitly analytical and an empirical, modern social-scientific mindset (other Analytical Marxists have included John Roemer, Samuel Bowles, Robert Brenner, Philippe van Parijs, and several less well-known figures).[19]

After almost two decades of intense work under this new Analytical-Marxist framework, many practitioners felt they did what they could and, underwhelmed by the results, stopped identifying with the label and moved on to other projects. As Jon Elster recounted in 2011 in a particularly pithy way,

> The flaws of Marxism as a theoretical enterprise were exposed so thoroughly by the "non-bullshit Marxist" group that *non-bullshit Marxism was revealed to be an empty set* (a rare case of intellectual autophagy). ... Marxist *theory* has nothing to contribute to empirical social science (which is not to decry the work of individual Marxist scholars).[20]

Analytical Marxists – both those who continue to accept the label or something like that and those who dropped it – recognize, and have done so for decades now, all of the following:

1 Marx's labour theory of value, which claims that labour-power is the only source of value, is finished.[21]
2 Canonical Marxist theory of history, according to which technological development propels history forward and moves it through definite stages, is a dead end.[22]
3 The classical Marxist notion of 'bourgeois revolutions' is wrong.[23]
4 Even absent ideological manipulation, large collectives such as the working class rarely spontaneously form and organize on the basis of its members recognizing and pursuing their individual interests due to pervasive (and rational) free-rider problems.[24]
5 The successful Marxist explanations, or at least Marxist conclusions, such as the fact that the average worker under capitalism tends to be exploited (at least to a degree) or that the state is structurally dependent on maintaining a favourable investment climate for business owners, and so on, are not specifically Marxist and have either been incorporated into mainstream social science or independently discovered by it.[25]
6 Mass liberal democracy – the regime with the most robust protections of civil and political rights of ordinary people – has never emerged, or been sustained, in a non-capitalist society.[26]
7 The Marxist insistence on the causal primacy of the economic aspect of societies in determining grand social phenomena is either wrong in its strong form or not special to Marxism in its weak form.[27]
8 The polarized Marxist class model, wherein societies are wholly or at least mostly split across the proletarian/capitalist divide, is obviously wrong, while more nuanced schemes introducing various middling strata are not specific to Marxism, even though certain specific causal mechanisms related to class retain a Marxist flair.[28]
9 In the medium- to long-term perspective, capitalism has massively increased material well-being for everyone, albeit inequality does remain a problem, but that is also a central claim in most contemporary non-Marxist literature.[29]

Why, then, do Wright and Chibber, for example, continue to adhere to the Marxist and anti-capitalist label? What survives of Marxism after the rightful analytical onslaught on it produced pretty meagre results?

Wright cites two particular reasons for, as he puts it, remaining 'stubbornly working inside of Marxism.'[30] First, he is clinging on to Marxism because he thinks its descriptive, explanatory 'diagnosis of capitalism as a system of oppression built around class and exploitation' remains indispensable. Second, he remains a Marxist because Marxism offers a distinct 'normative vision of a radically egalitarian democratic alternative to capitalism.'[31]

Chibber, for his part, concurs with both points. First, descriptively, Chibber says that it was 'Karl Marx [who] gave a very intuitive description of the process through which a capitalist goes about their business,' a process inevitably involving exploitation and oppression.[32] Second, and more normatively, he holds that

> as long as capital remains the arbiter of people's fate, any social movement with a real ambition for justice will have to find a way of gaining leverage against it … This simple fact has enormous implications, not just for "class" demands, but for the pursuit of social justice more generally, which includes the fight against other social oppressions.[33]

Here is how Wright fleshes out the first, descriptive point – the point I take to be most important for anyone maintaining the validity of Marxist theory specifically and radical anti-capitalist critique more generally. Take exploitation first. For Wright, capitalist economic structures inherently tend to generate exploitation of the economically vulnerable because, in capitalism, some own the means of production (the capitalists) and others do not (the workers). Those who own the means of production use them to generate as much wealth for themselves as possible, which implies they will want to extract as much work effort from the workers as possible while also paying them the least amount possible in return. Workers will accept the deal because they have no other realistic option – they are, after all, workers who lack the means of production and who therefore must work for a capitalist to get the income to survive. This, Wright says, is 'roughly … what is meant by "exploitation".'[34] And the tendency towards exploitation is structurally inherent because, in a competitive capitalist market, an entrepreneur simply *has to* make as much money as possible; otherwise, competitors will do so and will, for example, use the extra money to encroach on the entrepreneur's market share, thus driving him out of business.

Capitalism, however, is not only inherently exploitative but, says Wright, also produces constant economic anxiety for a large segment of the population. It does so because constant technological improvement is an inherent tendency of competitive markets, and technological change usually has disruptive effects on people's lives. Technological change 'continually renders skills obsolete, destroys jobs, and displaces workers.'[35] The result is a constant feeling of anxiety ('will my job be destroyed tomorrow, or in a few years?') and later on the result is even actual poverty – workers who become obsolete can struggle to find new work which pays the same as their last job, and sometimes they even struggle to remain employed at all. This is another issue for human well-being, another issue that is inherently generated by capitalist institutions if left to their own devices, and it can exist even independently of anyone being exploited.

Wright's complete list of capitalist 'bads' gets quite long. He explains how capitalism inherently creates – at least when there are no non-capitalist counter-vailing forces present – vast amounts of wealth and income inequality that can be translated into almost insurmountable political inequality of power within a soci-ety. He explains how private capitalist enterprises are actually mini-dictatorships where workers are constantly monitored from above, have no democratic say in how the firm is run, or what the precise nature of their own work is, and can only freely exit the current company they work at just to be forced by the raw necessities of life (having to eat, be sheltered, and so on) to seek work at a dif-ferent company.[36] He points to how inefficient markets are in the production of certain goods and services such as public goods or goods which have negative externalities. Capitalism, for instance, overproduces polluting goods as the costs of pollution are not spontaneously included in market prices, thus destroying the very environment people live in. Moreover, capitalism fuels militarism and imperialism, says Wright, and it corrupts our morals and values by pushing us into a consumerist, commodified mindset where solidarity and reciprocity are underappreciated and undermined.

As I will outline below and as will be demonstrated in much more detail in the following chapters, there is an interesting duality to the preceding critique. On one hand, some of the key claims it contains are correct, or at least ap-proximately correct. Capitalism does engender exploitation, it does disrupt some workers' lives, it can fuel inequality if left to its own devices, it has trouble with negative externalities, and so on. On the other hand, however, some of the above claims are very wrong, others are presented one-sidedly, and – importantly in light of Wright's descriptive reason to remain calling himself a Marxist – not a single one is *distinctively Marxist*.

To illustrate only the one-sided and wrong ones (I take up Marxism's dis-tinctiveness in the next section), it is simply not true that competitive markets have *only* a tendency for creating and increasing exploitation. In fact, they also tend to reduce it at certain times and in certain circumstances – especially if they are highly competitive – albeit of course not to zero. Wright then also correctly points out that in the *absence of countervailing forces*, capitalist markets tend not to do a perfect job in caring for the lowest economic rungs in a society, say the bottom 10%, many of whom do not even participate in the market. However, social-democratic capitalism which uses the generative power of markets and combines it with the redistributive power of the welfare state has little issue taking care of the least well-off, even though this is still capitalism we are talking about. Moreover, advanced capitalist economies today are among the most re-ciprocal societies where impersonal pro-sociality and generalized trust are the highest in the world. Lastly, it is simply not true that capitalism fuels militaristic and aggressive foreign policy attitudes, making war more likely. Actually, the opposite might be the case, as will be discussed in more detail in Chapter 5.

Marxism's correct – but not distinctively Marxist – insights

How unique are Marxism's main claims?

To me personally, one of the main intellectual attractions of Marxism (and its radical critique of capitalism) was the ostensible fact that, without being a Marxist, one could not hold to, and theoretically justify, the following crucial sociological claims.

i   *Structure and agency*: individuals, their behaviour and attitudes, are strongly shaped by the surrounding social environment and structure, not voluntarily determined by an individual's 'free will.'

ii *Exploitation*: in capitalist markets, workers are still exploited to an extent and will most likely continue to be in the future, just as they have been (even though to a much bigger extent) in pre-capitalist societies.

iii *Rising inequality*: capitalist markets have a strong, even though not necessarily constant or irreversible, tendency to increase starting inequalities in wealth and income.

iv *The antagonism between workers and capitalists*: owing to the different positions they assume in the economy in particular and society more generally, workers usually want something different than what capitalists strive for. For example, workers want higher wages, which is a cost to the capitalist, while capitalists want higher profits, which they can get by, among other things, lowering wages or not increasing them as much as they could in principle.

v   *Capitalism's incredible productivity*: capitalism is an immensely and inherently productive system due to its powerful internal engine of market competition that makes it rational – in contrast to pre-capitalist systems – both for owners and direct producers to constantly innovate and improve technology, thereby incessantly increasing labour productivity.

vi *Market failure*: capitalist markets sometimes engender destructive 'social dilemmas,' resulting in highly collectively irrational outcomes that flow from individually rational behaviour of economic actors (with environmental pollution and under-provision of public goods being only the most salient examples).

vii *Indirect subordination of the state to capital*: the state in capitalism is not wholly autonomous in its policy decision-making, but is in fact highly curtailed, dependent as it is for its own budget on the general will of capitalist owners to continue investing and driving economic growth. Put more concretely, if the capitalist owners do not like state's policies and decide to lower their own private investment activity, move production abroad, or go on an investment strike, the state is thereby indirectly threatened with financial paralysis as it cannot collect as much taxes as before.

viii *Direct subordination of the state to special interests, including entrepreneurs*: powerful economic actors – the capitalists most obviously, but unions and other groups as well – use their wealth to directly influence the halls of political power. They do so by making deals with politicians, by bribing them, by using wealth to finance politicians' electoral campaign, by personally entering politics with the help of money and networks the rich and powerful usually have, etc.

ix *Elite self-interestedness*: economic and political actors (succinctly, capitalists and politicians) are not primarily interested in the common good and public welfare but instead strive to line their own pockets and aim to maintain or improve their privileged positions in society.

x *The formal separation of the economic from the political*: capitalism increases the probability that mass democracy emerges because only in capitalism do the economic and the political sphere formally split, allowing economic elites to remain wealthy and economically powerful even if they lose their political power. This split increases the chances that elites assent to the relinquishment of their political power.

xi *Transition to capitalism*: the transition from feudalism to capitalism happened not merely due to expanding towns and markets, or the flourishing of Protestant values, but due to a radical, and quite conflictual, qualitative transformation of pre-capitalist markets (themselves not marked by widespread market dependence) into competitive capitalist markets in which the majority of the population became dependent on the market for survival.

xii *Conflictual theory of history*: the whole recorded human history is primarily, or at least in one crucial aspect, a history of struggle between various powerful and less powerful social groups (not necessarily *classes*) striving to improve their standing in society or at least hold on to power. Moreover, these struggles have unintended consequences that can result in either maintenance or transition to a different social order.

I judge all of these claims as true. It should, then, not be hard to see how when one thinks – as I did – that Marxism is the only (or most accurate) way to get at these truths, Marxism becomes quite attractive and powerful. The issue, of course, is that Marxism is simply not the only, or the most accurate, research programme which one can use to arrive at these conclusions. Even Wright now recognizes this. He says, 'While I continue to work in the Marxist tradition, I no longer conceive of Marxism as a comprehensive paradigm that is inherently incompatible with a "bourgeois" sociology.'[37]

To see this more clearly, let us go through the enumerated points on the list one by one.

Virtually all contemporary sociological and, more generally, social-scientific theories recognize the structured nature of agency in society. To give just a general example, rational choice theory is one widely used framework in social science that explicitly recognizes, and cannot even work without positing, the structure-agency divide.

Next, as I will demonstrate in Chapter 3, mainstream economics has no issue in the slightest, either theoretically or empirically, with recognizing the fact of exploitation on labour markets, especially those markets evincing monopsonistic or imperfectly competitive conditions.

The same goes for other points from the list. Especially in recent decades, inequality has been a primary research agenda for mainstream economics. Thomas Piketty wrote a bestselling, 800-page book on the topic in 2014. His colleagues Gabriel Zucman and Emmanuel Saez are superstar economists (with over 65,000 citations between them at the time of my writing) whose claim to fame was precisely the study of inequality. Looking at a recent representative sample of economists, it is clear that the vast majority of economists today agree even with the normative claim that 'Redistribution of income is a legitimate role for the US Government,' and only a tiny minority agrees with the claim 'The distribution of income and wealth has little, if any, impact on economic stability and growth.'[38]

Point (iv) flows straight from rational choice analysis and game theory. Points (v) and (vi) are the core of mainstream, neoclassical economics, so much so that Austrian economists chastise neoclassical economists for the latter's focus on market failures. In fact, detailed discussions of market failure figure prominently in all modern economics textbooks, even those that are characterized as having a strong right-wing slant (for example, Gregory Mankiw's famous introductory textbook).[39]

The fact that the state is financially dependent on private investment and that, consequently, even politicians personally and ideologically hostile to capitalists and capitalism are incentivized to maintain a comfortable business climate and shape their policies accordingly are also not lost on non-Marxist, neoclassical political economy, or for that matter anyone using rational choice theory to understand politics.[40] The same goes for the claim that capitalists and other economic actors make deals with political actors manning the state in order to seek rents through favourable regulation for their particular business, the issuing of subsidies, selective taxing of competitors, erecting various barriers to entry for new potential market participants, and so on. This claim and the various arguments underpinning it are public choice's claim to fame.[41]

Next, the general notion that actors, especially economic ones, are self-interested is infamously a part of mainstream economics, and the self-interestedness of political actors is a mainstay of both rational and public choice theory. Moreover, it was Milton Friedman, not only Karl Marx or the Marxist political theorist Ellen Meiksins Wood – and it was modernization theorists, not solely Marxists – who time and again claimed that in capitalism the economic social sphere becomes formally separate from politics and that capitalism structurally increases the probability of democratic transitioning because of that.

Lastly, historical points (viii) and (xi) are common to Marxism, rational choice theory, and new institutional economics.[42]

When one looks at it like this, Marxism rapidly (and rightly) starts losing a good deal of its appeal, radical nature, and overall substantive theoretical distinctiveness.

Is public choice theory Marxism's grand foe or potential ally?

At first glance, there is scarcely a body of theory that could be further removed from Marxism than the *public choice* variety of political economy. If anything, according to the critical (although also very flawed) historical treatise written by Nancy MacLean in 2017, the conservative public choice paradigm is a *complete inversion* of the radical Marxist programme.[43] Borrowing the words of the historian Richard Hofstadter, the prologue of MacLean's book is thus tellingly titled 'The Marx of the Master Class.'[44] However, I will argue – as is perhaps also unintendedly suggested by the phrase just cited – that there are actually quite a few explicit similarities between the two paradigms and several implicit affinities that suggest a productive, if in the end only partial, synthesis of the two.[45]

In a general sense, public choice theory is nothing more than the application of rational choice theory, as it was typically used in the analysis of markets and other economic phenomena, to the sphere of politics.[46] The starting question of public choice is: if economic actors, such as capitalists, consumers, and workers, are usually modelled as primarily self-interested actors – concerned with maximizing the profit/cost ratio, the satisfaction/cost ratio, or the wage/effort ratio, respectively – and if they are modelled as capable of making intentional and strategic decisions so as to successfully pursue these personal goals in different environments, then why do we not think of political actors similarly, instead depicting them as actors primarily altruistically concerned with the collective will of the public? Is it not more appropriate, on grounds of consistency if nothing else, to (i) *either* amend the usual starting analysis of markets by dropping the rational choice assumptions, treating all actors – including capitalists, consumers, and workers – as beneficent and collectivistic as politicians ostensibly are; (ii) *or* to amend the default characterization of political actors, putting their motivations and cognition in line with the rational capitalists, consumers, and workers? And if so, is it not the second option (ii) that is more justified, seeing as how politicians are simply people, just like economic actors are?

In this general sense, then, public choice theory is simply 'politics without romance.' It starts with the sensible assumption that, given an unpunished chance, the average political actor – just like the average economic actor – will primarily strive to take care of him- or herself and the people close to him or her instead of automatically (or likely) looking out for the welfare of total strangers. It follows from this that only when provided with the appropriate incentives can we count on politicians (or capitalists) to tend to also do what is in the interest of the public rather than just themselves. When the incentives are lacking, i.e. when corruption goes unreported by the media and unpunished by the public; when voters do not have a watchful eye over politicians because they are un- or misinformed; when powers are not separated; when a politician's last term is coming to an end, and so on, politicians (just like capitalists in cases of market failure) will tend to be much less benevolent towards the public in their actions. Put like this, public choice is not at all an esoteric theory, and it certainly is not the opposite of Marxism.

There are also more concrete ideas associated with public choice, ideas which again reveal certain affinities with Marxist intuitions. For instance, public choice analysis diagnoses the phenomenon of rent-seeking as a pervasive activity which, when successful, can result in regulatory capture and similar conspiracies against the public. Put more concretely, capitalists, trade unions, and other powerful economic actors strive to benefit themselves by influencing politicians and, through them, government policy. By making mutually advantageous deals, economic and political actors can enter into alliance and enrich themselves by impoverishing the public. Corporations try to tailor regulations in such a way that the prices of their goods and services, and therefore corporate profits, become artificially higher, while the public is burdened with the extra costs. Individual capitalists want to stifle, not encourage, their competition, and they make deals with politicians to make that happen. Trade unions strive to increase the wages of their workers by influencing politicians, even when such increases would be detrimental to consumers or non-unionized workers.

Marx and Engels famously wrote in *The Communist Manifesto* that 'The executive of the modern state is but a committee for managing the common affairs of the whole bourgeoisie.'[47] This is a tad reductive, and it forgets about non-bourgeois (but still powerful) groups that pressure the government to execute their will, but the slogan is in essence perfectly compatible with public choice analysis. Moreover, Marx's public choice leanings are palpably on display in the third volume of *Capital* where he characterizes capitalists not as a unified class but as 'hostile brothers' willing to – rationally – tear each other (and the whole capitalist class) apart in certain circumstances.[48] As he put it:

> So long as things go well, competition effects an operating fraternity of the capitalist class, as we have seen in the case of the equalisation of the general rate of profit, so that each shares in the common loot in proportion to the size of his respective investment. But as soon as it no longer is a question of sharing profits, but of sharing losses, everyone tries to reduce his own share to a minimum and to shove it off upon another. The class, as such, must inevitably lose. How much the individual capitalist must bear of the loss, i.e., to what extent he must share in it at all, is decided by strength and cunning, and competition then becomes a fight among hostile brothers. The antagonism between each individual capitalist's interests and those of the capitalist class as a whole, then comes to the surface [...].[49]

Far from thinking that capitalists only do what is good for the whole capitalist class (or capitalism in general), Marx was aware that, rational actors that they are, capitalists will be at each other's throats and will exploit government legislation to hurt their competitors and help themselves, come what may. Public choice analysis arrives at the same conclusion, and books in the broad ambit of that approach carry suggestive titles like *Saving Capitalism from the Capitalists* and *A Capitalism for the People*, noting how destructive capitalists (and, of course, other economic actors) can be to the very system they preside over.[50]

Given the foregoing, it should not be surprising that left-leaning political economists such as Mancur Olson, or even left-wing politicians such as Elizabeth Warren, have contributed to, and drawn on, public choice theory.[51] If not used in a biased way as a tool to solely bash the government and apologize for markets, public choice points as much to left-wing as to right-wing conclusions. This theory, as indeed goes for any theory, has sometimes been used in a very biased manner. But a consistent application of the general principles of rational choice theory on both market and political decision-making is beyond partisanship, and it organically leads one to arrive at both left-leaning and right-leaning conclusions in various cases. It reveals why markets fail and why governments fail. At the same time, it suggests how and when both markets and governments work more optimally.

Capitalism for realists: a neutral and common framework

This book does not explicitly position itself either in the Marxist or the anti-Marxist theoretical camp. Moreover, my main goal is not to defend or attack capitalism and its related phenomena. The central purpose of the book is to present detailed facts about capitalism and economic development, as well as facts about their impact on society, and to analyse capitalism by employing as bare-bones a theoretical framework as possible.

That is why the *capitalism-for-realists* approach that I advocate in this book involves two general moves. First, evidence-based, empirical conclusions about how capitalism performs are seen as of the utmost importance under this approach. Especially crucial is empirical evidence that commands wide assent in the cross-disciplinary literature and flows from widely used and recognized social-scientific methods. Grand theoretical defences or critiques of capitalism on the basis of first principles are not nearly enough, and where theoretical considerations are employed, they should be empirically well-grounded independently of theory.

Second, as far as theoretical analysis is concerned, it should be done – as far as possible – on the basis of broadly shared theoretical precepts and in a consistent manner. This is to say that if traditional theories favouring and critiquing capitalism share (either implicitly or explicitly) certain theoretical foundations, which are also independently, empirically plausible, then our theoretical analysis should be consistently based precisely on these foundations. No special pleading should be introduced without ample theoretical and evidentiary support.

This means that if capitalists are presupposed to be rational, selfish actors who maximize income and power, so too should politicians, citizens, or workers. In other words, one should avoid starting with the conclusion that workers (or whatever other social actors) engage in 'good,' pro-social, favourable behaviour in a given social system, and then trying to justify this *a priori*, politically motivated conclusion by a backwards stipulation of special, 'good,' pro-social, favourable behavioural, and motivational assumptions on the part of this actor (and this actor alone). Instead, one should apply the basic (broadly shared) theoretical axioms – for instance, the axioms of rational choice –, combine them with the accumulated evidence about the environment people live in and the performance of various systems and institutions, and see what conclusions naturally emerge from this exercise. If unfavourable, but theoretically and empirically justified conclusions emerge, then so be it.

Is seeking for a broadly shared theoretical bedrock among the various existing and rivalrous approaches to capitalism an impossible task? Fortunately, as has already been seen in previous sections, it is not. It seems then that one does not really have to choose between, say, Marxist sociology, public choice economics, or institutional economics. All of these approaches to political economy have, at their heart, the axioms of rational choice. All of them sensibly, although sometimes only implicitly, presume that social actors are to be thought of as responsive to incentives and prone to strategizing, with incentives flowing both from the current behaviour of other people as well as from entrenched institutions or structures. All of them presume social actors, including capitalists, politicians, bureaucrats, workers, consumers, feudal lords, peasants, and so on, are primarily – though not exclusively – concerned with improving their own lot in a society, not that of complete strangers.

Some would no doubt contest my claims. Some time ago, the Marxist political theorist Ellen Meiksins Wood, for instance, wrote a long critique of analytical Marxism – the flavour of Marxism which is self-consciously and explicitly rooted in axioms of rational choice – arguing against the use of methodological individualism and game theory in Marxist theorizing.[52] Ironically, however, it is precisely the work of Wood and her colleague Robert Brenner, on whose historical sociology she constantly draws, that demonstrates – even though this demonstration is sometimes only implicit – how reliant contemporary Marxists rightly are on rational choice.[53]

It is exactly Brenner's general theoretical schema, namely, the famous formula 'social property relations → rules for reproduction → social laws of motion,' that is arrived at by Brenner through standard rational choice analysis.[54] What Brenner does when explicating how feudalism or capitalism work as social systems – and what Wood endorses when relying on this explication in her work – is the following. He (1) describes the *institutional context* within which workers and capitalists, or feudal lords and peasants, find themselves; he (2) lays out the *rational, strategizing, self-interested actions* of the relevant actors (given the institutional incentives); and he then (3) deduces from those actions the larger *macrosocial patterns of development* (i.e. constant technical improvement and capital accumulation in capitalism, and chronic technical stagnation and political accumulation in feudalism). Such Marxist reasoning is actually rational choice analysis 101 and institutional economics 101. I will have more to say on this in the second part of Chapter 2.

Outline of the book

In the chapter immediately following this one, I first take a step back. I show how historically exceptional the modern, self-sustaining, capitalist type of economic growth we are all accustomed to today is, and ask why the first society a few centuries ago finally managed to break out of humanity's millennia-long economic stagnation.

I present and examine three prominent and influential cultural explanations of the European transition from feudalism to capitalism (Weber's, Henrich's, and Mokyr's). I focus most extensively on Max Weber's classical sociological claim that Protestantism caused the transition, and on the recent 'WEIRD' hypothesis proposed by Joseph Henrich who argues that Christianity and the Church unintentionally produced, between 500 CE and 1500 CE, a wholly novel psychological and behavioural set of dispositions in European populations that then triggered the transition to the modern economy. I use simple descriptive statistics to demonstrate empirical flaws burdening at least parts of these explanations, and I also draw, where appropriate, on more sophisticated existing quantitative studies examining the various hypotheses.

I find these prominent cultural explanations at least moderately lacking, so in the second part of the chapter I move on to an alternative materialist explanation that is more consistent with the presented data. Drawing on older and recent historiography, new institutional economics, and sophisticated modern Marxist historical sociology, I explain why agrarian capitalism at first started emerging only in the English countryside around the 15th and 16th century, and why this was − *contra* Marx − a very unlikely historical occurrence, not one prefigured by the grand sweep of history. Moreover, conflict, violence, and expropriation emphasized by Marx and Marxists were only one part of the transitional process, not the only one. On the other hand − *contra* the culturalists − I show the process had more to do with structural economic change, power, interests, rationality, and conflict among the main economic actors of the old social regime than with shifting cultural norms and attitudes.

In Chapter 3, I turn to the (contemporary) economic issues capitalism ostensibly engenders. I first explain what is at stake, theoretically and empirically, in the controversy over poverty and capitalism that recently flared up, and I take a closer look at it through the scholarly dispute between the anthropologist Jason Hickel and economist Max Roser. I review the dispute, find some common ground between the two rhetorically polarized sides, and resolve the remaining disagreement (as much as possible) by using the latest data and new approaches to measuring historical absolute poverty. I show Hickel's popular critical treatment of the topic to be on the lacking side.

Next, I show that capitalist markets as they currently exist do evince a certain amount of worker exploitation and that, consequently, simple economics 101 reasoning about (perfect) competition is far from sufficient. However, at the same time I demonstrate this conclusion without relying on the discredited Marxist labour theory of value, staying within the standard rational choice perspective and grounding my argument in mainstream economics evidence about market concentration, search costs and frictions, and employment impacts of minimum wage.

Lastly, I disentangle income and wealth inequality trends in different (groups of) countries and at different levels (especially world inequality, between-country inequality, and within-country inequality). In contrast to the popular claim that inequalities are skyrocketing virtually everywhere, I demonstrate a much more mixed picture, especially in Europe and Latin America and especially after the year 2000. I then consider why inequalities are, and are not, increasing, and – by means of conceptual investigation and a review of the empirical literature – what economic, social, and political dangers they could, or are not likely to, pose.

Having thoroughly examined the general economic issues with capitalism in the previous chapter, I move to more concrete and more explicitly political issues in Chapter 4. In it, I first demonstrate the incoherence of the term 'neoliberalism' as typically employed. I then ask how one could define and operationalize it more fruitfully so as to empirically (and systematically) examine the popular claim that the world has been getting more neoliberal for the past 40 years and that, on average, this is a worrisome development. I present two options. One is to simply look at the movement of economic freedom of the world (utilizing, for example, the Fraser Institute's index of economic freedom). I consider various objections to this method and respond to them. The other is to break neoliberalism down into more specific aspects, indicators, and domains which can be explored for the world, in general, and individual countries in particular. For example, one can look at the size of government spending and social spending, the degree of economic regulation, the rate of unionization, the rate of taxation, openness of international trade, and so on. A somewhat mixed picture emerges, as some of these have increased and others decreased.

The Washington Consensus (WC) is one narrow way in which neoliberalism can be defined. Thus, I review both older and most recent (up to 2021) empirical literature on the economic effects of WC and uncover three distinct waves of WC research (primarily positive, primarily negative, and then moderately positive). On the whole, the record seems to be mixed as WC has had mostly negligible effect on growth, on average, before 2000, but significant positive effects after 2000. Here, I also consider the most prominent theoretical case against unqualified free trade for developing economies – the infant industry protection argument. I investigate both theory and evidence its proponents (such as Ha-Joon Chang and Joe Studwell) mobilize in favour of it, and

I compare this state-led case for development to government failure theory and contrary evidence collected by free trade proponents (such as Arvind Panagariya and Douglas Irwin).

Lastly, I show Milton Friedman's ostensibly controversial, partisan statement that there exists a non-trivial causal affinity between capitalism and political democracy and that politics and economics become two distinct, separate social spheres only under capitalism, to be perfectly justified on the grounds (among other things) of standard, and even Marxist, historical sociology research.

Chapter 5 takes up the pervasive claim that modern market societies reinforce and increase various negative social behaviours and attitudes, such as aggressiveness, selfishness, corruption, and mistrust. Reviewing recent experimental and statistical evidence coming out of behavioural economics, psychology, and international relations, I examine these claims and show them to have little support. I also demonstrate, theoretically, why stronger market integration and interdependence should in most circumstances actually lead to less mistrust and more impersonal reciprocity (and when this might break down).

At the same time, I point to the various nuances empirical research has revealed. It is not true, as some pro-capitalist reviewers have recently said, that capitalism always and in virtually all respects contributes towards moral social behaviours and attitudes. For instance, one element of economic freedom, namely small government size, is negatively correlated with trust, and it seems to boost homicide rates. Nevertheless, there is an abundance of evidence that, in other respects, capitalism and economic growth are consistent with and, indeed, positively causally connected to pro-social outcomes.

Chapter 6 is the book's conclusion. This shorter chapter is entirely devoted to the environmental issue. In it, I take up the question of whether global climate change is solely the responsibility of capitalism, or if the issue of responsibility is more complicated, with *industry* (not particularly capitalism) being the chief cause. I present climate change as a large-scale collective action problem, and I question whether – paradoxically – further economic development might help *ease* climate change. For that purpose, I investigate the empirical literature on existence of a Kuznets-curve relationship between development and climate change.

Notes

1 Rosling (2018) reports that even people from highly educated countries (across the world) are deeply mistaken when answering questions about basic trends of poverty reduction, rates of child vaccination, levels of economic development in various parts of the world, and so on. As he puts it, 'Everyone seems to get the world devastatingly wrong. Not only devastatingly wrong, but *systematically* wrong. By which I mean that these test results are not random. They are worse than random: they are worse than the results I would get if the people answering my questions had no knowledge at all.' Ibid., Introduction.
2 Roser and Ortiz-Ospina (2013).
3 Roser et al. (2013).

4 Ibid.
5 Wright (2019).
6 Robinson (2019); Sunkara (2020).
7 Wright (2010, xviii).
8 The Conversation (2021).
9 Saad (2019).
10 Heyward (2017).
11 Fukuyama (1989; 1992).
12 Wright (2019).
13 Ibid.
14 Ibid.
15 Chibber (2018, 3).
16 Ibid., 7.
17 Ibid., 34.
18 Cohen (1978).
19 For more on the history of Analytical Marxism see Levine (2003), Chapter 5; Wright (2006).
20 Elster (2012, 163). Emphasis in original.
21 Cohen (1979); Gintis (1992, 114); Wright (2000, 1560); Przeworski (2003); Chibber (2014, 622). Note, though, that Gintis says he is not an outright Analytical Marxist (he also denies the traditional Marxist label).
22 Elster (1985); Levine et al. (1992); Chibber (2011; 2014, 622).
23 Brenner (1989); Chibber (2013; 2014, 622).
24 Przeworski (1986); Elster (1985).
25 Przeworski (2021); see also next section.
26 Wright (2010); Przeworski (2021).
27 Wright (1983).
28 Wright (1985; 2009).
29 Wright (2019). Chibber is somewhat contradictory on this topic, but see Chibber (2018). For non-Marxist literature start with Piketty (2014).
30 Wright (2006, 342).
31 Ibid.
32 Chibber (2018a, 13).
33 Chibber (2018b, 30).
34 Wright (2010, 28).
35 Ibid., 29.
36 For a non-Marxist argument advocating the 'business as dictatorship' thesis see Anderson (2017).
37 Wright (2009).
38 See the survey results in Geide-Stevenson and La Parra Perez (2021).
39 See the study by Eyzaguirre et al. (2016), who also demonstrate that, if anything, economics textbooks devote *far more attention* to market failure than government failure. The same conclusion is reached by Fike and Gwartney (2015). For a good economics textbook that covers both market and government failure in detail see Cowen and Tabarrok (2015).
40 For example, Adam Przeworski cites the following non-Marxist research in support of this claim: Barro (1990); Bertola (1993; 1996). See Przeworski (2021).
41 For introductions to public choice theory see Simmons (2011); Butler (2012); Holcombe (2016).
42 See North et al. (2009); Acemoglu and Robinson (2012).
43 For a highly critical but judicious treatment of MacLean's book and her actions towards her opponents see Teles and Farrell (2017).
44 MacLean (2017).
45 My thinking on this matter was partially inspired by Munger (2020).
46 See footnote 41 for introductory literature on public choice.

47 Marx and Engels (2008 [1848], 36).
48 Marx (2010 [1894], 252).
49 Ibid.
50 Rajan and Zingales (2003); Zingales (2012).
51 See Farrell (2019) for more on this.
52 Wood (1995).
53 See, on this, Carling (1995).
54 Brenner (2007).

References

Anderson, Elizabeth. 2017. *Private Government: How Employers Rule Our Lives (and Why We Don't Talk about It)*. Princeton: Princeton University Press.

Barro, Robert J. 1990. 'Government Spending in a Simple Model of Endogenous Growth,' *Journal of Political Economy* 98, S103–S126.

Bertola, Giuseppe. 1993. 'Factor Shares and Savings in Endogenous Growth,' *American Economic Review* 83, no. 5, 1184–1198.

Bertola, Giuseppe. 1996. 'Factor Shares in OLG Models of Growth,' *European Economic Review* 40, no. 8, 1541–1560.

Brenner, Robert. 1989. 'Bourgeois Revolution and the Transition to Capitalism,' in A. L. Beier, David Cannadine and James M. Rosenheim (eds.), *The First Modern Society: Essays in English History in Honour of Lawrence Stone*, 271–304. Cambridge: Cambridge University Press.

Brenner, Robert. 2007. 'Property and Progress: Where Adam Smith Went Wrong,' in Chris Wickham (ed.), *Marxist History-Writing for the Twenty-first Century*, 49–111. Oxford: Oxford University Press.

Butler, Eamonn. 2012. *Public Choice – A Primer*. Westminster: The Institute of Economic Affairs.

Carling, Alan. 1995. 'Rational Choice Marxism,' in Terrell Carver and Paul Thomas (eds.), *Rational Choice Marxism*. Basingstoke: Macmillan, 31–78.

Chibber, Vivek. 2011. 'What Is Living and What Is Dead in the Marxist Theory of History,' *Historical Materialism* 19, no. 2, 60–91.

Chibber, Vivek. 2013. *Postcolonial Theory and the Specter of Capital*. London: Verso.

Chibber, Vivek. 2014. 'Making Sense of Postcolonial Theory: A Response to Gayatri Chakravorty Spivak,' *Cambridge Review of International Affairs* 27, no. 3, 617–624.

Chibber, Vivek. 2018a. *The ABCs of Capitalism: A – Understanding Capitalism*. Brooklyn: Jacobin Foundation.

Chibber, Vivek. 2018b. *The ABCs of Capitalism: C – Capitalism and Class Struggle*. Brooklyn: Jacobin Foundation.

Cohen, Gerald A. 1978. *Karl Marx's Theory of History: A Defence*. Princeton: Princeton University Press.

Cohen, Gerald A. 1979. 'The Labor Theory of Value and the Concept of Exploitation,' *Philosophy & Public Affairs* 8, no. 4, 338–360.

Cowen, Tyler, and Alex Tabarrok. 2015. *Modern Principles of Economics*. New York: Worth.

Elster, Jon. 1985. *Making Sense of Marx*. Cambridge: Cambridge University Press.

Elster, Jon. 2012. 'Hard and Soft Obscurantism in the Humanities and Social Sciences,' *Diogenes* 58, no. 1–2, 159–170.

Eyzaguirre, Hugo, Tawni Hunt Ferrarini, and J. Brian O'Roark. 2016. 'Textbook Confessions: Of Failures, Markets, and Government,' *Journal of Economics and Finance Education* 15, no. 2, 60–71.

Farrell, Henry. 2019. 'Socialists Will Never Understand Elizabeth Warren,' *Foreign Policy*, December 12. Accessible via: https://foreignpolicy.com/2019/12/12/elizabeth-socialist-understand-capitalism-pro-market-leftist/.

Fike, Rosemarie, and James Gwartney. 2015. 'Public Choice, Market Failure, and Government Failure in Principles Textbooks,' *The Journal of Economic Education* 46, no. 2, 207–218.

Fukuyama, Francis. 1989. 'The End of History?' *The National Interest* no. 16, 3–18.

Fukuyama, Francis. 1992. *The End of History and the Last Man*. New York: Free Press.

Geide-Stevenson, Doris, and Alvaro La Parra Perez. 2021. 'Consensus Among Economists 2020 – A Sharpening of the Picture,' Working Paper. Accessible via: https://www.aeaweb.org/conference/2022/preliminary/paper/HBhGyFD7/.

Gintis, Herbert. 1992. 'The Analytical Foundations of Contemporary Political Economy: A Comment on Hunt,' in Bruce Roberts and Susan Feiner (eds.), *Radical Economics*, 108–116. New York: Springer.

Gintis, Herbert. 2018. 'Economic Theory and Social Policy: Where We Are, Where We Are Headed,' *Evolutionary Studies in Imaginative Culture* 2, no. 1, 1–10.

Heyward, Anna. 2017. 'Since Trump's Victory, Democratic Socialists of America Has Become a Budding Political Force,' *The Nation*, December 21. Accessible via: https://www.thenation.com/article/archive/in-the-year-since-trumps-victory-democratic-socialists-of-america-has-become-a-budding-political-force/.

Holcombe, Randall G. 2016. *Advanced Introduction to Public Choice*. Northampton, MA: Elgar.

Levine, Andrew. 2003. *A Future for Marxism? Althusser, the Analytical Turn and the Revival of Socialist Theory*. London: Pluto Press.

Levine, Andrew, Sober, Elliott, and Erik Olin Wright. 1992. *Reconstructing Marxism: Essays on Explanation and the Theory of History*. London: Verso.

Marx, Karl, and Friedrich Engels. 2008 [1848]. *The Communist Manifesto*. London: Pluto Press.

Marx, Karl. 2010 [1894]. *Capital Volume III*. Electric Book: Lawrence & Wishart.

Munger, Michael. 2020. 'Was Karl Marx a Public-Choice Theorist?' *The Independent Review* 24, no. 4, 509–520.

Piketty, Thomas. 2014. *Capital in the Twenty-First Century*. Harvard: Harvard University Press.

Przeworski, Adam. 1986. *Capitalism and Social Democracy*. Cambridge: Cambridge University Press.

Przeworski, Adam. 2003. *States and Markets. A Primer in Political Economy*. Cambridge: Cambridge University Press.

Przeworski, Adam. 2021. 'What Have I Learned from Marx and What Still Stands?' *Politics and Society* 49, no. 4, 1–18.

Rajan, Raghuram, and Luigi Zingales. 2003. *Saving Capitalism from the Capitalists: Unleashing the Power of Financial Markets to Create Wealth and Spread Opportunity*. Princeton: Princeton University Press.

Robinson, Nathan J. 2019. *Why You Should be a Socialist*. New York: All Points Books.

Roser, Max, Ritchie, Hannah, and Bernadeta Dadonaite. 2013. 'Child and Infant Mortality,' *Our World in Data*. Accessible via: https://ourworldindata.org/child-mortality/.

Rosling, Hans, with Ola Rosling and Anna Rosling Rönnlund. 2018. *Factfulness: Ten Reasons We're Wrong about the World – and Why Things Are Better Than You Think*. New York: Flatiron Books.

Saad, Lydia. 2019. 'Socialism as Popular as Capitalism among Young Adults in U.S.,' *Gallup*. Accessible via: https://news.gallup.com/poll/268766/socialism-popular-capitalism-among-young-adults/.

Simmons, Randy. 2011. *Beyond Politics: The Roots of Government Failure*. California: The Independent Institute.

Sunkara, Bhaskar. 2020. *The Socialist Manifesto: The Case for Radical Politics in an Era of Extreme Inequality*. New York: Basic Books.

Teles, Steven M., and Henry Farrell. 2017. 'When Politics Drives Scholarship,' *Boston Review*. Accessible via: https://bostonreview.net/articles/henry-farrell-steven-m-teles-democracy-chains-response/.

The Conversation. 2021. 'Meet BreadTube, the YouTube Activists Trying to Beat the Far-Right at Their Own Game,' *The Conversation*, March 8. Accessible via: https://theconversation.com/meet-breadtube-the-youtube-activists-trying-to-beat-the-far-right-at-their-own-game-156125/.

Wood, Ellen Meiksins. 1995. 'Rational Choice Marxism: Is the Game Worth the Candle? (with a Postscript 1994),' in Terrell Carver and Paul Thomas (eds.), *Rational Choice Marxism*, 79–135. Basingstoke: Macmillan.Wright, Erik Olin. 1983. 'Giddens' Critique of Marxism,' *New Left Review* I/138, Mar/Apr.

Wright, Erik Olin. 1985. *Classes*. London: Verso.

Wright, Erik Olin. 2000. 'Class, Exploitation, and Economic Rents: Reflections on Sorenson's "Sounder Basis",' *American Journal of Sociology* 105, no. 6, 1559–1571.

Wright, Erik Olin. 2006. 'Falling into Marxism, Choosing to Stay,' in Alan Sica and Stephen Turner (eds.), *The Disobedient Generation: Social Theorists in the Sixties*, 325–349. Chicago: University of Chicago Press.

Wright, Erik Olin. 2009. 'Understanding Class,' *New Left Review* 60, Nov/Dec, 101–116.

Wright, Erik Olin. 2010. *Envisioning Real Utopias*. London: Verso.

Wright, Erik Olin. 2019. *How to Be an Anti-capitalist in the 21st Century*. London: Verso.

Wright, Erik Olin, Levine, Andrew, and Elliott Sober. 1992. *Reconstructing Marxism: Essays on Explanation and the Theory of History*. London: Verso.

Zingales, Luigi. 2012. *A Capitalism for the People: Recapturing the Lost Genius of American Prosperity*. New York: Basic Books.

2

HISTORIC ORIGINS

More political-economic in nature than cultural

Introduction: understanding the 'hockey-stick' graph

Throughout human history, centuries and even millennia had gone by without any significant, self-sustaining economic development occurring. This fact has nowadays become almost a cliché not worth explicitly mentioning, even though it remains one of the most important facts in all of human history. Almost any contemporary book dealing with economic history and progress either describes in some way or reprints the famous 'hockey-stick' graph, which shows world *per capita* income completely flat in the period from year 0 up until 1800 and then shooting up vertically in mere 200 years.[1] For that reason, I will not dwell on this fact but to mention, at the outset, that the emergence of capitalism in centuries around 1800 is primarily responsible for this radical change, which means that one has to understand why capitalism historically came to be (and why it appeared only so late in human history), if one wants to *understand* – not merely know – one of the most important historical facts.

In the 19th century, two classical sociological rivals, Karl Marx and Max Weber, offered two iconic and competing explanations of how the pre-capitalist world turned into a capitalist one. Marx saw the violent expropriation of the small peasantry of their customary landholdings, the rise of merchants and rich tenant yeoman farmers, and the enclosure of the commons as the most important social development responsible for the epochal transition. The country which experienced the transition in this ostensibly classic form most fully was, for him, England. 'And the history of this,' claimed Marx in volume one of *Capital*, 'is written in the annals of mankind in letters of blood and fire.'[2] So, Marx emphasized the causal role of *conflict* ('blood and fire') between a rising entrepreneurial farmer and bourgeois class wanting to trade and use free wage labour in production, and the ruling feudal class of aristocracy and monarchy reliant for their wealth on bonded labour and sinecures.

DOI: 10.4324/9781003305811-2

This conflictual and materialist explanation stands in sharp contrast to the more pristine and culturalist hypothesis advanced by Weber. Although Weber is, like Marx, one of the most important classical conflict sociologists, he nevertheless saw a sudden change in values and attitudes through the incidental emergence of Protestantism as the key causal variable responsible for the transition from feudalism to capitalism. He agreed that England was where capitalism rose in its most worked-out form, and he did not ignore the expropriation of the peasantry as an important background condition in the transition, but for him cultural-religious change after the end of the Middle Ages was the key missing ingredient.

We know much, much more today about the transition than either Marx or Weber did (and could) know. Nevertheless, the competing materialist and culturalist explanations for the emergence of the modern economy are still with us, albeit in an updated form. Which is closer to the truth? What brought capitalism into existence? In this chapter, I first present and examine three prominent and influential cultural explanations of the transition – besides Weber's I also look at the recent important theses proposed by Joseph Henrich and Joel Mokyr. I use simple descriptive statistics to demonstrate empirical flaws burdening the explanations, and I also draw, where appropriate, on more sophisticated existing quantitative studies examining the various hypotheses. I find these prominent cultural explanations at least moderately lacking, so in the second part of the chapter, I move on to an alternative materialist explanation that is more consistent with the presented data.

Drawing on older and recent historiography, new institutional economics, and contemporary Marxist historical sociology, I explain why agrarian capitalism at first started emerging only in the English countryside around the 15th and 16th century, and why this was – *contra* Marx – a very unlikely historical occurrence, not one prefigured by the grand sweep of history. Moreover, conflict and expropriation were only one part of the transitional process, not the only one. On the other hand – *contra* the culturalists – I show the process had more to do with structural economic change, power, interests, rationality, and conflict than with shifting cultural norms and attitudes. Lastly, I offer, in a similar political-economic vein, a structural geopolitical explanation for the spread of capitalism during the 19th century from its initial birthplace to other countries, such as France, Germany, and Japan. Again I show that cultural change could not have had much to do with the transition, at least not as an original prime mover.

Capitalism as a creature of culture

The 'beloved myth' of Protestantism and capitalism[3]

'In a theory that could only have been thought up by an assimilated German Jew,' writes Steven Pinker in *Enlightenment Now*, 'the sociologist Max Weber proposed in 1905 that capitalism depended on a "Protestant ethic".'[4] Pinker snide remark might be apposite, but the idea that the Protestant cultural revolution radically transformed the behavioural dispositions of West European populations after the end of the Middle Ages has nevertheless been one of the most iconic sociological theses of the past two centuries.[5] We cannot ignore it, no matter what its peculiar socio-psychologic genealogy. In fact, it was in the past and continues to be today one of the central starting, if not ending, points in many attempts – sociological or otherwise – to explain the origins of the modern economic system.

Weber's idea is simple and intuitively plausible, which is perhaps what explains its staying power. He argued that Protestant values and beliefs, especially asceticism and the notion of predestination, influenced believers in such a way that they worked harder and were more prone to saving money and reinvesting profits into production, instead of spending most of it on unproductive conspicuous and luxury consumption.[6] Protestants worked harder, Weber argued, because under this new religious framework one's work was thought of as a nothing less but a service to God himself. They were also more frugal and reinvested surpluses, instead of spending them, because for Protestants there is great value in denying oneself the pleasures of this world. Perhaps most importantly, Calvinists thought that by working hard – and succeeding in business adventures – one can find out whether one has been chosen by God to be saved when rapture comes. Although the notion of predestination posits that God has already picked the chosen ones, surely the Almighty would not have picked those who fail at what they do. So, how does one resolve the anxiety felt by the burning question of whether one has, or has not, been chosen for salvation? By opening a business and (consciously or not) doing everything possible not to turn out a failure.

Thus, Weber argued, a new set of cultural values and beliefs that have been adopted in certain countries after the 16th and 17th century unintendedly produced a new set of economic behaviours, a completely new economic rationality. Markets had existed for millennia in virtually all civilizations. But this exotic new way – a capitalist way – of participating in market affairs had not been known before. And these incipient capitalist behaviours were what paved the way for the various capitalist practices, institutions, and phenomena which puzzled early sociologists and political economists, but which come as second nature to us today. Phenomena such as constant and significant yearly increases in GDP (gross domestic product) per capita, constant improvement of labour productivity, the Industrial Revolution, market competition, etc. So, Weber's proposed causal chain is simple: (1) changing norms and beliefs due to the appearance of Protestantism → (2) changing economic behaviour → (3) the emergence of capitalist macrosocial trends of development.

Now, Weber was careful not to argue that Protestantism was the only, or even the only important, factor in the transition to capitalism. He famously criticised Karl Marx for his one-sided materialism, which Weber warned was not to be replaced by an equally naïve and one-sided idealism. But both he and the prevailing sociological interpretation of his thesis were quite clear that Protestantism was, at least at the beginning of the emerging capitalist world, one of the crucial necessary conditions for the transition. And, indeed, a superficial glance at history suggests he might have been right. After all, Protestant England was the first capitalist economy in Early Modern Europe. It was also the birthplace of the later Industrial Revolution. Moreover, outside Europe, the Protestant English colonies in North America, which later became the United States of America, were also a somewhat early example of capitalism. (Critics, it is true, are quick to point to the decidedly non-Protestant examples of thriving capitalism from the second half of the 20th century such as Hong Kong, Singapore, Taiwan, Japan, or South Korea. In *Why Nations Fail*, for example, Acemoglu and Robinson chastise Weber in such a way.[7] Surely this settles the debate? Alas, it does not, at least not wholly; Weber primarily used his thesis to explain the *early* transitions, and he allowed non-religious factors to be the main reasons responsible for later transitions.)

Unfortunately, even though Weber provided these and other interesting impressionistic evidence in favour of his thesis, he did not subject it to any kind of systematic quantitative interrogation. Fortunately for us, several such investigations have been conducted in the past three decades, and we can now use them to scrutinize his idea more thoroughly.

Most of the existing studies find no historical effect of Protestantism on the emergence of capitalism, or, to be more precise, on modern economic development.[8] One team of sociologists measured the effect simply by examining how much the GDP per capita of different countries – majority Protestant and majority Catholic – had grown in the centuries following the Protestant revolution.[9] The correlations they uncovered do point in the right direction but are not statistically significant (p value is above 0.05).

A sophisticated recent study looked at the impact of Protestantism on economic growth in the Holy Roman Empire between 1300 and 1900.[10] This test seems especially appropriate, as large religious differences existed between the various cities of the empire, which can now be statistically exploited as a natural experiment. In fact, the cities under examination were either entirely Protestant or entirely Catholic after 1500. The study finds 'no effects of Protestantism on economic growth ... the growth performances of Catholic and Protestant cities are virtually indistinguishable.'[11]

Another paper is unfortunately mostly limited to the 19th century but looks at variety of development measures, such as GDP per capita, bank deposits per capita, savings per capita, date of founding of the stock exchange, extension of railroad networks, and the share of male labour force in agriculture and industry.[12] If Weber is correct, one would expect all these measures to be highest in the most Protestant European countries and much lower in Catholic countries. However, except for the correlation between Protestantism and savings per capita, there are no other significant statistical relationships. As the authors conclude, there is precious little evidence that 'Protestantism caused, facilitated, or was in any way instrumental in the development of industrial capitalism.'[13]

In a famous paper, Acemoglu and colleagues find that their main result, which is that whether particular European colonies economically developed or not was dependent on the mortality faced by the settlers and the institutions they set up, remains the same even when controlling for religion.[14] This does not tell us much about how and why the first European countries became capitalist after the Middle Ages, but it does suggest that Protestantism could not have much to do with why North America and Australia adopted capitalism, while South America and Africa did not.

Nevertheless, there are a few temporally and spatially limited studies suggesting that, even though Protestantism is not either the necessary or sufficient condition of development pointed to by Weber, there are some (late historical) religious correlates of development in certain places. One recent study focuses on Western Switzerland in the late 19th century. It found Protestants to be more likely than Catholics to migrate from the countryside to the cities, which is a measure of economic development.[15] Another study covers late 19th-century Prussia, and it found Protestantism to have an effect on economic development.[16] The authors also managed to tease out a possible mechanism linking the two. Interestingly, it turns out not to be Weber's asceticism, frugality, hard work, or predestination – rather, the mechanism is the increased literacy rates found among Protestants as compared to Catholics.

These latter positive studies notwithstanding, there are other empirical (and theoretical) issues that cast a large shadow of doubt over Weber's thesis. For example, some of the business practices that Weber argued could only have been ideologically legitimized by Protestantism actually already existed in Catholic Mexico all the way back in the 16th century.[17] To be more specific, despite the Church's strictures against the sins of commerce, 'Mexico developed early an active system of credit and loans.'[18] More fundamentally, the sheer timing and nature of virtually all Western European transitions to capitalism (except, perhaps, for the English case) suggest Protestantism simply could not have been the, or even a, crucial variable. However, before delving into this objection, let us first turn to an illustrious 21st-century reworking of Weber's cultural explanation for capitalism, which is both more theoretically complex and more intricately empirically corroborated.

How the church shaped Western psychology ... and led to modernity?

Joseph Henrich is one of the most important interdisciplinary social scientists of the past decade. He is a prominent proponent of cultural evolutionary theory (very briefly explained below) and is, perhaps, most recognized for his 'WEIRD hypothesis.'[19] WEIRD is an acronym for Western, Educated, Industrialized, Rich, and Democratic. These are the main five (historically peculiar) social characteristics most Western populations have now possessed for a few centuries. More importantly, these characteristics, uncommon in world history and even in most of the world in the 20th century, have been implicitly taken for granted in almost all psychological studies of human behaviour. For Henrich, two important implications flow from this fact. First, owing to their spatial and temporal rarity, WEIRD minds are not really representative of the average human, so psychological studies performed on WEIRD minds – and almost all are – should not be taken as telling us much about human behaviour in general. Second, we must explain how one tiny corner of the world suddenly, and very late in human history, became WEIRD.

Henrich's hypothesis about the rise of modernity in the West can be broken down into five key causal steps.[20]

First, since around the year 500 CE, the Church started radically transforming the prevailing norms around family life and kinship ties in Europe. Specifically, polygamy was forbidden and monogamy imposed instead. Cousin marriages, and later on even marrying one's more distant kin, were forbidden practices. The formation of neo-local residences was encouraged, meaning that new couples now had to move away from their parents' households and had to set up their own separate homes.

Second, in the following centuries, the European populations under the auspices of the Church slowly started adopting these new norms. Henrich suggests this was primarily achieved through unconscious psychological imitation. Cultural evolutionary theorists in general hypothesize that humans possess a variety of psychological mechanisms that can ultimately be traced back to processes of genetic selection, but the proximal operation of which is highly sensitive to existing cultural contexts. These mechanisms induce people to behave in various ways. One mechanism is called 'prestige bias,' and it induces people to copy the beliefs and actions of prestigious social actors such as community leaders, elders, priests, and kings. For Henrich, the Church was one key prestigious social actor imitated by the common folk due to prestige bias.

Third, all these normative and later behavioural changes started, over time, transforming the broader social environment populated by Europeans. Lowered rates of cousin marriages and increased rates of neo-local residences meant that people increasingly had to interact with (complete) strangers. They had to look beyond the family in order to marry. They found themselves living in a different village or town when they moved away from their parents. They were more likely to (have to) turn to a stranger – instead of a family member or a close friend – if they needed help in this new environment. The same was true if they wanted to be successful in life, or if they simply wanted to carry out a project requiring cooperation of multiple people.

Fourth, this new social environment of increasing interactions with strangers led to new radical changes in norms and behaviour. For example, people started becoming increasingly impersonal and universalistic in their worldviews and actions. They were less and less likely to support, sanction, and enact particularistic norms which function to protect and benefit one's kin, close friends, and the local community. Instead, they were more likely to evaluate the world with less of an obvious bias, applying the same general norms to most, or even all, people in a country or region. In the changed social landscape, particularism ceased being as ecologically rational as it had been before. Moreover, feelings of trust were no longer limited solely to family and friends but were themselves becoming more universalistic. Generalized social trust started emerging. Even more fundamentally, conformism started going down so that people no longer merely copied what family and friends were doing but were becoming more individualistic and creative in how they acted.

Lastly, the normative and behavioural shifts from the previous point are, for Henrich, the key to understanding why after 1500 Europe, but not Africa or Asia, firmly set its sights on modernity. Rapid urbanization ensued, and markets and commerce were spreading far and wide. Capitalism – requiring constant impersonal interactions with strangers – was being born. What is more, modern politics started taking shape. Nepotism was looked down upon, corruption was increasingly viewed as illegitimate, and democratic practices, where the voice of each individual counts equally, were taking root. Thus, between 1500 and 1800, Europe started sharply diverging from the rest of the world.

In contrast to Weber, Henrich has impressive quantitative data corroborating his causal story.[21] To my mind, two pieces of evidence are crucial. First, strong correlations have been uncovered between, on the one hand, the years of exposure of a region to the Church's influence from 500 to 1500 and, on the other, the various measures of how impersonal, universalistic, and trusting people of that region are. The more Church exposure a region got in the past, the more impartial and trusting people are today. These correlations are not only strong but also robust, holding even when one statistically controls for a variety of possible hidden variables. Second, if one compares the map showing kinship intensity of various ethnolinguistic groups around the world in 1900 to the map depicting the historic territorial reach of the Church, one is struck by how visually tight the relationship is. The majority of Europe, North America, South America, and Australia – the Church's territory – are marked as having the lowest kinship intensity. On the other hand, Africa, the Middle East, and most of Asia (excepting Russia, Japan, and Thailand) have middling-to-highest kinship intensity.

Henrich is careful not to explicitly argue that Church exposure was the *only* thing that mattered in the transition. He admits that other factors 'may have played some role, even if minor in some cases.'[22] But he claims outright that it was the 'psychological changes [that] fostered … the subsequent development of impersonal markets, competing voluntary associations, … [and] representative governance.'[23] It is not precisely clear what he means by 'fostered': were they just one of the myriad causes of no particular importance; one of the more prominent causes; one of the most important causes; the most important cause? However, he obviously significantly prefers his hypothesis to the others and, given how important it is to his book, assigns it a crucial, key explanatory role. Indeed, it is hard not to get the impression from his book that his suggested cultural causes are the *primum mobile* of the whole story.

It can hardly be doubted that the Church tried to impose radically new norms and beliefs upon European populations after the year 500. It also cannot seriously be doubted that the Church was at least partially, if not mostly, successful in doing so, nor that people started behaving at least somewhat differently when they adopted the new norms, which is certainly not causally unimportant for explaining the rise of Europe. Some historians, such as Charles Freeman, do argue forcefully that Henrich is quite mistaken on several counts, and in certain respects the critics may turn out to be right in the end.[24] To my mind, however, the main weakness of Henrich's cultural-religious explanation of the transition to capitalism lies elsewhere.

Given that Henrich insists on the Church's influence being at least a key importance in the transition, 'fostering' it, one would expect capitalism to spring up more or less concurrently in the most affected European countries. Henrich's own data of bishopric exposure indicate that England, Germany, France, Italy, the Netherlands, Belgium, and Switzerland had identical, i.e. the longest, exposure to the Church's normative influence between 500 and 1500. A very long exposure is also reported for Spain, Portugal, Denmark, Sweden, Scotland, Ireland, and Austria. Here, we seem to have a clear testable implication of Henrich's theory: we should expect all these countries, especially the first group, to move to capitalism early and roughly simultaneously. The trouble is, this is not the case at all.

Figure 2.1 shows the movement of GDP per capita between 1400 and 1800 in a sample of countries from both groups for which we have reliable long-term data.[25] Of the sampled countries, only England evinces signs of modern, capitalist economic development after 1600. It, but not the others, shows a clear

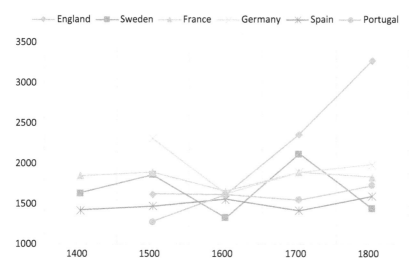

FIGURE 2.1 GDP per capita of selected European countries between 1400 and 1800 (adjusted for inflation and differences in purchasing power across countries).

Source: Maddison Project Database (Broadberry et al. 2015; Schön and Krantz 2015; Ridolfi 2016; Krantz 2017; Palma and Reis 2019; Bolt and van Zanden 2020) via Our World in Data (Roser 2013).

trend of continuous, self-sustaining economic growth. The other countries are completely separate from England, demonstrating only signs of pre-modern economic stagnation all the way up to 1800.

Figure 2.2 shows a similarly dual trend in the movement of agricultural labour productivity.[26] England stands alone, moving away from the others after 1600. The other countries show no significant positive changes in productivity from 1500 up to 1800, only stagnation. In fact, after three centuries of opportunities for improving productivity, all countries, but England, were at a lower level in 1800 than they had been in 1500.

That the growth of English productivity really took off after 1600, while before that – say between 1250 and 1550 – even England itself had been exhibiting the same stagnant Malthusian trend in productivity as the rest of Europe is also confirmed by very recent quantitative research and new estimates.[27]

Other indicators of capitalist development paint a similar comparative picture.

Take, first, the ratio of income received by labourers to the price of basic subsistence goods, an important indicator of the rate and quality of economic development. After 1600, the ratio is continuously climbing in London, while in Vienna and Florence, it is falling. Moreover, the ratio's level in Vienna and Florence is comparable to the ratio's level in the clearly pre-capitalist Delhi and Beijing.[28]

Second, we can take a look at the incredible transformation of the agricultural population in England. In these terms, England again moves completely away from almost all of continental Europe between 1500 and 1800.[29] In 1500, the share of agricultural population in England was 74%, making England one of the more backward European countries according to this criterion.[30] In the

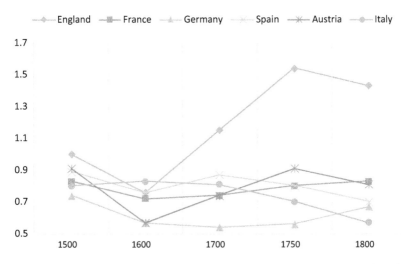

FIGURE 2.2 Agricultural labour productivity (output per worker) in selected European countries between 1500 and 1800. England in 1500 is indexed as 1.
Source: Allen (2000).

following three centuries, however, the share more than halved to 35%.[31] No other country, apart from the Netherlands, comes even close to this.[32] In 1500, peasants made up about 75% of the population in Germany, France, Austria, and Poland. In 1800, the shares still stood at around 60% in all these countries. In Italy and Spain, where in 1500 the share was comparatively lower (62% and 65%, respectively), nothing much changed in the next three centuries. In 1800, the Italian and Spanish shares dropped only by a few percentage points.

Lastly, compare how around 1600 the price of labour (the wage) had been in a 1:1 ratio with respect to the price of capital in England, France, and Austria.[33] After 1600, the ratio started shifting in England, such that the price of labour soon outstripped that of capital and was continuously rising higher, reaching a ratio of 1.75:1 around 1800. The ratio in France and Austria stayed the same (1:1) for the whole 200-year period.

These data suggest that, first, Henrich's Europe-wide story does not hold up at least as far as the emergence of capitalism and modern economic growth go. Capitalism *did* come about soon after the Middle Ages had ended; but, it did so *only in England* (and, in the Netherlands, but this case of early capitalism is extremely complicated and uneven; see note 43). Moreover, other candidate countries such as Germany, France, Italy, Sweden, and Spain started moving in the capitalist direction *only after 1800*, well into the 19th century. (And they did so quite abruptly and for geopolitical, not normative reasons, a point which will be dealt with later on.) This is a date far removed from the one claimed by Henrich's Church thesis, according to which significant economic shifts should have been occurring in the whole of Western Europe already in 1500, 1600, and 1700.

The data also suggest, second, that something exceptional started happening in England around the end of the Middle Ages, something which has to be investigated further.

Neither Protestantism nor Christianity, but a culture of innovation?

Weber and Henrich notwithstanding, all is not yet lost for the family of cultural explanations of capitalist development. In *Enlightenment Now*, for example, Steven Pinker points to a different cultural-ideational explanation of the transition, one that has been specifically applied to the English case. So, why was *England* – not Europe, nor even Western Europe – exceptional? As Pinker tells us, 'The most obvious cause was the application of science to the improvement of material life, leading to what the economic historian Joel Mokyr calls "the enlightened economy."'[34]

Mokyr's hypothesis is that the Scientific Revolution of the 16th and 17th century and the Enlightenment movement of the 18th century were the key detonators of modern economic growth, itself most clearly exemplified by the British Industrial Revolution around 1800. It was by using reason, thinking scientifically, and experimenting that people finally found an inexhaustible source of practical solutions to the challenges of the human condition. Reason and controlled observation, paired with a belief in the improvability of mankind, opened the doors to rapid technological innovation, ushering in capitalist industrial development and growth hitherto unimaginable. In short, the British Industrial Revolution was created by individual inventors and entrepreneurs, such as James Watt, Richard Arkwright, or Thomas Newcomen, who ostensibly worked or communicated with the leading scientists of the era.

At first glance, this is a plausible story. But, the economic historian Robert Allen examined the background of 79 important British inventors in the 17th and 18th century.[35] He finds that although around half of them had 'some connection' to scientists and the Enlightenment, the connections are sometimes tenuous and industry specific. As he says,

> The importance, therefore, of Enlightenment links depends on which industries one thinks were central to the Industrial Revolution. Steam, of course, was important in the long run, and in that context Enlightenment links mattered. In the late eighteenth and early nineteenth centuries, however, textiles and metals had much greater economic impact. Using that yardstick, the Industrial Enlightenment did not matter much.[36]

However, Mokyr's case does not wholly rest on the claim that the Enlightenment mattered via personal contacts. The claim is also made that British inventors – having a scientific and Enlightenment background or not – most definitely used experiments to get at their inventions. This, I think, is undoubtedly correct, and it could then be claimed further that this itself is evidence of the Scientific Revolution and Enlightenment being key to economic development. Such reasoning, however, is not perfectly sound. Inventions in any time and place are rarely made but through experimentation. So, the very fact that inventions were occurring in Britain during the Industrial Revolution could not – even absent Enlightenment – have happened without significant experimentation. Therefore, this fact by itself cannot be evidence for Mokyr's hypothesis. Of course, we can still ask whether British inventors used experiments *because* they were influenced by Enlightenment culture. Perhaps they did. Or perhaps they did not. The mere fact that they experimented and innovated does not, itself, resolve this issue.

Most importantly and lastly, even though Mokyr's hypothesis is presented as specifically designed to account for the economic rise of Britain, one is again struck as before by the fact that the Scientific Revolution and the Enlightenment were *Europe-wide phenomena*, certainly reaching countries like Germany, France, and Italy. (Indeed, as he himself shows, many key scientific ideas and experiments applied in England *originated in France*.) How can these two intellectual movements be the most important cause of modern economic growth, in general, and the Industrial Revolution, specifically, if the latter two happened between 1600 and 1800 only in England, while at the same time other Enlightenment countries economically stagnated or declined? The timeframe fits, but the territory does not.[37]

Moreover, how come the British were busy experimenting and innovating, and most importantly *applying these breakthroughs in production*, in the 17th and 18th century, but the similarly enlightened Frenchmen and Germans were not? Perhaps economy-wide experimentation in production and rapid technological innovation does not flow necessarily (or even likely) out of the Enlightenment movement. Something more structural is needed that actively incentivizes economic actors to be willing to constantly innovate and improve production technology, thereby effecting modern economic development and industrialization.

A contemporary materialist explanation of the transition

Mainstream historiography, new institutional economics, and Marxist historical sociology all teach us a crucial lesson about development.[38] Modern, post-Malthusian, capitalist economic growth has been, for completely rational reasons, tremendously exceptional in human history. Only under very specific and (up until now) rare social conditions – i.e. when capitalist structures and institutions prevail – are the main economic actors in a society both willing and able to engage in the type of economic behaviour that results in capitalist economic development.

Now, it is (approximately) true that most people everywhere and in any historical period behave as they do because they are pursuing their interests. Based on this simple observation, one would have thought that, because strong economic development is so obviously in people's interests, they will spontaneously act in such a way as to bring it about. But this overlooks the crucial sociological point that people are always pursuing their interest *within a social environment*, an environment which dictates what precisely they have to do in order to secure their interests. The general causal framework through which societal dynamics should be understood schematically looks like this: (1) existing structures/institutions → (2) incentives for behaviour → (3) microsocial behaviour → (4) macrosocial patterns and outcomes.

When, for example, people live under (1) capitalist structures and institutions, i.e. secure property rights, market-dependent subsistence, and strong market competition which increases the possibility of going out of business, they are faced with (2) specific capitalist incentives. These incentives make it rational for them to, for example, (3) accumulate surpluses and plough them back into production to create even more (because now these surpluses will remain safely in their own hands and will not be expropriated away) and to constantly strive to raise labour productivity through technological innovation (because otherwise they will not be able to cut costs, lower prices, and attract customers but will be outcompeted by other producers and become bankrupt). Over time, this results in (4) the tendency towards industrialization and modern economic development of a society, as producers constantly search for new, more efficient methods of production and labour-shedding, productivity-increasing technological innovation. Moreover, increasing (agricultural) specialization and productivity, which slowly result in an abundance of food per capita, release people from the need to engage in farming themselves, which further enables them to move from the countryside to the city. It also enables them to start producing non-agricultural, industrial goods.

Consider, on the other hand, a pre-capitalist society where the vast majority of direct producers – usually peasants – are politically tied to a small plot of land, are pushed to bare subsistence by the daily political exploitation they face, and are not entitled to the full fruits of their labour.[39]

In such a society, people are, first, not dependent for their subsistence on the market but can instead themselves work the small plot of land they have in order to survive. Thus, they are under no external competitive pressure to cut costs to stay in business through innovation, increasing efficiency, and raising of the productivity of their labour. Moreover, given the vicissitudes of pre-modern agriculture, the typical small peasant is not likely to voluntarily (absent the competitive pressure emanating from the market) risk becoming market-dependent by trying to specialize and bet his whole livelihood on one crop which he could, in principle, produce more efficiently if he abandoned the typical strategy of diversified subsistence production. In short, pre-capitalist direct producers, if they are rational, tend to adopt a 'safety-first' production strategy, which involves diversifying, not specializing production.

Second, they know that even if they wanted to create more output by mechanizing production and being more efficient, this extra surplus would likely be stolen by the exploiting political elite, i.e. the king and aristocracy. Moreover, highly exploited peasants simply do not have the capability, seeing as how they are dirt-poor, to save up and invest in new machinery. Such feudal, or pre-capitalist, incentives being what they are, not much surplus accumulation, investing, saving, or innovating will be done by the masses. Under the circumstances, this is simply not a rational course of action.

Meanwhile, in this same society where the king and aristocracy need not work, be productive, or constantly scramble to stay in business in order to live lavishly – instead, given the prevailing social structure, they can simply use the power of the sword and take from the peasants what they produce or coerce them into working for free on lands of the elite – they too will not behave as a capitalist would. They will accumulate surpluses but then primarily invest them in military resources, luxury goods, and political ventures instead of in economic production and innovation. Such 'political accumulation' enables them to take even more from the poor (and from other members of the ruling class) in the future.[40] After all, why bother producing stuff and cutting costs when you are not dependent on the competitive market for survival?

Even the main market participants, such as merchants and traders, are under no compulsion to innovate and cut costs in pre-capitalist societies because the ruling class grants them state-sanctioned trading monopolies. In the past, traders were typically able to 'buy cheap and then sell dear.'[41] They moved goods from where they could be bought cheaply to places where they could be sold at a higher price. Strong market competition and free entry of new participants into the market, two institutions that would have made such a zero-sum trading practice much less ubiquitous, were unfortunately absent.

In short, in pre-capitalist societies, neither the masses nor the middle class, let alone the ruling class, has a robust, systematic incentive to behave productively in the medium to long term, so one should not expect modern economic development to be unleashed in such a society even as centuries and millennia go by. And because this stagnant pre-capitalist society is in equilibrium, no one has a rational reason to unilaterally deviate from how they are behaving.

Stickiness and change in social orders

This brings us to an interesting theoretical puzzle, which will detain us in the following sections. The puzzle is how a society whose structure is such that the majority of economic actors have no strong, persistent incentive (or ability) to act in a way that would result in sustained economic development, over time nevertheless manages to have its structure transformed so that vastly different incentives form and, consequently, vastly different economic behaviour ensues. In short, how did a stable, equilibrated *feudal* England turn into a stable, equilibrated *capitalist* England?

A general, superficial answer is that people – either the elite or the masses – at some point in time have to press for change in the social structure. One would think that if, or when, people demand a transition from feudalism to capitalism, it will probably happen. But, this is a very unsatisfactory answer. Note, again, that societies tend to be in equilibrium, which means that a fundamental structural change is unlikely to happen spontaneously at any point in time. Those who would benefit from change and so have, at least abstractly, an interest in change are simply too weak to enact it, while those who would be hurt by it, and thus do not want it, are powerful enough to resist it.

One solution to the puzzle emerges when we turn our attention to sudden, unexpected, and powerful exogenous shocks.[42] Deadly epidemics, deep economic (or ecological) crises, destructive civil or interstate wars, or even just a credible threat of invasion are all phenomena that can almost in an instant importantly change the balance of power currently existing between different groups and, through that, their structural incentives and capacities.[43] Thus, exogenous shocks can, for a period of time, knock a society out of its equilibrium, which can, in turn, lead social actors to behave in a way they otherwise would not have pursued. For example, if the balance of power in society is significantly shifted following a shock (due, perhaps, to the elite losing an important source of income), the masses might be momentarily empowered to press for change such as the abolition of serfdom, universal suffrage, and civil rights. Even without a significant reordering of power-relations, exogenous shocks can incentivize social actors to behave in a way they, otherwise, would not have. For example, significant economic or political reforms that would increase the welfare of a society or take the whole social structure of the society in a very different future direction, but which for rational, selfish reasons members of the elite presently do not want to enact, are more likely to be passed if the elite is threatened by the geopolitical pressure of a foreign power. The unintended, long-term consequences of the novel way in which the elite (or other social actors) react to a shock can be profound.

It is crucial to understand that the same exogenous shocks need not have the same social impact in two different societies.[44] The nature of the impact is itself conditioned by the various (even small) endogenous differences that, owing to historical randomness, can emerge and persist between societies for decades or even centuries before a shock hits. For example, as will be seen below in much more detail, the fact that English feudalism – in comparison to French feudalism – started out with a much higher degree of political centralization and a much higher proportion of land under direct elite control had an immense influence on how the same exogenous shock – the Black Death in mid-14th century – affected both societies and their future transformation. The French and English feudal elites reacted to the shock differently because the starting endogenous character-istics of French and English feudalism had been different.[45]

Capitalism emerged in the English countryside

Serfdom in England was being steadily abolished only around the year 1400, a whole century after it had already disappeared in France.[46] Facing a more unified and powerful ruling class, English peasants in the past were simply too weak to resist their lords in such a fashion as their French counterparts had been able to do within the context of a more anarchical, more characteristically feudal France in the 13th century. And even though the famous 1381 Peasants' Revolt in England was put down in the end, this great rebellion was a sign of changing times on the island.

After the early 14th-century famines and especially after the Black Death ravaged through Europe around 1350, many peasants had died, which increased the peasant class' bargaining power vis-à-vis the lords. This was especially crucial in England. Labour was becoming a scarce and coveted resource, as peasants in the past had been the main source of lordly income both through the institution of serfdom, whereby serfs were required to work for free on their lord's demesne for a few days per week, and through regular rent-extraction and labour hiring. Thus, the death of so many peasants hurt the English lords financially. Moreover, dead peasants left behind vacant land, which, in turn, significantly increased the otherwise strongly restricted migratory chances of the still living peasants, tied as they typically were to the land by their landlords. They now suddenly became much more mobile and could, thus, credibly threaten their landlords with flight if the latter did not acquiesce to the former's demands. As the 1381 Peasants' Revolt exemplifies, English peasants were well aware of these changing circum-stances and used them to try and get rid of serfdom by pressuring the aristocracy through collective action. They succeeded around 1400, and now the English lordly class was faced with two critical issues: how to replace this important source of income with a new one, and what to do with their own enormous demesne lands which now laid unworked by their former serfs.

Even though this was not their absolutely preferred course of action, they opted to engross their already historically large demesnes (now unworked by the serfs) by adjoining newly vacant land to them. Then they leased this lordly land to the richer stratum of peasants and other relevant actors.[47] This was one way in which they could recuperate income losses from the abolition of serfdom. Moreover, it enabled them to sidestep the novel issue, in light of massive population decline, of high and rising price of labour-power they would need to hire to work the fields in a more voluntary way. The sheer amount of land they held enabled them, but not, for instance, the comparatively weaker French ruling class, to avert the looming income crisis simply by renting out land (and not, as in the French case, by building and being absorbed by an absolutist tax-office state).[48] In the early 15th century, English demesnes 'amounted to between two and three times the amount of demesne in France which was only around eight to ten percent of the land.'[49]

And, indeed, this is what had happened. As the famed historian Christopher Dyer writes in a new historiographical account,

> farming and farmers were not entirely new around 1400. There was novelty, however, in the leasing of some thousands of demesnes, varying in size between 100 and 500 acres, and amounting to a quarter or a fifth of the land in lowland England.[50]

The historian Spencer Dimmock describes it similarly, claiming,

> English lords were compelled to lease out their demesnes in order to maintain themselves as lords in the late fourteenth and early fifteenth century … This entailed the transference … of between one-fifth and one-third of all cultivable land in England to peasants, merchants and lesser gentry, although the vast majority of it went to wealth peasants.[51]

This was nothing short of revolutionary. '[T]aking on a lord's demesne,' writes Dyer,

> transformed their whole way of life and economic behaviour. The peasants who made up the majority of the new generation of farmers had previous experience of managing a holding of perhaps 30 acres. Overnight they found themselves having to run an enterprise of 300 acres.[52]

What was so revolutionary at this point was not just the extraordinary amount of transferred land but also that the leases were economic, or negotiated, in nature – and temporary.[53] That meant that the lords started leasing them to those peasants who were willing to pay the most, promising the peasants they can keep the surplus generated above the rent, and it also meant that peasants knew the offer will be made again in a few years' time. This was crucial because it set up two new structural incentives. First, if the lords wanted to get rid of their lands, they had to compete with each other in the market for land, offering the land at competitive prices. Second, if the peasants who received the land wanted to keep it down the line, when the temporary contract ended, they had to compete with each other in the market for agricultural products so as to be able to offer lords the highest amount in the next 'auction' and reap the reward.

Now, by mid-to-late 15th and early 16th century, a rising number of rich peasants (called yeomen) started facing a very different economic environment, one in which efficient specialization in a single crop (instead of inefficiently diversifying production to meet all of one's own subsistence needs directly) had become much more attractive than before. And with specialization came market-dependence. Tenant farmers now needed to buy basic subsistence goods on the market because, due to specialization, they stopped themselves producing everything they needed to survive. Market-dependence induced them to behave more efficiently, seeking new ways (and technologies) of production in order to secure enough income to be able to buy everything they needed on the market from others. As Dyer describes it,

> The most important adjustment required of the farmers came from their exposure to the full forces of the market, as they moved from a holding in which most of the crops were absorbed in the subsistence of the tenant's household, to one so large that at least three-quarters of its produce was sold.[54]

The incredible shift underway, first in the economic structure and consequently in economic behaviour, can be gleaned from how the average farm sizes in England changed in this period. No longer was land being held in the form of small subsistence plots, and no longer was it being constantly subdivided and fragmented further, as is otherwise the (rational) rule for peasants in pre-capitalist societies. If the average farm in 1279 amounted to less than 14 acres (a typical smallholding), this had increased to 72 acres by the year 1600. In other words, the farms tended to be consolidated and had grown to very significant sizes (much later, around 1800, the average size shot up even further to 151 acres).[55] Crucially, farms up to 60 acres can be worked without depending on external, hired labour, while 'farms above 60 acres would ... have had to rely on ever-larger supplies of wage labour.'[56] In pre-capitalist China, to make a stark comparison, the average farm in 1400 had amounted to 4.2 acres, which then slowly *declined* throughout the centuries so that, by 1850, the average size was only 2.5 acres.

Even historians who disagree among themselves on particular details, such as Brenner and Robert Allen, concur 'that by the 16th century the yeoman class had acquired a substantial proprietary interest in the land, and thus an incentive to innovate.'[57] To be sure, Dyer warns we cannot claim that by 1550 England had already been fully capitalist (which is also obvious from Figures 2.1 and 2.2).

But, at the same time, the first key, fundamental structural changes were very much occurring at that time. With especially the first two legs of the classic capitalist triad – made up of the capitalist landlords, capitalist tenant farmers, and the working class – slowly emerging in the mid-to-late 15th and early 16th century, the path towards capitalism had been unintentionally laid down in the English countryside. The historian Bruce Campbell agrees, pointing out how in that time

> tenures became "contractual" rather than "manorial" and rents began to become "competitive" rather than "customary". … Thereby the way was opened to the establishment from the close of the middle ages of a new and economically more fruitful working relationship between lords, tenants, and semi-landless labourers. Already the foundations had been laid for the precocious emergence of agrarian capitalism ….[58]

Following these initial, but crucial, property developments in the century after the Black Plague, landlords and yeomen made another crucial, and this time more intentional, step. They started expropriating the small peasantry and enclosing the common land. Seeing how the economically leased land has been farmed more efficiently and generated high returns both for tenants and landlords, the latter now

> sought to dispossess small, customary tenants of their rented land, which was farmed in strips, and let it out in large units on "economic" leases rather than customary copyhold; to appropriate part of the commons and similarly let it out. … This was bitterly resisted.[59]

Over time, landlords working with the monarchy were able to crush the small peasantry. This was the bloody and fiery process of 'primitive accumulation' Marx emphasized – *overemphasized* – in his account of the transition from feudalism to capitalism.

Dimmock concurs with this assessment and himself discusses acts of land enclosure, engrossment, and peasant rebellion in the mid-15th and 16th century in a new case study of medieval Kent and Lydd, demonstrating the advancing of capitalism.[60] Overall, this was a conflictual period. As another source reports, 'Early enclosures (15th and early 16th centuries) involved brutal evictions and depopulation of manors.'[61] By actively expropriating the peasantry and enclosing the commons, the landlords were slowly creating a new class of landless labourers, the working class, which had to work for a tenant farmer in order to survive.[62] At that time, in late 16th, early 17th century, the first – agrarian – stage of the transition to capitalism in England had, to a very significant extent, already been carried out.

> By the end of the Tudor era the transition had been completed, the new class structure was in place, and the way was set for the stark opposition, in the countryside, of agricultural proletariat and capitalist employer in alliance with a powerful capitalist landlord class.[63]

It should, of course, be added – *contra* Marx – that the creation of proletarians through expropriation was not always a violent and conflictual, nor even intentional, process. Many workers were brought into being, as former farmers, through the bitter market process of bankruptcy and land loss.

In the 17th century, the expropriation and enclosure movement continued and was even more significant than in the 15th, meeting substantial resistance and overcoming it.[64] According to perhaps the most influential historiographical review on this matter, up to 70% of English land had already been enclosed by 1700.[65] Thus, unsurprisingly, the extent of English agrarian capitalism significantly deepened and spread in the 17th century, its macrosocial economic effects finally clearly visible at the aggregate level in Figures 2.1 and 2.2. From then on, the working class grew even more, and in the late 18th century, the Industrial Revolution had finally been triggered precisely in the capitalistically precocious England, not pre-capitalist Germany or France.

It is virtually impossible to imagine that, for example, Christianity, the Scientific Revolution, Enlightenment culture, the Glorious Revolution of 1688, England's propitious geographical location and access to the Atlantic, and many other commonly proposed factors did not *in some way* contribute to the rise of English capitalism and the Industrial Revolution. However, given the specific timing of England's exceptional agrarian economic take-off already in early 17th century, and given the momentous early structural transformation of the English countryside from 1400 to 1550 described above, this latter fact has to be seen as the key originating cause – absent elsewhere in Europe – behind English economic exceptionalism. It was also a necessary, if not by itself sufficient, cause of the later Industrial Revolution. Indeed, the authors of a fresh quantitative study of English productivity between 1250 and 1870 conclude that their findings – a continuous rise in productivity starting around 1600 – 'support the idea that broad-based economic change *preceded* the bourgeois institutional reforms of the 17th century England and may have contributed to causing them.'[66]

War, more than culture, spread capitalism across Europe and beyond

Now that one puzzle is solved, another one opens up. If feudalism really is a sticky, stable system capable of reproduction throughout the ages, and so capitalism emerged out of feudal England not by near certainty but virtually by historical happenstance, how can we explain its spread throughout the Western world in the 19th century? In the first half of the 19th century, France and Germany started modernizing their economies, which was followed in the second half of the 19th century by Russia, Japan, and other Western powers. Was all of this also mere throw of historical dice, just the right initial endogenous social conditions meeting the right exogenous shock?

Well, in a general way, yes. Everything that happens in history happens due to preceding sufficient conditions being present for it happening. But more specifically, no, it was not chance alone. In a *wholly pre-capitalist world*, feudal and absolutist societies were, indeed, sticky and capable of continuous, uninterrupted reproduction. Chance was needed to break one of them apart. But in a world with one or two capitalist powers already emerging (themselves the result of historical chance), powerful new structural pressures were about to be unleashed on pre-capitalist societies, making *their* transition more a necessity than mere historical chance.

Once a relatively unimportant geopolitical backwater, England – now a dynamic, industrial capitalist society – quickly started becoming the most powerful military force in the world around mid-18th and beginning of 19th century. Its rapidly increasing wealth per capita could now be used both to finance its own war machine more thoroughly and sustainably than had been the rule in stagnant pre-capitalist societies and to fund its allies and make them stronger. Moreover, the constant stream of technological innovations flowing from its competitive market economy, and most radically exemplified in the Industrial Revolution, was not just a powerful economic boon but could also directly be applied in the military sphere.

Continental geopolitical behemoths, such as 18th-century France, could no longer ignore the epochal changes that were afoot. England – or, after 1707, Britain – thoroughly beat France in the Seven Years' War (1754–1761). And although it did not manage to subdue the United States, allied with France, in the American Revolutionary Wars (1775–1783), this latter war bankrupted France and opened the door to the French Revolution. While now, at the end of the 18th century, pre-capitalist France was undergoing a radical ten-year long civil upheaval, capitalist Britain stood strong and continued growing both militarily and economically. At the beginning of the 19th century, Napoleonic Wars (1803–1815) followed, but again Britain had in the end emerged victorious.

French ruling elites were influenced by all of these dramatic events and started realizing that a stagnant pre-capitalist economy will no longer cut it, militarily. Already between 1766 and 1771, ministers backed a slew of early policies designed to create a capitalist mentality of 'agrarian individualism.'[67] The policies included clearing wasteland, enclosure of the commons, and restrictions on free grazing.[68] The ensuing effects were negligible, but the policies were quite revealing of elite fears and intentions. Then, in 1776, the finance minister Robert Jacques Turgot tried his hand at more daring capitalist reforms, most famously the abolition of artisan guilds.[69] However, predictably, '[t]he edict was once more rapidly retracted after it had ignited growing insubordination among artisans and strong dissatisfaction among large section of French elites (including a large proportion of merchants).'[70] Due to the 'political replacement effect,' elites are afraid and hesitant of backing otherwise beneficial, modernizing reforms.[71]

Thus, up until the eve of the French Revolution, the state's attempts of igniting a transition from feudalism to capitalism have been short-circuited. This is most vividly on display in the following figures:

> in its cotton trade, England had [at the time] 260 spindles per 1000 inhabitants against 2 in France. There were 900 spinning jennies in France against 20,000 in Britain and no more than a dozen mule-jennies in the former country against 9000 in the latter.[72]

Even in the years after the revolution, capitalism had still been absent in France.[73] In contrast to the pervasive myth of a 'bourgeois revolution,' in which the bourgeois representatives of the Third Estate ostensibly threw off the feudal yoke and installed capitalism in its stead, the French Revolution did not actually birth capitalism – although a few important economic changes had been made.[74] However, in the years and decades following the Napoleonic Wars, French elites were more and more recognizing the imperative of change. The

> French state felt strong pressure to modernize and develop the country's industrial sector so as to support its geopolitical standing. Not all sectors of French elites agreed with this project, however, and many were still attached to their ideal of a rural and non-industrialized France.[75]

Crushing the resistance, Napoleon III finally made key changes around mid-century.[76] Monopolies were being disbanded, market competition was being introduced more and more, protectionism was slowly reduced, and modern transport infrastructure was laid down.[77] The state did everything in its power, including offering low interest loans to firms willing to modernize, to ignite capitalist industrialization from above. This was the start of French capitalism proper.

The German defeat in Napoleonic Wars was even more sobering for the Prussian elites than the later defeat of France will have been for French elites. When Prussia was traumatically defeated and lost a large proportion of its territory to France in 1806 – it was also strongly financially punished by France – the elites got to work reforming the economy already in the following year. Serfdom, which was still going strong in Prussia centuries after it had been abolished in France and England, was the first to go. Its abolition was decided on in 1807 with the reasoning that this would open the pathway towards a more productive economy, which would then enable Prussia to militarily stand up to its enemies in a new, uncertain world of emerging capitalist powers.[78] In the next years and decades, all the way up to mid-century, the famous 'Stein-Hardenberg' reforms were underway, modernizing the German economy. The state was easing its protections of peasant smallholdings, and the lords were more and more allowed to enclose the commons and to engross their demesnes.[79] Peasants lost between a third and half of all their land. In the second half of the 19th century, the Prussian Junker elite 'ceased to be a feudal landlord class and became a class of capitalists farmers.'[80]

As before in France, the transition to capitalism in Germany was anything but smooth. There was conflict, hesitancy, and a significant degree of reform blocking on the part of elites afraid of losing their power due to modernization, especially before 1850. But, the external pressure emanating from Britain (and now France) was strong and getting stronger. 'The threat from the rapidly industrializing Britain and France and from the 1848 wave of revolutions may have … been important for the change in the attitudes toward industrialization, adding some element of defensive modernization to the German case.'[81] The final step was made in 1871, after the Franco-Prussian War (1870–1871) ended. Bismarck united the German princely states and Prussia, creating Germany as we know it today. A strong wave of state-led industrialization swept over Germany and set it on the path to become one of the strongest economies and military powers in the world.

With a bit of a lag, Russia and Japan were also on their way to modernizing in the second half of the 19th century. Here again, external geopolitical threat seems to be the primary inducement for change. Russia got its modernizing message with the defeat at the hands of the British and French in the Crimean War (1853–1856). Already in 1861, tsar Alexander II tried abolishing serfdom and revoking some of the aristocratic tax privileges burdening the state budget. The most significant industrializing boost happened in the last decade of the century under the auspices of finance minister Sergei Witte. The Russian path to capitalism was then famously disrupted by the revolutionary upheaval of 1917, after which Russia did industrialize further but in a distinctly non-capitalist fashion.

Japan started significantly modernizing soon after the Americans pried it apart with the arrival of Matthew Perry's battleships in 1853 and 1854.[82] Even before that, in the First Opium Wars (1839–1842), the Japanese had the opportunity to witness the awesome military strength of an industrial capitalist power when Britain defeated China despite China committing ten-times as many soldiers as Britain to the fight. But after Perry's coercive offer of a trade treaty, the Japanese elites knew time for complacency had passed. In the 1870s, efforts at state centralization have been made and were successful, the existing feudal-absolutist social structure was being dismantled, the samurai warrior class was abolished, and the legal, military, and financial systems were reformed.[83]

In the 18th century and especially 19th century, Britain – a state underpinned by a dynamic capitalist economy never seen before – started posing a wholly new, structurally different military threat (and model of imitation) to other European powers. Change-averse elites in pre-capitalist societies knew that in these new times the old order is no longer viable and has to be transformed. Reluctantly, and through many conflicts, various elite groupings in several countries did what they had to do and initiated a state-led transition to capitalism, dismantling many (though not all) old structures.

Marx famously claimed in the *Communist Manifesto* that the

> cheap prices of commodities are the heavy artillery with which [capitalism] batters down all Chinese walls … It compels all nations, on pain of extinction, to adopt the bourgeois mode of production; it compels them to introduce what it calls civilisation into their midst, i.e. to become bourgeois themselves. In one word, it creates a world after its own image.[84]

Marx's suggestion that it was the direct price efficiency of the capitalist market that (peacefully) compelled pre-capitalist societies to adopt it so as to reap its price benefits sounds plausible at first blush. However, given that pre-capitalist societies were existing in a pre-capitalist world with a pre-capitalist world market, the direct producers living in those countries did not feel the pressure of market competition which, had it existed, would indeed have compelled them to imitate the British 'bourgeois' mode of production for direct economic reasons of survival on the market. In short, with the rise of British capitalism, the world did not suddenly become market dependent and so was not forced to produce optimally, i.e. capitalistically. Instead, as we have seen, it was more the *actual*, physical – not metaphoric or economic – heavy artillery of rising capitalist powers that pressured pre-capitalist societies to adopt the modern economy.

Conclusion

The influential pristine cultural explanations of the emergence of capitalism I reviewed in the first part of the chapter are all burdened by at least moderate empirical weaknesses. What is more, as we have seen, there exists a more conflictual and materialist perspective on the transition to capitalism in Europe (and elsewhere) that is itself not undermined by the empirical facts burdening the cultural explanations, and is also positively corroborated by a variety of fine-grained historical evidence. In fact, given all the structures and institutions that have to be transformed in a feudal society for capitalism to start forming, and given how (rightly) fearful elites are of significant economic change, it is hard to even theoretically imagine how a mere shift in norms, attitudes, and ideas could have done the necessary heavy lifting.

To be clear, by saying this I am not advancing the vulgar Marxist claim that ideas simply do not matter in social causation. Rather, as a moderate materialist, rational choice sociologist I am only suggesting that ideational changes cannot have a strong and persistent effect on how the average person behaves in society, without the underlying structural environment or power relations, and the incentives flowing from it, also having been changed in the meanwhile (due either to a preceding ideational cause or other non-cultural causes).[85] This is true at least in instances when the ideational changes are such that the action they recommend people take is in sharp conflict with the action that structural social incentives are pointing people toward. When lofty ideas and existing structures *clash*, structure usually wins out. This is why, for example, I am somewhat doubtful in an *a priori* way – i.e. on theoretical grounds – of Weber's and similar claims that the sudden appearance of Protestant values in certain *feudal* European societies was able to motivate people to suddenly start acting in a *capitalist* way even though such capitalist behaviour had still been incongruent with the prevailing feudal structures of the day.[86]

Even defenders of ideational explanations, such as Vlad Tarko, express a similar concern to the one I have. Critiquing a particular cultural explanation of the emergence of modernity provided by the eminent economist Deirdre McCloskey, he sensibly points out in a recent paper that

> explanations such as McCloskey's … are, *at best*, only proximate explanations. Suppose that 'bourgeois virtues' [or Protestant values] have indeed

played a critical role in the emergence of the modern world. The reason why such a belief about what constitutes 'virtue' has spread cannot itself be cultural. A change in the costs and benefits of holding such beliefs is also a necessary part of the explanation for why all of the sudden this particular moral belief has had an advantage over other competing beliefs.[87]

This is precisely what I have tried to do in this chapter. On the materialist account above, a 'bourgeois,' 'capitalist' mentality took root in England (but not France or Germany) after the end of the Middle Ages, *because the economic structure of England had been changing before that* and because with this structural change the costs and benefits of 'capitalist behaviour' and 'feudal behaviour' had also shifted significantly. Culture is thus not denied, but structurally contextualized and provided with an ultimate instead of just proximate explanation.

Notes

1 Here is just a short, but ideologically varied list: McCloskey (2011); North et al. (2013); Fukuyama (2014); The CORE Team (2017); Pinker (2018); Brennan and van der Vossen (2018); Kenworthy (2020).
2 Marx (1983 [1867], 669).
3 The phrase 'beloved myth' was first used in Delacroix and Nielsen (2001).
4 Pinker (2018).
5 Delacroix and Nielsen (2001).
6 Weber (2001 [1930]).
7 Acemoglu and Robinson (2012, 60).
8 Delacroix (1992); Delacroix and Nielsen (2001); Acemoglu et al. (2001); Sanderson et al. (2011); Cantoni (2015).
9 Sanderson et al. (2011).
10 Cantoni (2015).
11 Ibid., 562.
12 Delacroix and Nielsen (2001).
13 Ibid., 543. Note that the study is temporally quite removed from the end of the Middle Ages, so it could be argued in Weber's defence that Protestantism was influential only at the beginning of the transition to capitalism, while its effect later faded as he himself allowed.
14 Acemoglu et al. (2001).
15 Spater and Tranvik (2019).
16 Becker and Woessman (2009).
17 Cummins (1988).
18 Ibid., 440.
19 Henrich et al. (2010).
20 Henrich (2020).
21 Ibid.
22 Henrich (2020, 435).
23 Ibid.
24 Freeman (2020).
25 Data are from Roser (2013) who relies on the Maddison Project Database 2020.
26 Allen (2000).
27 Bouscasse et al. (2021).
28 Allen (2015).
29 Allen (2009).

30 Ibid., 17.
31 Ibid.
32 Ibid.
33 Allen (2011, 31).
34 Pinker (2018).
35 Allen (2009, 243).
36 Ibid., 252.
37 Compare this to Gregory Clark's points in his critical review of Mokyr's thesis, Clark (2012).
38 North et al. (2009); Acemoglu and Robinson (2012); Brenner (2007); Dimmock (2014).
39 Brenner (2007). In recent years, revisionist historians have quite convincingly shown that, at least in England in the century prior to the Black Death, villeins (unfree peasants) were actually not as extremely economically oppressed as had once been thought (by, amongst others, Robert Brenner). Legally speaking, they were, as always, subject to numerous arbitrary fines, labour services, and other lordly powers, but these were less arbitrary and effective in practice. For an overview of the literature and revision, see Hatcher (2015). Nevertheless, the revisionists themselves recognize that, even in this exceptional time and place, 'It is not difficult to understand why impoverished villeins struggled to retain as much as they could of their product in an age of rising prices and falling wages and employment opportunities, when even low rents could threaten the subsistence of those with holdings too small to feed their families.' Ibid., 138. Moreover, 'if rents and charges on villain land did not increase much in the inflationary thirteenth century it follows that they must have been extremely onerous in earlier times and the ability of lords to impose them commensurately greater.' Ibid.
40 Brenner (2007).
41 Meiksins Wood (2001).
42 Brenner (2007); North et al. (2009); Acemoglu and Robinson (2012).
43 With regards to the impact of ecological crises on rapid and unexpected social change see the following explanations: de Vries and van der Woude (1997); Brenner (2001). These explanations deal not with the English transition to capitalism which I will look at in this chapter, but with the early economic take-off of Holland, a different case of an early capitalist transition that – unlike the English case – stalled later on.
44 Acemoglu and Robinson (2012, 96–101).
45 My account of the transition is significantly shaped by the 'Brenner Debate' in general and by Brenner's contribution to the debate in particular. For more on the 'Brenner Debate', see Aston and Philpin (1985) and Dimmock (2014).
46 Brenner (2007, 96–97); Dimmock (2014, 26); Isett and Miller (2017, 75).
47 Campbell (2006, 235–236); Dimmock (2014; 2019); Isett and Miller (2017, 75). It would have been, of course, more beneficial for them to have retained access to either serfs or cheap free labour. Moreover, they did not know what exactly to expect from the leases. As Dyer reports, 'We can sense the reluctance of many lords, who leased out part of the demesne, or who tentatively began with a short-term letting for perhaps six years, or who experimented with a period of leasing and then took the land back temporarily into their own hands again.' Dyer (2005, 197).
48 Brenner (2007, 97).
49 Dimmock (2014, 92).
50 Dyer (2005, 195).
51 Dimmock (2014, 27).
52 Dyer (2005, 197).
53 '[M]ost fifteenth-century demesne leases were based on negotiated contracts, reflecting the forces of the market.' Ibid., 198. See also Campbell (2006, 236); Dimmock (2014); Isett and Miller (2017, 75–76).
54 Dyer (2005, 199); see also Campbell (2006, 235–236).

55 Brenner and Isett (2002, 620).
56 Brenner (2001); see also Allen (1992).
57 Bouscasse et al. (2021, 22).
58 Campbell (2006, 236).
59 Byres (2009, 40).
60 Dimmock (2014, 272–345).
61 Bouscasse et al. (2021, 22).
62 Žmolek (2013).
63 Byres (2009, 41).
64 Žmolek (2013); Isett and Miller (2017, 79–80).
65 Wordie (1983).
66 Bouscasse et al. (2021, 1). Emphasis added.
67 Jones (2012, 246).
68 Ibid.
69 Lafrance (2019, 114).
70 Ibid.
71 Acemoglu and Robinson (2006).
72 Lafrance (2019, 115).
73 Jones (2012); Miller (2015; 2019).
74 Miller (2008); Chibber (2013, 66–75).
75 Lafrance (2019, 124).
76 Ibid., 125.
77 Ibid., 126–127.
78 Byres (1996, 106).
79 Ibid., 111.
80 Ibid., 115.
81 Acemoglu and Robinson (2006, 127).
82 Moore (1966); Anievas and Allinson (2010).
83 Ibid.
84 Marx and Engels (2008 [1848], 39).
85 Compare Singh et al. (2017).
86 In comparison to Weber's explanation, Henrich's theoretical account is much more sophisticated as it ties normative change to environmental structural change, positing a plausible mechanism of mutual interaction.
87 Tarko (2015, 18).

References

Acemoglu, Daron, and James A. Robinson. 2006. 'Economic Backwardness in Political Perspective,' *American Political Science Review* 100, no. 1, 115–131.
Acemoglu, Daron, and James A. Robinson. 2012. *Why Nations Fail: The Origins of Power, Prosperity, and Poverty.* London: Profile Books.
Acemoglu, Daron, Johnson, Simon, and James A. Robinson. 2001. 'The Colonial Origins of Comparative Development: An Empirical Investigation,' *The American Economic Review* 91, no. 5, 1369–1401.
Allen, Robert C. 1992. *Enclosure and the Yeoman.* Oxford: Oxford University Press.
Allen, Robert C. 2000. 'Economic Structure and Agricultural Productivity in Europe, 1300–1800,' *European Review of Economic History* 4, no. 1, 1–25.
Allen, Robert C. 2009. *The British Industrial Revolution in Global Perspective.* Cambridge: Cambridge University Press.
Allen, Robert C. 2011. *Global Economic History. A Very Short Introduction.* Oxford: Oxford University Press.

Allen, Robert C. 2015. 'The High Wage Economy and the Industrial Revolution: A Restatement,' *The Economic History Review* 68, no. 1, 1–22.

Anievas, Alexander, and Jamie Allinson. 2010. 'The Uneven and Combined Development of Meiji Restoration: A Passive Revolutionary Road to Capitalist Modernity,' *Capital & Class* 34, no. 3, 469–490.

Aston, Trevor H., and C. H. E. Philpin (eds.). 1985. *The Brenner Debate: Agrarian Class Structure and Economic Development in Pre-Industrial Europe*. Cambridge: Cambridge University Press.

Becker, Sascha O., and Ludger Woessmann. 2009. 'Was Weber Wrong? A Human Capital Theory of Protestant Economic History,' *The Quarterly Journal of Economics* 124, no. 2, 531–596.

Bolt, Jutta, and Jan Luiten van Zanden. 2020. 'Maddison Style Estimates of the Evolution of the World Economy. A New 2020 Update,' Accessible via: https://www.rug.nl/ggdc/historicaldevelopment/maddison/publications/wp15.pdf/.

Bouscasse, Paul, Nakamura, Emi, and Jón Steinsson. 2021. 'When Did Growth Begin? New Estimates of Productivity Growth in England from 1250 to 1870,' SSRN working paper. Accessible via: https://papers.ssrn.com/sol3/papers.cfm?abstract_id=3814612/.

Brennan, Jason, and Bas van der Vossen. 2018. *In Defense of Openness. Why Global Freedom Is the Humane Solution to Global Poverty*. Oxford: Oxford University Press.

Brenner, Robert. 2001. 'The Low Countries in the Transition to Capitalism,' *Journal of Agrarian Change* 1, no. 2, 169–241.

Brenner, Robert. 2007. 'Property and Progress: Where Adam Smith Went Wrong,' in Chris Wickham (ed.), *Marxist History-writing for the Twenty-first Century*, 49–111. Oxford: Oxford University Press.

Brenner, Robert, and Christopher Isett. 2002. 'England's Divergence from China's Yangzi Delta: Property Relations, Microeconomies, and Patterns of Development,' *The Journal of Asian Studies* 61, no. 2, 609–662.

Broadberry, Stephen, Campbell, Bruce M. S., Klein, Alexander, Overton, Mark, and Bas van leeuwen. 2015. *British Economic Growth, 1270–1870*. Cambridge: Cambridge University Press.

Byres, Terence J. 1996. *Capitalism from Above and Capitalism from Below: An Essay in Comparative Political Economy*. Basingstoke: Palgrave Macmillan.

Byres, Terrence. 2009. 'The Landlord Class, Peasant Differentiation, Class Struggle and the Transition to Capitalism: England, France and Prussia Compared,' *The Journal of Peasant Studies* 36, no. 1, 33–54.

Campbell, Bruce M. S. 2006. 'The Land,' in Rosemarx Horrox and W. Mark Ormrod (eds.), *A Social History of England, 1200–1500*, 179–237. Oxford: Oxford University Press.

Cantoni, Davide. 2015. 'The Economic Effects of the Protestant Reformation: Testing the Weber Hypothesis in the German Lands,' *Journal of the European Economic Association* 13, no. 4, 561–598.

Chibber, Vivek. 2013. *Postcolonial Theory and the Specter of Capital*. London: Verso.

Clark, Gregory. 2012. 'A Review Essay on "The Enlightened Economy: An Economic History of Britain 1700–1850" by Joel Mokyr,' *Journal of Economic Literature* 50, no. 1, 85–95.

Cummins, Victoria Hennessey. 1988. 'The Church and Business Practices in Late Sixteenth Century Mexico,' *The Americas* 44, no. 4, 421–440.

de Vries, Jan, and A. van de Woude. 1997. *The First Modern Economy. Success, Failure, and Perseverance of the Dutch Economy, 1500–1815*. Cambridge: Cambridge University Press.

Delacroix, Jacques. 1992. 'A Critical Empirical Test of the Common Interpretation of the Protestant Ethic and the Spirit of Capitalism,' Paper presented at meetings of Int. Assoc. Business & Society, Leuven, Belgium.

Delacroix, Jacques, and François Nielsen. 2001. 'The Beloved Myth: Protestantism and the Rise of Industrial Capitalism in Nineteenth-Century Europe,' *Social Forces* 80, no. 2, 509–553.

Dimmock, Spencer. 2014. *The Origin of Capitalism in England, 1400–1600*. Leiden: Brill.

Dimmock, Spencer. 2019. 'Expropriation and the Political Origins of Agrarian Capitalism in England,' in Xavier Lafrance and Charles Post (eds.), *Case Studies in the Origin of Capitalism*, 39–62. New York: Palgrave.

Dyer, Christopher. 2005. *An Age of Transition? Economy and Society in England in the Later Middle Ages*. Oxford: Oxford University Press.

Freeman, Charles. 2020. 'Henrich's Central Argument and Its Offshoots are Not Supported by Historical Fact,' a review published on Amazon. Accessible via: https://www.amazon.com/gp/customer-reviews/R28QL9PWWETSD6/ref=cm_cr_dp_d_rvw_ttl?ie=UTF8&ASIN=B07RZFCPMD/.

Fukuyama, Francis. 2014. *Political Order and Political Decay. From the Industrial Revolution to the Globalization of Democracy*. New York: Farrar, Straus and Giroux.

Hatcher, John. 2015. 'Lordship and Villeinage Before the Black Death: From Karl Marx to the Marxists and Back Again,' in Maryanne Kowaleski, John Langdon, and Phillipp R. Schofield (eds.), *Peasants and Lords in the Medieval English Economy: Essays in Honour of Bruce M. S. Campbell*, 113–145. Turnhout: Brepols.

Henrich, Joseph, Heine, Steven J., and Ara Norenzayan. 2010. 'The WEIRDest People in the World?' *Behavioral and Brain Sciences* 33, no. 2–3, 61–83.

Henrich, Joseph. 2020. *The WEIRDest People in the World: How the West Became Psychologically Peculiar and Particularly Prosperous*. New York: Farrar, Straus and Giroux.

Isett, Christopher, and Stephen Miller. 2017. *The Social History of Agriculture: From the Origins to the Current Crisis*. Lanham: Rowman & Littlefield.

Jones, Peter M. 2012. 'Agriculture,' in William Doyle (ed.), *The Oxford Handbook of the Ancien Régime*, 236–251. Oxford: Oxford University Press.

Kenworthy, Lane. 2020. *Social Democratic Capitalism*. Oxford: Oxford University Press.

Krantz, Olle. 2017. 'Swedish GDP 1300–1560: A Tentative Estimate,' *Lund Papers in Economic History: General Issues* 152. Accessible via: https://ideas.repec.org/p/hhs/luekhi/0152.html/.

Marx, Karl, and Friedrich Engels. 2008 [1848]. *The Communist Manifesto*. London: Pluto Press.

Marx, Karl. 1983 [1867]. *Capital, Volume One*. London: Lawrence and Wishart.

McCloskey, Deirdre N. 2011. *Bourgeois Dignity. Why Economics Can't Explain the Modern World*. Chicago: Chicago University Press.

Miller, Stephen. 2008. *State and Society in Eighteenth-Century France: A Study of Political Power and Social Revolution in Languedoc*. Washington: Catholic University of America Press.

Miller, Stephen. 2015. 'Ralph Kingston on the Bourgeoisie and Bureaucracy in France, 1789–1848,' *Historical Materialism* 23, no. 3, 240–252.

Miller, Stephen. 2019. 'Peasant Farming in Eighteenth- and Nineteenth-Century France and the Transition to Capitalism Under Charles de Gaulle,' in Xavier Lafrance and Charles Post (eds.), *Case Studies in the Origin of Capitalism*, 87–109. Cham: Palgrave Macmillan.

Moore, Barrington Jr. 1966. *The Social Origins of Dictatorship and Democracy: Lord and Peasant in the Making of the Modern World*. Boston: Beacon Press.

North, Douglass C., Wallis, John Joseph, Webb, Steven B, and Barry R. Weingast. 2013. 'Limited Access Orders: An Introduction to the Conceptual Framework,' in Douglass C. North, John Joseph Wallis, Steven B. Webb, and Barry R. Weingast (eds.), *In the Shadow of Violence. Politics, Economics, and the Problems of Development*, 1–23. Cambridge: Cambridge University Press.

Palma, Nuno, and Jaime Reis. 2019. 'From Convergence to Divergence: Portuguese Economic Growth, 1527–1850,' *The Journal of Economic History* 79, no. 2, 477–506.

Pinker, Steven. 2018. *Enlightenment Now: The Case for Reason, Science, Humanism, and Progress*. New York: Viking.

Ridolfi, Leonardo. 2017. 'The French Economy in the Longue Durée. A Study on Real Wages, Working Days and Economic Performance from Louis IX to the Revolution (1250–1789),' Accessible via: http://e-theses.imtlucca.it/211/1/Ridolfi_phdthesis.pdf/.

Roser, Max. 2013. 'Economic Growth,' *Our World in Data*. Accessible via: https://ourworldindata.org/economic-growth/.

Sanderson, Stephen K., Abrutyn, Seth B., and Kristopher R. Proctor. 2011. 'Testing the Protestant Ethic Thesis with Quantitative Historical Data: A Research Note,' *Social Forces* 89, no. 3, 905–911.

Schön, Lennart, and Olle Krantz. 2015. 'New Swedish Historical National Accounts since the 16th Century in Constant and Current Prices,' *Lund Papers in Economic History* 140. Accessible via: https://lucris.lub.lu.se/ws/portalfiles/portal/5872822/8228142.pdf/.

Singh, Manvir, Wrangham, Richard, and Luke Glowacki. 2017. 'Self-Interest and the Design of Rules,' *Human Nature* 28, 457–480.

Spater, Jeremy, and Isak Tranvik. 2019. 'The Protestant Ethic Reexamined: Calvinism and Industrialization,' *Comparative Political Studies* 52, no. 13–14, 1963–1994.

Tarko, Vlad. 2015. 'The Role of Ideas in Political Economy,' *Review of Austrian Economics* 28, 17–39.

The Core Team. 2017. *The Economy: Economics for a Changing World*. Oxford: Oxford University Press.

Weber, Max. 2001 [1930]. *The Protestant Ethic and the Spirit of Capitalism*. London: Routledge.

Wood, Ellen Meiksins. 2001. *The Origin of Capitalism: A Longer View*. London: Verso.

Wordie, J. R. 1983. 'The Chronology of English Enclosure, 1500–1914,' *The Economic History Review* 36, no. 4, 483–505.

Xavier, Lafrance. 2019. 'The Transition to Industrial Capitalism in Nineteenth-Century France,' in Xavier Lafrance and Charles Post (eds.), *Case Studies in the Origin of Capitalism*, 111–137. New York: Palgrave.

Žmolek, Michael Andrew. 2013. *Rethinking the Industrial Revolution. Five Centuries of Transition from Agrarian to Industrial Capitalism in England*. Leiden: Brill.

3

A NUANCED LOOK AT POVERTY, EXPLOITATION, AND INEQUALITY

Introduction: contemporary vindications of Marxism?

There exists a well-known, yet nevertheless continuously striking graph that seemingly demonstrates at a single glance the incredible amount of exploitation that workers suffer in contemporary capitalism. The *Economic Policy Institute* (EPI) has compiled official government data showing a gaping divergence between two crucial economic indicators: worker *productivity* (output per worker) and worker *compensation* (wages and benefits).[1] The graph shows that, since around 1973, worker productivity has grown tremendously, increasing by 73.7% between 1973 and 2016. The graph also shows that, in the same time period, hourly worker compensation has been very sluggish, almost stagnant, rising only by 12.3% between 1973 and 2016.

In short, workers are ostensibly producing more and more with their labour (per hour) every year but are not being paid more for it. Without getting into the intricacies and technicalities of normative philosophy, this seems pretty exploitative on the face of it, and a strong vindication of the traditional Marxist charge that capitalism is inherently exploitative.[2] As we shall see later, such simple statistics actually belie a much more complex reality, and taking them at face value as indicating exploitation is simply wrong. But, let the point stand for now.

What is less well known, oddly, is that in 1820, when capitalism still only existed in a just few countries, the whole world had been mired in extreme poverty. According to a now infamous graph compiled by Max Roser at *Our World in Data*, between 84% and 94% of world population could be said to have lived in extreme poverty in the third decade of 19th century.[3] But then, during the initial slow introduction of modernity, capitalism, and the industrial revolution in Europe through the 19th century, the global share of those in poverty started dropping. By the end of the century, it had dropped to between 70% and 85%.

DOI: 10.4324/9781003305811-3

With the spread of modern economic institutions throughout the world in the 20th century, extreme poverty was reduced even more significantly, standing at under 10% in the second decade of the 21st century. So, capitalism might be very exploitative, but it does seem to have almost vanquished extreme poverty. If nothing else, does this latter fact not point against capitalism's critics and in favour of the modern economy?

Not necessarily. Surprisingly, the poverty data might even provide a certain kind of vindication of Marxism – or, to put it more accurately, they are not strong evidence *against* Marxist theory – as Karl Marx himself declared in his various works that capitalism will not increase absolute misery.[4] It was more the *relative* immiseration – that is, inequality – that Marx worried about in the infamous 25th chapter of his *Capital*, a point we will get to later on. Contemporary critics of capitalism, however, are not as convinced. Some of them are more in line with the Marx of the *Communist Manifesto*, where the absolute immiseration thesis is quite clearly on display. The economic anthropologist Jason Hickel, for example, disputes the data and (almost) denies the two-century long reduction in extreme poverty.[5] Moreover, he claims that rather than vanquishing it, capitalism (and colonialism) created extreme poverty where there was none before.

But perhaps the clearest economic downside of capitalism today is the seemingly exploding rate of inequality all over the world. Inequality, even more so than poverty or exploitation, is said to be the main issue of the modern economy. Over the past decades, we have been inundated with media reports of extreme wealth possessed by the rich. Today's top world billionaires, such as Elon Musk, easily pass the $100 billion wealth benchmark.

Contemporary inequality, however, is not only about world's top billionaires being extraordinarily rich. One *Forbes* headline from October 2020 reads 'Top 1% of U.S. households Hold 15 Times More Wealth Than Bottom 50% Combined.'[6] Relying on the latest data provided by the US Federal Reserve, the article reports that the top 1% of Americans have a combined net worth of almost $35 trillion, while half of all American citizens combined possess less than $2 trillion.[7] Of course, inequality is not solely to provenance of the US – although US inequality is among the highest in OECD countries. The world in general is also highly unequal. According to *Oxfam*, 'the world's richest 1% have more than twice as much wealth as 6.9 billion people.'[8] Who constitutes this global top 1%? In 2018, it was any individual with a net worth of $871,320 (net worth is the household's value of stocks and other financial assets and the value of real assets, such as housing, minus any debt).[9]

Such reports tend to paper over one important fact. The latest data on income inequality show that, between 1980 and 2016, the real income of the world's bottom half population has grown by 94%, which is quite impressive.[10] True, even here significant inequality is still on display. The income of the world's top 1% grew by 101% in the same period, while that of top 0.001% increased by extraordinary 235%. On the other hand, income growth for the people between the bottom half of the world and the top 10%, 1%, or 0.001%, say the 60th, the

70th, or the 80th world percentile, has been more modest. These percentiles, which represent the *European* or the *American* bottom 50% and middle 40% – i.e. the middle and working class of the developed world – grew on average by just 43%. So, some inequalities are increasing, other decreasing – a point I will develop in much more detail later on – but on net, there still seems to be plenty of inequality to go around today.

The purpose of this chapter is to thoroughly investigate both theory and data on the relationship between poverty, exploitation, inequality, and capitalism. As we shall see in each of the following sections on poverty, exploitation, and inequality, respectively, the relationship is much more complex than usually presented in simplistic accounts provided either by defenders or by critics of the modern economy.

The dispute over poverty and capitalism

In January 2019, just a few days before the start of the *2019 World Economic Forum Annual Meeting* in Davos, Bill Gates tweeted a picture containing 6 graphs compiled by *Our World in Data* (OWID), saying that it was one of his favourite infographics. The graphs depict how the past two centuries have seen a significant increase in basic education, literacy, vaccination, and democracy. They also depict a sharp reduction in child mortality. But what proved to be the most controversial is the graph showing a fall in extreme poverty from 94% in 1820 to 10% in 2015.

Aside from the expected Twitter firestorm that followed that post, the radical economic anthropologist Jason Hickel wrote a column for the *Guardian* bluntly titled 'Bill Gates says poverty is decreasing. He couldn't be more wrong,' which sparked a global debate that in the end drew in, among others, the *OWID* director Max Roser and the former *World Bank* lead researcher Branko Milanović.[11] In the column and various later publications, Hickel presented a suite of ostensibly fundamental issues that, as he claims, falsify virtually any triumphant claim about significant poverty eradication in the past two centuries.[12] He is especially critical of a claim which Gates and social scientists such as Steven Pinker are gesturing towards when writing about poverty, namely that the rise of capitalism in the 19th and 20th century is one of the key social-structural reasons for extreme poverty eradication.

The following list captures the most important critical points presented by Hickel and other sceptics:

1 The data on poverty going back in time further than the 1981 mark when the World Bank started collecting the data, are – as he puts it – 'extremely sketchy' and even 'meaningless.'[13] This is so because the typical poverty data going back in history beyond 1981 are based on GDP estimates, which ostensibly do not take into account various non-market commodities and sources of wealth people relied on in the pre-capitalist past. Moreover, the

data for many countries are missing and so have to be regionally interpolated, which is too speculative. In short, data for the past unintentionally overstate poverty to such an extent to be of no use.

2 The emergence of capitalism through the 19th and 20th century did not reduce poverty, but rather caused it. Colonization of the Global South and the European enclosure movement in these centuries expropriated former subsistence peasants of their land and robbed them of their access to the commons which they used in the past to survive. Capitalism forced former peasants who previously had no need of money to live in a moneyed economy, thus introducing them to poverty as they were transformed into landless low-wage workers.

3 Apart from the previous points, the poverty measure itself is wrong. Extreme poverty as depicted by the OWID graph is defined as living on less than $1.9 a day, but that bar is much too low. If a person earned less than $2 in the past and then started earning more, that does not mean she escaped extreme poverty. Moreover, a single poverty line for the whole world across two centuries, even corrected for differences in purchasing power, is much too blunt of an instrument.

4 The proper extreme poverty baseline should be much higher, say around $5 a day or $7.4 a day, or even higher. And when we use this bar to measure poverty, we are presented with a much less impressive drop in poverty.

5 Moreover, it is not that the world as a whole has seen a sharp reduction in poverty. It was mostly China that accounted for the bulk of poverty reduction.

6 But China is not a typical capitalist economy, or one embodying the neoliberal Washington consensus. So, Chinese poverty reduction cannot be used for the capitalist triumphalism narrative.

The first point from the list is incorrect, or at least significantly misleading. It is not the case that the 19th-century extreme poverty rate as proxied by GDP measurements leaves out non-market sources of wealth, thus vastly overstating poverty.[14] It is true that most people two centuries ago and in the past were peasants endowed with customary plots of land, who engaged in subsistence production of grain and other foodstuffs on their plots of land, had access to the commons, and so on. But economic historians responsible for past GDP reconstructions use a variety of methods to correct for the fact that in the pre-capitalist past people held a significant amount of their wealth and income in non-commodity forms. Historians measure these sources of wealth and consumption by, for example, estimating the amount of arable (and other) land in use, average crop yields, livestock numbers, even when these had nothing to do with markets or money.[15] These material estimates then get converted into monetary figures, and from those GDP estimates are constructed. A lot of work goes into making sure pre-capitalist GDP figures expressed in money reflect non-monetary, material wealth of pre-capitalist populations, which means that past poverty estimates that are based on GDP also do not simply ignore non-market wealth.

It is true that data on global poverty in the 19th century are indirect and so less reliable compared to the direct data that exist for the 20th century, especially after 1950. It is also correct that poverty measures for world regions as a whole have to be interpolated, i.e. the various individual countries for which data exist are used to create an estimate of overall poverty within a region. However, this does not mean that only a few countries, or only Western countries, are used to make the imputation, as critics falsely intimate. In 2021, for instance, Michail Moatsos presented data on extreme poverty for the OECD within a new approach – Robert Allen's 'cost of basic needs' approach, which tracks the share of world population that was not able to meet basic needs (i.e. minimal adequate nutrition and heated shelter) in particular historical timeframes.[16] According to this measure, the picture of extreme poverty in the 19th century that emerges is almost the same as the one produced by standard GDP estimates. In 1820, 76% of the world was not able to eat enough or have adequate shelter.[17] The percentage dropped to 74% in 1850, to 59% in 1900, 53% in 1950, 28% in 2000, and it now stands at 10% in 2018.[18] Crucially, even for the (early) 19th-century regional imputations, Moatsos uses data from more than 40 countries across the world.[19]

A central part of the second point from the list is undoubtedly correct. Subsistence peasants in Europe and abroad were expropriated and their access to the commons was restricted in the process of either colonization or the emergence of capitalism. However, to take capitalism first, the material living standards of former subsistence peasants – now landless workers – then rose dramatically as capitalism emerged and developed further. Almost all subsistence peasants lived in extreme poverty in pre-capitalist societies in 1820. Then, as we have just seen, the proportion steadily (although slowly) started dropping during the 19th century. It was reduced even more significantly in the 20th century, especially its second half, so that today only a small fraction of the world population lives in extreme poverty. It is not that, as Hickel presents it, most people in the past lived materially comfortable lives, never coming close to extreme poverty, and then with the creation of capitalism most of them were suddenly pushed into starvation.

To the contrary, Moatsos' 'cost of basic needs' estimates of extreme poverty demonstrate how the quickest and most significant reduction tended to happen in those countries that were most exposed to capitalist industrialization early: Great Britain, Germany, Australia, Canada, and the US. By 1900, extreme poverty in these countries had dropped from around 70% or more (in 1820) to less than a third of the population (in Australia and the US, it was even less than 10%).[20]

Turning now to colonization, it is completely true that this was an unimaginably violent and immoral practice, one that bequeathed serious, structural impoverishment to the colonized.[21] It is also undeniable, as Hickel intimates, that colonization is a historical part of modernity and that many states with a capitalist economy engaged in it. However, Hickel and critics err when suggesting this practice has a special, distinctive connection to modernity and capitalism. In fact, colonization was a constant in recorded human history. Moreover, according to contemporary Marxist historical sociology influenced by the work of Robert Brenner, political accumulation and territorial aggrandizement are, if anything, the sine qua non of *pre-capitalist* modes of production, which were unable to economically grow in a sustained fashion through continuous productivity increases.[22] In short, it is unclear why Hickel points to colonization to dispute the statistics on extreme poverty reduction or the claim capitalism and industrialization helped reduce extreme poverty.

It is not correct, as the third point on the list claims, that the standard extreme poverty measure (living with less than a $1.9 a day) tells us nothing important about people's lives, or that when a person moves beyond the threshold they are virtually just as badly off as they were before. This is so for two reasons.

First, the standard measure of extreme poverty strongly tracks Allen's new 'cost of basic needs' measure, so it clearly is not arbitrary but adequately reflects the bare minimum people need to survive. There is no issue here either of 'dollar arbitrariness' because the measure does not rely on a monetary threshold, nor is there any issue of creating a single, homogenizing poverty line for all countries and all time. As Moatsos say,

> The goal of this chapter is to provide global, regional and country estimates of a specific measure of extreme poverty for (almost) all present-day countries of the world as if they were sovereign in 1820. ... In this approach, poverty lines are calculated for every year and country separately, rather than using a single global line.[23]

Second, if a person lives under the standard extreme poverty threshold and then just barely moves beyond it, her life is indeed undoubtedly still very miserable, and one should not tout this as incredible progress. However, now she is at least able to survive when before she was barley doing that (or not at all). That is at least the necessary first step on the way to progress.

Hickel and the other critics are wrong that the $1.9 a day threshold is arbitrary or irrelevant for assessing improvement in people's ability to satisfy their most basic survival needs. Nevertheless, they are correct that other thresholds, say $5 a day, exist and that they sensibly posit much higher thresholds which, if they are reached, suggest much more meaningful progress.[24] Unfortunately, there is no longitudinal historical data for these higher thresholds. But the data that exist are clear. As Figure 3.1 shows, all measures of absolute poverty from the lowest to the highest show a steady, although admittedly less significant and slower, decline.[25] In 1981, 57.39% of the world population lived on less than $3.2 a day. That share has declined to 24.25% in 2017. For $5.5, the drop has been from 66.54% (in 1981) to 43.53% (in 2017). In 1981, 75.06% of the world lived on less than $10, while in 2017 the share has decreased to 62.35%.

The fifth point claims that China singlehandedly drove virtually all of the poverty reduction in previous decades. The suggestion is that *global* poverty was not really reduced. Instead, it was (almost) all concentrated in a single country.

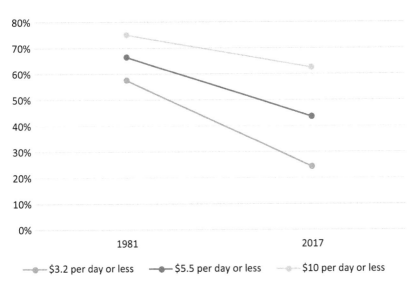

FIGURE 3.1   Share of world population living in poverty according to more demanding poverty measures (adjusted for differences in purchasing power across
countries and inflation).
Source: PovcalNet World Bank via Our World in Data (Roser 2021).

Now, it is true that China, since it started introducing market reforms and since
it has liberalized, was responsible for a large part of poverty reduction since the
1980s. When we exclude China, global extreme poverty has fallen from 29% in
1981 to 18% in 2008.[26] If we include China, the reduction was from 42.2% in
1981 to 18.1% in 2008.[27] After 2008, the two rates overlap each other virtually
completely. So, China was a very important, albeit far from the only, contributor
to world poverty reduction until 2008. This fact should not be surprising (or
presented in a dismissive tone in discussions of global poverty reduction) since
China after all accounts for a fifth of humanity. Be that as it may, it is simply not
true that the last decades of poverty reduction have essentially been solely due
to China's economic growth. After 2008, China contributed nothing to world
extreme poverty reduction, while in the decades before that around half of the
reduction was due to countries other than China.

In fact, *all regions of the world* (save for one) have been on a clear and continuous
downward extreme poverty trend since the last decades of the 20th century.[28]
Between 1990 and 2019, extreme poverty in Latin America and the Caribbean
has fallen from 15.2% to 3.7%.[29] In South Asia, poverty has been reduced from
just under 50% in 1990 to 15.2% in 2014. In West Africa, the figures are 56.5%
(in 1990) and 34.5% (in 2019). In Sub-Saharan Africa, the share in poverty was
55.1% in 1990, while it stood at 40.4% in 2018. In East Africa, the reduction has
been modest, but still palpable: around 60% of the population lived in extreme
poverty in the early 1990s, and 43.7% lived in poverty in 2018. The fall was most
impressive in East Asia and the Pacific: in 1990, 60.9% were mired in poverty,

while in 2019, 1% struggle to survive. Only in the Middle East and North Africa is the trend more complicated. In 1990, poverty stood at 6.5%. It then increased in the following year to 10.2% and then started falling steadily from a high of 10.2% to a low of 2.1% in 2013. Then, it started increasing again so that in 2018 it was at 7%. The same downward trends for world regions appear if we use higher measures of absolute poverty, such as $3.2 or $5.5.

Taking up the last point from the list, Hickel is clearly correct that the Chinese economy is not a free-market capitalist economy based on the strict adherence to the policies and institutions recommended by the Washington consensus.[30] However, he brushes over an important fact. Namely, that China's miraculous growth and poverty reduction has only happened since it started dismantling collectivised farming, protectionism, and state-planned pricing, and replacing them with market mechanisms, private property, and the private sector.[31] China definitely demonstrates that hundreds of millions of people can be lifted out of extreme poverty without neoliberal shock therapy or wholesale dismantling of the state. In short, it shows that capitalism with strong statist features has no problem of dealing with extreme poverty. But China of the past few decades is still clearly a capitalist society. Between 1980 and 2018, its economic freedom score has increased from a low of 3.91 to a more respectable, if still below-average, 6.21.[32] Significant gains were made in all five areas tracked by the Fraser Institute's *Economic Freedom Index*, i.e. government, property rights, sound money, international trade restrictions, and regulation, with the biggest gains registered in trade restrictions and regulation area.[33]

What the market alone does, and does not do, for poverty

It is not just the general timing of the transition to capitalism and extreme poverty reduction that suggests the former had something to do with the latter. The data show a clear and strong correlation between increases in wealth of a society (GDP per capita), for which capitalism is primarily responsible, and poverty reduction. The global average of extreme poverty has steadily declined as GDP per capita increased: see Figure 3.2.[34] As the world moved from a GDP of just over $1.000 (in 1820) to $5.000, extreme poverty (as measured by the 'cost of basic needs' approach) had dropped from around 75% to less than 50%. It then fell to 25% as the world moved to a GDP per capita of $10.000. As it passed the $15.000 mark between 2010 and 2017, the share of poverty declined further to 10%.

The same pattern holds for every region of the world, including Sub-Saharan Africa, although the GDP thresholds are somewhat different for each region as there are various endogenous and exogenous reasons – reasons having to do with the speed of development (i.e. early versus late developers), geopolitics and war, foreign aid, the timing of economic crises, and so on – for why poverty is reduced earlier or later.[35] In Sub-Saharan Africa, for example, extreme poverty was almost 90% in 1820. As the region moved to a GDP per capita of $2.000, the share fell to 50%. It now approaches $5.000, and the share is 37% (as of 2017). The correlation

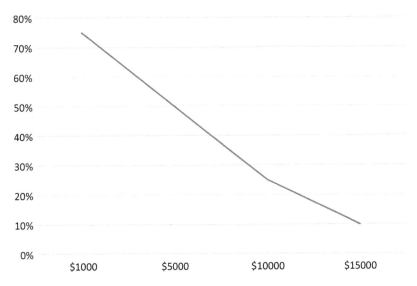

FIGURE 3.2 Share of world population living in extreme poverty (defined as 'cost of basic needs') at different levels of world's economic development (expressed in GDP per capita, adjusted for inflation and differences in purchasing power across countries).

Source: Moatsos 2021 and Bolt and van Zanden 2021 via Our World in Data (Roser 2021).

coefficient between GDP growth and share in extreme poverty for the almost 200-year period between early 19th and early 21st century is, on a typical year, stronger than −0.5 (the average for the whole period is −0.59), which means that, statistically speaking, sheer economic growth explains a substantial part of poverty reduction.[36]

Apart from this longitudinal perspective, it is also clear that today societies with greater overall economic freedom (one measure of how capitalist a society is) enjoy the lowest poverty rates in the world. If we group them under four quartiles, we can see that the various poverty rates in first quartile (where economic freedom is highest) were 1.7% (living with less than $1.9 a day), 4.37% (less than $3.2 a day), and 9.84% (less than $5.5 a day) between 2000 and 2018.[37] Even just moving to the second quartile, holding inflation and purchasing power constant, the population shares for the various poverty thresholds were much higher: 9.4%, 19.02%, and 33.59%, respectively. They were higher still in the third quartile and even higher in the fourth quartile. Moreover, in 2018, the absolute level of income earned by poorest 10% of population in most economically free societies was significantly higher than in societies of the second, third, or fourth quartile. On average, the bottom decile in countries classified as belonging to the first quartile by economic freedom received more than $12.000 a year, compared to almost $5.000 a year received by the bottom decile in the countries of the second quartile, slightly over $2.500 in the third, and slightly over $1.500 in the fourth.

These measurements, again, control for inflation and differences in purchasing power across countries.

All of this is very suggestive of capitalism and economic development in general having something important to do with poverty reduction. However, we must be careful not to hastily conclude that the capitalist market, and especially free markets without a welfare state, are the solution to global poverty everywhere and for all times. Modern markets are, undoubtedly, the chief source of wealth creation and, therefore, have to be implicated in how much the typical person's material standards have increased over the past two centuries. In fact, in an extremely poor and economically undeveloped society, simply successfully unleashing economic growth through market reforms typically does wonders for the material well-being of the poor. However, especially if we are concerned about the fate of poor people in advanced, developed societies, sheer economic growth is usually not enough for their livelihoods to keep improving. Of course, markets in advanced capitalist societies remain the main mechanism of wealth creation, but they are no longer a robust mechanism of improving poor people's lives. When it comes to *distribution* of the wealth generated by the market, the modern welfare states play an important role.

Lane Kenworthy has shown that as the advanced economies' GDP per capita increased between 1979 and 2007, incomes of the poorest (the lowest decile) have also notably risen in the majority of cases (11 out of 17).[38] 'Growth is good for the poor,' says Kenworthy.[39] However, if we look at the specific source of the poor's income growth, we see that in the majority of these cases (though not all) it was not their earnings and other market income that were mainly responsible for their improvement.[40] Primarily, it was net government transfers. In countries like the Netherlands and Switzerland, earnings were also rising, but this is not the typical case. Moreover, there are a few countries, such as the US, Germany, Australia, and Canada, where the poor saw little or no growth either of their earnings or government transfers. In these atypical cases, GDP per capita increased, but the average income of the bottom decile remained more or less stagnant.

Growth is still good for the poor – even in the advanced capitalist societies. Without growth, the amount of government transfers would not have increased in the majority of advanced countries in Kenworthy's sample. 'Where net government transfers increased, this was underwritten by economic growth. None of these countries significantly raised the share of GDP going to transfers during this period.' But growth is good for the poorest of the poor in these advanced societies *primarily 'if social policy passes it on.'*[41] It was not the market alone that helped the bottom 10% in these countries. It was the market in conjunction with a generous welfare state. As Kenworthy notes, this conclusion should not be surprising as many in the bottom decile are simply unable to work and so cannot afford to live off the market:

> For this bottom 10 percent there are limits to what employment can achieve. In all of these countries, 5 percent or more of working-age households have

no employed adult. Some people have psychological, cognitive, or physical condition that limit their earnings capability. Others are constrained by family circumstances. At any given point in time some will be out of work due to structural or cyclical unemployment. And in all rich countries a large and growing number of households are headed by retirees.[42]

In conclusion, capitalism does not create absolute immiseration, as at least some contemporary critics of capitalism such as Hickel still intimate. In fact, absolute immiseration was, and still is, impressively *reduced* with the transition to the modern economy.

Capitalism tames exploitation but does not eliminate it completely

The theoretical case for and against the existence of exploitation in capitalism

But, if not immiserated, are workers under capitalism nevertheless exploited? Are the fruits of their labour taken from them without appropriate remuneration? For Marx and the Marxists, the answer is obvious and clearly affirmative. In the past, still relying on the discredited labour theory of value, the argument was simple. Labour-power is the source of all value, and given that capitalists – who themselves do not work (or work only a little) – capture a large fraction of the generated value in the form of profits at the end of the production-sales cycle, it follows that at least some amount of value created by workers must have been appropriated without pay by capitalists.[43] What the capitalist pays a worker in return for the worker performing labour for him – the wage – cannot be fully commensurate with the value the worker created for the capitalist in the production process. Hence, the worker is necessarily exploited under capitalism.

The fact that the central premise above – and a crucial part of the labour theory of value – namely that labour-power is the source of all value has been thoroughly discredited since the Marginalist Revolution in the late 19th century does not really undermine contemporary Marxists' charge of capitalist exploitation. Without reliance on the old theory, contemporary Marxists such as Wright and Chibber make the following case.[44] Capitalists want to keep their production costs as low as possible so as to maximize the amount of profit they generate for themselves by selling products on the market above production costs. Now, labour is one key production cost for capitalists. They have to pay wages to workers; otherwise, the latter do not show up for work. So, capitalists will among other things strive to pay their workers as little as possible, i.e. just enough for the workers to show up, while also extracting the highest amount possible of work-effort from them so that workers produce as much as possible for a given amount of payment. 'This, roughly, is,' says Wright, 'what is meant by "exploitation".'[45]

He does not make this explicit, but I suspect the following is the reason for calling the situation 'exploitative' (which is a normative charge usually relating to unjustly unequal exchange). The reason is that there is a general expectation that in many cases the above dynamic will lead to workers being paid less than what their actual contribution to the firm was (or would have been) worth if capitalists were not able to drive down the wages so low. And they are able to drive them down because market conditions are not a levelled playing field. Here, Chibber is more explicit – although, interestingly, he does not mention the word exploitation. A capitalist can make the worker work for a low wage that strikes us as unfair in some way (or exploitative, non-reciprocal, etc.) because the power relation between the two is unequal. The capitalist 'has the power to hire and fire – and the worker is rarely in a position to afford losing her job.'[46] The worker works at the mercy of the employer (this is the asymmetric power point), which usually means that the latter will be able to extract more from the former than would be just and commensurate under more symmetric bargaining conditions (this is the exploitation charge).

For a long time, mainstream, neoclassical economics was perceived to strongly disagree with this Marxist analysis and its conclusions. More to the point, basic introductory economics is seen by many as providing an unambiguous, law-like apologetic explanation for why capitalism is simply *incompatible* with exploitation. This is so because the 'perfect competition' introductory model ineluctably proves that capitalist competition will eliminate any existing exploitation. In a perfectly competitive labour market – where movement from job to job is frictionless, all actors are price-takers and are completely rational and informed – workers receive a wage identical to their productivity, or the amount of value they contribute to the firm. In more technical terms, in the model the wage is equal to the 'marginal product' created by the worker (i.e. the added benefit the firm received by employing one more worker).[47]

Why should that be? Intuitively, the mechanism that ensures this theoretically pans out in the model looks as follows. If worker A is capable (due to her own human capital and due to the existing level of technological sophistication in an industry) of creating $10 worth of value, but her current employer X is only willing to employ her at a $5 wage (exploiting the employee at a rate of 100%), other employers who are also in need of an extra worker are now presented with a lucrative profit opportunity. If they manage to lure the worker away from employer A to instead work for them, they will be able to exploit her and reap similar additional profits just like the first exploitative employer is currently doing. For example, employer Y should be willing to offer the worker a higher wage, say $6, so as to motivate her to switch employment from X to Y. If employer Y is successful in luring the worker away from X, employer Y now has an additional worker (worker A) who creates $4 extra benefit for Y ($10-$6). This is less than the $5 the first employer was able to extract but still clearly profitable and thus beneficial for Y. However, observe what has happened to the level of exploitation experienced by the worker. It went down. Her wage has increased (from $5 to $6) and the unpaid value extracted from her has been reduced.

Now imagine what the incentive for the next employer Z is. Employer Z is now motivated to lure the worker away from Y by offering her an even bigger wage, say $7, to gain a net benefit of $3 (which is a smaller amount than before but definitely better than the $0 of additional profits Z is currently enjoying). The exploitation experienced by the worker is decreasing with each offer. And, according to the perfect competition model, it should decrease further still as other employer have an incentive to bid up the wage of worker A right up until the point where they cannot capture any additional benefit from having her employed – i.e. up to the worker's productivity or marginal product ($10). Thus, one should expect perfectly competitive capitalist markets not only to not increase exploitation and keep it high (as per the Marxist critique) but actually decrease it and even completely eliminate it.

Capitalism's critics might accept this theoretical account as suggestive or even internally coherent, but they would also (correctly) point out that conditions stipulated by the perfect competition model simply do not obtain in the real world. Markets are *not* perfectly competitive. This is so because economic actors are not simply price-takers, and they are not wholly rational and informed.

For example, in the real world, there might exist market concentration which can give firms price-setting power as Wright and Chibber gestured above. In such conditions, employees do not have an easy time exiting the current firm and getting (better) employment elsewhere because there simply are not that many competitors to which they could turn. Moreover, even when market concentration is not a problem and there are lots of alternative options, workers simply do not have all the information about which particular employers exist and are looking for additional workers, or how high the wages they are willing to offer are. After all, becoming informed about one's choices is costly in terms of time and energy expended, so workers might remain imperfectly informed even for rational reasons. So, being imperfectly informed, they might overlook beneficial employment offers, and then the whole bidding-up logic outlined in the previous paragraph gets short-circuited. As a result, exploitation persists in the market and does not get eliminated. Lastly, workers might intentionally tolerate some exploitation at their current employer if they have developed certain emotional attachments to the firm, such as deep friendships with colleagues, and so on. This is one more reason why wages are not guaranteed to equal workers' marginal product in capitalism. In sum, there are many real-world conditions, such as the existence of market concentration or market power and search costs/frictions, that make the logic and conclusions of the perfect competition model inapplicable outside the textbook.

Now, is this enough to (1) indict economics? Is it enough to (2) conclude the Marxists are correct? Does it (3) corroborate their reliance on the simple EPI graph to empirically demonstrate (rising) exploitation? One must tread lightly here.

First, the perfect competition model is only *one* economics model, not the *only* one. In fact, the same students who started out with perfect competition in their first year of college quickly learn of a different model which turns out to be more applicable in the real world. That is the 'monopsony' or 'monopsonistic competition' model. The model assumes stifled competition or search frictions, and it elegantly demonstrates how under such imperfectly competitive conditions wages will not equal workers' marginal product. In a word, it demonstrates exploitation. (At least if we take exploitation to be, roughly, the discrepancy between the benefit a worker added to the firm and the pay he got in return for that benefit).

Contrary to a pervasive myth, mainstream economics is not – especially not today – apologetic of capitalism. In fact, it provides the very basis upon which a powerful theoretical account of the various shortcomings of the capitalist economy as it exists right now can be launched. As the former Marxist economist Herbert Gintis observed, 'Most of my radical economist friends [argued] ... that standard economic theory is simply an apology for free market capitalism ... The truth is quite the opposite. ... Standard economic theory provides the proper framework for analysing market failure.'[48] It is true, of course, that economics provides reasons to be sceptical not only of markets (due to market failure) but also of state intervention (due to government failure). Nevertheless, a judicious reading of economics and economics textbooks does not easily lend itself to unqualified free-market dogma as charged by critics.[49]

Second, Marxists are correct that exploitation persists in capitalism, but they miss or underemphasize two important points. First, capitalism – as opposed to pre-capitalist and socialist societies – has a built-in market mechanism, i.e. competition, that tends to tone down exploitation to a certain extent even under fairly general conditions. It does not completely eliminate it, but it does reduce it. Second, Marxists seemingly miss the fact that exploitation is not a binary but a spectrum. One is not simply exploited or not exploited. Workers are exploited to a higher or lower degree. And, as already intimated, one would expect even imperfect market competition to put most workers on the lower end of the spectrum.

Indeed, currently existing empirical measures of exploitation suggest workers are paid about 20% less than what their marginal product is (lower estimates put the share at 15%, higher estimates at 25%).[50] This is important and a rather strong vindication of the Marxist exploitation charge against capitalism. But it also flies in the face of various Marxist gestures that exploitation is either extremely high (that would probably mean that it exceeds 40%, 50%, or 60%) or that it is inherently rising under capitalism.

Third, the use of the EPI graph to claim enormous exploitation belies a much more complex reality. There are many issues here. For example, the size of the gap between productivity and pay changes significantly depending on the different price deflator one uses. More fundamentally, the gap cannot be solely – or even primarily – attributed to employers exploiting workers. There is robust evidence that sluggish growth of the median wage after 1973 is in large part a function of skill-biased technological change, which has nothing to do with worker exploitation.[51] In contrast to workers at the median or lower down, workers with above-average education who are employed in sectors where computing and communications technology figures heavily *have* seen their wages rise significantly in the past decades. The wages (real weekly earnings, which are not even the whole compensation received by workers from employers) of male workers with a Bachelor's degree have increased by 40% between 1964 and 2012.[52] Those with education higher than an undergraduate degree have seen their wages grow by more than 90% in the same period.[53]

This is because, in recent decades, technological innovation which raises labour productivity has significantly affected primarily the more skilled jobs, but not the jobs in other sectors that require less skill. Janitors or store clerks, for example, have seen their wages stagnate not necessarily because of increasing exploitation (i.e. their marginal product ostensibly increasing but their wages not tracking that increase) but rather because they have simply not become much more productive over the decades. They perform tasks which have not been made significantly more productive by new technology, so their marginal product remains relatively small. The EPI graph thus hides the heterogeneity of productivity (and wage) growth *across different sectors*. In reality, some workers have become much more productive and their wages roughly tracked the increase, while other workers are just as productive today as they were in the seventies and their (stagnant) wages are tracking that fact.

Technological change also had other effects that can help explain why, for some workers, wages have been sluggish, stagnant, or even falling. For instance, some jobs have been wholly automated away due to technical innovation, which means that the demand for a certain worker and his skill set has plummeted, stifling wage growth or putting it in reverse for that subset of the workforce.

Next, the booming of global trade since 1980s is another factor apart from technological change (or domestic exploitation of workers) that has negatively affected a section of Western workers with lower education. Outsourcing and cheap imports from China and elsewhere have destroyed certain jobs in the US, forcing workers to try their hand at retraining and finding employment elsewhere.[54] Some of them struggled to do that and got hired primarily in sectors with much lower wages than their previous manufacturing job offered. So, as the output of goods per worker (i.e. productivity) increased *in general* in the previous decades, wages of *particular groups* of workers did not reflect that change simply because these workers were not tied to productivity growth. Exploitation is a separate issue that is orthogonal to all of that.

Of course, as I have already pointed out and as will be discussed in more detail below, workers *are* exploited in capitalism and that is one of the reasons for the divergence between productivity and pay. But it is not the only or the primary reason. After all, if we took the graph as direct evidence of exploitation, then we would have to say that there was no worker exploitation in American capitalism between 1948 and 1973 when the graph shows no divergence between productivity (it rose by 96.7%) and compensation (it rose by 91.3%).[55] That seems unlikely and definitely not something Marxists would take kindly to.

Empirical evidence for imperfect competition and monopsony: minimum wage research and market concentration

We have seen, theoretically, why and how imperfectly competitive markets engender a degree of exploitation. I have also pointed to two recent empirical studies estimating the extent of exploitation in real-world, imperfect capitalism. Defenders of capitalism are usually not really convinced by the outlined critique. For example, in her recent book *Private Government*, the philosopher Elizabeth Anderson presented an insightful critique of capitalist firms along similar lines. The economist Tyler Cowen wrote a critical, if also generally appreciative, response. In it, he focused specifically on her charge of monopsony exploitation. This is his rebuttal:

> Many corporate critics, including Anderson at the tail end of her piece, postulate the existence of 'monopsony' – namely, that a single company has a good deal of market power of the workers it employs. I am worried she, like others, doesn't offer much evidence to back up her portrait, save for one footnote to an adequate but not very influential book. In contrast to her treatment, the best study I know finds that Walmart – the largest private sector employer in America – does not have significant monopsony power in most regions, some parts of the rural south and center excepted.[56]

In what follows, I respond to Cowen's scepticism by presenting both indirect and direct evidence of at least a moderate amount of monopsony in particular and imperfect competition more generally in the US economy.

Turning first to indirect evidence, the recent explosion of rigorous minimum wage research shows quite conclusively that at least a modestly high minimum wage – and modest minimum wage increases – typically does not have significant dis-employment effects. For example, 23 studies published between 2000 and 2013, which contain hundreds of quantitative estimates, reveal two important insights.[57]

First, that on several occasions increases in the minimum wage result either in significantly higher unemployment or significantly *lower unemployment*. Contrary to expectations that the minimum wage *always* increases wages above workers' marginal product and that it should, therefore, *always* result in employers laying off overpaid workers, it actually motivates additional employment in several cases. As I explain below, this is exactly what we would expect if at least certain markets are not perfectly competitive.

Second, the studies reveal that the single most common effect of a moderate minimum wage increase on employment is almost zero – more precisely, it is slightly negative (−0.03). This number denotes elasticity, and it means that a 25% increase of the minimum wage increases unemployment by only 0.75%. This is, again, a somewhat (though not completely) unexpected result if markets are thought of as perfectly competitive. But it is a matter of course if competition in the real world is less than perfect.

Other literature reviews reveal a slightly more negative but still quite mixed and, in general, unexpected picture.[58] Two conclusions are usually made. First, that unless the minimum wage is increased to above around 60% of the median wage in a country, then dis-employment effects are modest and lower than what the perfect competition model would predict. Second, that significant heterogeneity in the effects of the minimum wage on employment obtains in different locations – strongly negative, modestly negative, neutral, and even positive. What can we draw from all of this?

Let us first walk through the standard economic argument for why an even modestly high minimum wage should negatively affect employment.

If the labour market is perfectly competitive, such that workers are paid exactly the amount of their marginal product, a high minimum wage stipulating that employers pay their workers in excess of their marginal contribution to the firm will cause employers to start losing money. Employers will realize that under these new conditions some of their least productive workers contribute, say, only $5 worth of value an hour while costing them, the employers, $7 an hour (stipulated by the increased minimum wage). In other words, they will realize that they should let some workers go. After all, minimum-wage laws do not require employers to *keep* the currently employed workers. Therefore, some low-productivity workers will be fired, and employers will try to compensate the loss of labour by either hiring a more productive worker instead (one whose marginal product is not below the minimum wage) or by automating production (seeing as how machines are not affected by minimum-wage laws). Neither of these two options is good for the employment rate of low-productivity workers who would much rather be employed for $5 an hour without minimum-wage laws than not be employed at all (with $7 minimum-wage laws in place).

This is the standard argument against the minimum wage, and it seems quite convincing (and normatively pro-labour) in the context of perfectly competitive markets. But what if we drop the unrealistic assumption? What if workers are not paid their marginal product on the labour market? What if we look at the effects of minimum wage through the monopsony model? In this case, and if the minimum wage is not too high, employers will not likely be motivated to fire their workers. This is so because, if the marginal product of a worker (say, $5 an hour) had already been higher than what he was paid (say, $3.5 an hour) before the minimum wage was introduced or raised, then a modest increase of the latter (say, to $4.5 or $5 an hour) should not exceed his marginal product. In this case, the employer will have no incentive to fire the worker. Moreover, not only will employers not have an incentive to fire workers, instead certain previously unemployed workers might now, with the introduction of a minimum wage which pushes wages in line with workers' marginal product, be willing to seek employment. Under imperfect competition, a minimum wage increase does not necessarily increase unemployment but can, in fact, even lower it.

In this sense, contemporary minimum-wage research by itself indirectly suggests that many markets are quite imperfectly competitive and monopsonistic, which, in turn, means that a certain degree of exploitation is quite possible and, indeed, likely. That the former actually holds and is not just idle speculation is attested to by a recent study by Azar and colleagues.[59] As they put it:

> While increases in the minimum wage are found to significantly decrease employment of workers in low concentration markets, minimum wage-induced employment changes become less negative as labor concentration increases, and are even estimated to be positive in the most highly concentrated markets. *Our findings provide direct empirical evidence supporting the monopsony model as an explanation for the near-zero minimum wage employment effect documented in prior work.*

There is also plenty of other direct evidence, not having to do with the minimum wage, for either monopsony in particular or imperfect competition more generally in the US economy. One of the most systematic inquiries into the phenomenon I know of is a recent meta-analysis that looked at estimates of labour supply elasticities provided by 53 existing studies.[60] The main finding of the meta-analysis is that the current empirical literature 'provides strong evidence for monopsonistic competition,' which 'implies sizable markdowns in wages.'[61]

In 2016, the *Council of Economic Advisers* (CEA) issued a brief in which they warned of declining competition in the US. The CEA brief points to three key pieces of evidence for this: '1) increasing concentration across a number of industries, 2) increasing rents, in the form of higher returns on invested capital, across a number of firms, and 3) decreasing business and labor dynamism.'[62] Both market and government failures can be pointed to as the principal sources of this unappealing decline in the competitiveness of the US economy.

Unpacking (1), the CEA brief reviews studies which reveal that revenue shares of the largest firms in various sectors (and loan market shares of top banks) have been steadily increasing in the past decades, roughly between 1980 and 2010. This is a pretty good indication that market concentration has been rising at the end of the 20th century.

Demonstrating (2), the CEA brief points to how 'the 90th percentile firm sees returns on investments in capital that are more than five times the median. This ratio was closer to two just a quarter of a century ago.'[63] This means that top firms in multiple industries are receiving very large (and rapidly increasing) rents. Market competition, it seems, is not healthily eroding above-average profits – perhaps because market competition is actually *declining*.

Lastly, (3) the CEA brief demonstrates that the annual rate of new firm openings has been steadily falling between 1977 and 2013, while firm closures have remained the same.[64] Likewise, the churn of workers – 'the frequency of changes in who is working for whom in the labor market' – has also declined in the same timeframe. Such increased market concentration and decreased dynamism are by themselves suggestive of stifled competition. And, indeed, other studies explicitly link rising labour market concentration with declining wages and increased market power.[65]

Similar to the CEA brief, Germán Gutiérrez and Thomas Philippon report two broad recent findings about the US corporate sector that they present as 'important stylized facts.'[66] First, 'there has been a broad decrease in turnover and a broad increase in concentration across most US industries.'[67] In short, competition is weak. Second, 'corporate investment has been unexpectedly weak in recent years ... the cumulative under-investment is more than 10% of capital.'[68] In short, investment has also been weak, at least relative to Tobin's Q, which is a ratio of the market value of a company to its assets' replacement cost. What is most important for my case here is that Gutiérrez and Philippon provide evidence in their paper that the first fact – decreasing competition and increasing market concentration – is what helps account for the latter.

In another working paper, Jan de Loecker and Jan Eeckhout provide wide-ranging data that show increasing market power (proxied by rising markups, the ratio of a product's price to its costs of production) *across the world* between 1980 and 2016, but mostly in North America and Europe.[69] They suggest this could account for the decrease in labour's share of revenue in the past decades.

There are other recent studies that also point to surprising developments in the US economy, such as Stansbury's and Summers' latest contribution.[70] Chief among them, again, is that Tobin's Q has risen since the 1980s (as have corporate profits), while – unexpectedly – investment is weak. Stansbury's and Summer's preferred explanation is more centred on 'declining worker power' as a result of a decline in unions or increase in corporate management ruthlessness than on the standard monopoly/monopsony power argument proffered by sources cited in previous paragraphs. However, all these different explanations can be complementary and all point firmly toward imperfect competition, market power, and (consequently) worker exploitation.

We can clearly see that neither mainstream economists and their empirical research, nor neoclassical economic theory, are apologetic of contemporary capitalism. Exploitation is a reality in capitalism as it was, although to a much more significant extent, in pre- or non-capitalist societies. One does not need to rely on old discredited economic theories and dubious ideological claims to demonstrate or acknowledge this fact.

Inequality rising?

In the first section of the present chapter we have seen that, historically, capitalism simply cannot be indicted on the count of absolute poverty. Robust, competitive markets and secure property rights alone are enough to bring people out of extreme forms of poverty. Absolute poverty *in advanced capitalist societies* presents a more mixed picture, but still one in which capitalist markets play a significant and positive role. While economic growth does significantly increase material standards of the whole population compared to what came before, it does so primarily in the beginning (and unequally, of course). At later, post-industrial stages, market incomes for some (either the bottom 10% or a more expansive group of low-income earners) can be and are increasing only slowly, stagnate, or even decline somewhat in different time periods and countries. This can be significantly offset by countervailing non-market forces such as the welfare state. These tap into the enormous amounts of wealth created by markets and redistribute them more equitably.

The status of exploitation under capitalism is more mixed. Current (and realistically achievable) markets evince some amount of exploitation due to various factors that should be expected to either persist under realistic conditions or be only somewhat reduced, never perfectly eliminated. Market competition, which should in theory destroy exploitation, is imperfect. Both government meddling, embodied in bad regulations generated by rent-seeking and regulatory capture, and standard market failures are responsible for this imperfect state of affairs. However, this was much worse in past history when market competition and secure property right were much more absent than they are today. Moreover, it is virtually inconceivable that exploitation could be wholly eliminated under any system, either various forms of capitalism or (future) non-capitalist societies, unless we assume perfectly altruistic and informed agents. The question then becomes to what extent can exploitation be eliminated under different conditions. And one crucial condition is exactly market competition. Currently, it is in part due to not enough competition – i.e. due to market concentration – that exploitation persists.

At first blush, then, inequalities seem to be a starker and much more obvious problem in capitalist societies than either poverty or exploitation. No sophisticated analysis is required to recognize the existence of inequality and its rise in the past decades. In the US, the share of society's total income going to the top 1% of earners has increased from a low of 11–12% in the 1970s to around 20% in the 21st century.[71] The Gini index of market income, where 0 means total equality and 1 total inequality, rose from an already high 0.43 in 1979 to 0.53 in 2013.[72] (This measure excludes the effects of redistributive policies. The Gini index of *disposable income* is significantly lower and rose to a lesser degree, indicating again how the welfare state can offset market-generated inequalities and even tone down their rate of increase. Disposable income Gini was 0.31 in 1979 and 0.38 in 2013.) Taking a broader perspective, between 1985 and 2008, income inequality has increased not only in the US but in many – though not all – OECD countries.[73]

This, however, is not the only or the most important development. *Wealth inequality* is (and was) even higher than income inequality, and it is also on the rise in recent decades. According to Thomas Piketty, the share of total wealth going to the top 1% in the US was slightly lower than 30% in 1970, while in 2010 it was already approaching 35%.[74] The Gini index of wealth inequality in the US in 1950 stood at 79 (on a scale from 0 to 100) and then increased to 88 in 2010.[75] Europe is more egalitarian. The share of total wealth going to the top 1% was 20% in 1970 and 25% in 2010.[76] European wealth Gini is also more egalitarian in comparison to that of the US – but is nevertheless high – with such diverse

European countries as Great Britain, Italy, Sweden, Spain, Poland, and Russia having a Gini index of 69, 63, 73, 67, 58, and 78, respectively, in 2010.[77]

In this section, we have two tasks in front of us. First, we must examine in greater detail and with a longer-term perspective what the dynamics of inequality are in different regions of the world. Although inequalities are increasing in many countries, this is not everywhere the case. Moreover, viewed in historical perspective, contemporary inequalities are less worrying than is usually claimed. Capitalism has not been steadily increasing inequalities from an allegedly low starting point in pre-capitalist times to new highs every next decade.

Second, because in contrast to poverty and exploitation inequality is not immediately and by itself welfare reducing, we must explore the likely *indirect* deleterious effects that high, and rising, inequality can have on society over time. In other words, even though it makes for a good political slogan, it is important to note that high and rising inequality does not necessarily, simply by definition, mean that the rich are getting richer *while the poor are getting poorer*. That is a misconstrual of what (rising) inequality is. In fact, as we have seen in the first section on poverty, most advanced economies have seen the incomes of their poorest 10% grow between 1979 and 2007, even though inequalities were also increasing in the same period. Even in the US, where the poorest of the poor really were economically stagnant in the past decades and where inequalities are highest compared to the rest of the developed world, the average person nevertheless saw their income grow. Both the real median family income and personal income have risen by around 40% between 1974 and 2019.[78]

That is why we must carefully consider how high and rising inequality nevertheless might be injurious to the less privileged in ways other than directly lowering their living standards. Some tend to skip this important step. The economist Deirdre McCloskey, for example, claims there is nothing serious to worry about in regards to increasing inequality, as long as poverty is also not increasing. As she acerbically puts it, critiquing Piketty,

> What is worrying [him] is that the rich might possibly get richer, even though the poor get richer too. His worry, in other words, is purely about difference, about the Gini coefficient, about a vague feeling of envy raised to a theoretical and ethical proposition.[79]

McCloskey's critique notwithstanding, we will see that there is more to inequality than just a 'vague feeling of envy.'

Inequalities are not high and rising everywhere and in all contexts

Income inequality

Is the world getting more unequal? In one sense, the answer is definitely 'no' – despite the previously cited figures. *Global income inequality*, i.e. inequality between all individual citizens of the world, has indeed been on the rise between 1820 and 1950, as the world Gini index rose from 55 to more than 70. But then inequality more or less *stagnated* after World War II, and around 1980 a slow *decline* was already in effect.[80] At the beginning of the 21st century, global inequality declined sharply in a short span of time so that in 2013 world Gini index stood at 65, which is around what it had been in 1900. Therefore, it was higher in 2013 than before, and still very high in an absolute sense, *but also lower than at any other point in the 20th century.* The decline has continued in recent years all the way up to the present (2020).[81] This happened primarily (but not solely, especially not in recent years) due to the spectacular economic rise of China since 1980 and India somewhat later.[82]

Income inequality *between countries*, i.e. the difference in average income across different societies, has also been on a downward trend lately. Depending on the particular measure (weighting countries by their populations or not), between-country income inequality has been modestly falling either since 2001 (to a Gini of around 54 in recent years) when unweighted between-country inequality reached a historic peak (Gini of 57), or already since 1990, when weighted between-country inequality started sharply declining from a high Gini of around 62 (after a two-decade long stagnation that has been going on since the early 1970s) to a significantly lower Gini of around 50 in late 2000s, even dipping to 45 in the last decade.[83]

In recent decades, there are even societies that have seen their *within-country* inequality fall. This means that differences in income between people of the same society have been reduced. For instance, since the 1990s – but particularly since the early 2000s – income inequality has been reduced within almost all Latin American countries.[84] Just between 2002 and 2012, the Gini coefficient of Brazil, Mexico, El Salvador, Peru, Argentina, Nicaragua, and Bolivia declined between 6% and 16% (in Chile it declined by slightly less than 5%).[85] Of course, this decline cannot be simply attributed to the successful performance of competitive markets, the main engine of capitalism. The welfare state was also a key proximal mechanism of inequality reduction.[86] Moreover, Latin American income inequality, which has historically been very high, remains high today and is much higher than, say, inequality in Europe. However, the notable inequality decrease in almost all Latin American countries shows that at least a social variety of the capitalist economy can prevent increases in inequality and that the gap between rich and poor need not inherently, inevitably rise within a modern economy.

How about within-country inequality outside Latin America? Between 2004 and 2019, the Gini coefficient in the EU has remained roughly stagnant, on average, and it has stayed at a low level (below a Gini of 35) throughout.[87] However, a broader perspective, which includes other developed countries outside the EU and looks further back in time, shows that income inequality has actually *risen* in many OECD countries at the close of the 20th century. Between 1985 and 2008, for example, Mexico, the US, Israel, Australia, Canada, New Zealand, Norway, and even EU countries such as the UK (now a former member), Italy, Finland,

Sweden, Denmark, and the Netherlands have all seen their Gini coefficient rise by several points.[88] Some, such as France, Hungary, and Belgium have stayed put in the same time period, while others, such as Greece or Turkey (outside EU), have actually lowered their inequality slightly.[89]

A different measure of within-country inequality, i.e. the share of total societal income received by the top 1% of earners, also provides important evidence of the evolution of inequality. According to this measure, inequality has been significantly rising for several decades between 1980 and 2014 in the US and in other English-speaking countries such as Ireland, Australia, Canada, and the UK.[90] On the other hand, however, this same measure of inequality has remained virtually stagnant in France, Japan, Spain, the Netherlands, and Denmark over the same three decades.[91] In these latter countries, the share of income received by the top 1% remains similar in 2014 (even if measured before taxes and redistribution) to what it was in the 1960s or 1970s, i.e. around a tenth (or lower) of the whole societal income.[92]

Across the whole of Europe, the share of income captured by the top 10% – which, note, is a different measure of inequality than the top 1% income share from the previous paragraph – has risen somewhat between 1980 and the late 1990s but has then remained *stagnant* between the late 1990s and late 2010s, not increasing any further.[93] China has seen a more pronounced increase since 1980 (from under 30% to over 40%) and no later stagnation, while in India the share has almost doubled from 30% to over 55% in the same period.[94] On the other hand, The Middle East and Brazil registered a decline since 1990, and Sub-Saharan Africa has stagnated.

Lastly, if we average it across the whole world, *within-country* income inequality measured with the Gini coefficient actually turns out to have been remarkably stable in the second half of the 20th century (1950–1990), fluctuating between 38 and 39.[95] From 1990 onward, however, it suddenly significantly increased, mostly on account of China.[96]

To conclude, the evolution of *global, between-country,* and *within-country* inequality does not point in the same direction. Even the exact trends of each of the three inequality measures, respectively, are highly dependent on the time period and geographical location under study. Any simple, straightforward conclusion about the evolution of inequality under capitalism is unfounded.

Wealth inequality

Inequalities of wealth also present a more complicated picture than is usually claimed. The Gini coefficient of wealth inequality in Britain, France, Germany, Italy, and Sweden was *lower* in 2010 than in 1950 and 1960, and it was either lower or the same in 2010 than in 1970.[97] Looking further back in time, the wealth Gini for Britain, France, Italy, and Sweden (the only countries we have historical data for, apart from the US) in 2010 was *significantly lower* than in 1820 (when it was around 90) or 1900 (around 90) or even 1920 (around 90).

Looking at the share of total societal wealth owned by the richest 1%, the richest Americans do possess a significantly larger percentage of wealth in 2010 than they did in 1950–1970. According to Piketty's data, the percentage in 2010 comes to about 34%, or 4 percentage points more than in 1970.[98] But even this is still much lower than it had been in 1920 or 1910 when the US top 1% wealth share stood at around 45%.[99] According to Gabriel Zucman's research, the increase has been somewhat more steep, approaching 39% in recent years but currently stagnating, which is comparable to the early 20th century.[100]

Piketty's data show that the top 1% in Europe in 2010 owned around 25% of total wealth, which is 5 percentage points more than in 1970 or 1980.[101] Relative to that point, wealth inequality is clearly increasing. However, the wealth share was much, much higher in the past: almost 40% in 1950, 55% in 1920, and more than 60% in 1910. Even in 1810, when almost no European society was capitalist, the top 1% wealth share was higher than 50%. Relative to that point, European inequality today is much lower.

The same trends are evident if we look at individual European countries for which we have deep historical data.[102] In Denmark, France, Finland, UK, Norway, and Sweden, the top 1%'s share of total wealth at the beginning of the 21st century is a few percentage points higher than what it had been in the early 1980s. It moved from under 20% to over 20%. However, this contemporary level of inequality is substantially lower compared to the 1950s or 1960, and *doubly or triply lower* compared to early 20th or the whole of 19th century. At the end of 18th century, wealth inequality in pre-capitalist European societies was already high. It then rose even higher in the 19th and early 20th century (with the exception of Norway and Denmark), and it declined sharply in mid-20th century, bottoming out at historically unprecedented levels around 1980. After that, it increased again, but it did so extremely modestly, viewed in this broader historical perspective.

Lastly, Zucman has constructed a proxy measure for world distribution of wealth by combining the top 1% wealth shares in China, Europe, and the US.[103] In the 1980s, this proxied global top 1% had a wealth share of around 27%. Between 2010 and 2017, the share stood at around 32%–33%, which is a notable increase. Interestingly, however, the biggest increase occurred in the 1990s. Indeed, looking at the period between the late 1990s and 2017, one is struck by the now two-decade long *stagnation of the top 1% wealth share.*

The fact remains that considered over a longer time period – say, half a century – within-country income and wealth inequality have risen in many countries. This should not be ignored or underemphasized. With that in mind, let us turn to the potential (and actual) pernicious social effects of inequality.

Inequality is not just about envy

None of the above observations should be seen as recommending complacency. Rising inequality, and especially a high level of inequality (which, fortunately, is currently not characteristic of most OECD countries), can have various deleterious effects on society. Employing simple rational choice analysis, it should be easy to see how inequality might theoretically cause the following, to mention just a few general possibilities: (i) broad political instability in a society, (ii) increased possibility for the rich to engage in more rent-seeking and corruption, or (iii) rising educational inaccessibility.

To be more specific, (i) political instability can be caused by inequality due to potential resentment and polarization of the less well-off as they compare their slower rate of improvement with the much faster rate of improvement of those more well-off. Inequality can also (ii) increase rent-seeking and corruption because the faster rate of material improvement for the rich causes them to possess a greater amount of resources with which they can influence the political process in comparison to the poor and ordinary citizens, whose resources are growing at a slower rate. (iii) If costs of education keep increasing at the current enormous rates, if public education spending is not keeping pace with these increases, and if the rich grow faster than other segments of the society, then poor and ordinary citizens will not be as able to climb as high on the education ladder as the rich.

These hypothetical developments are worrying already by themselves, but they also lead to further social problems down the line. Most importantly, the three consequences of inequality outlined above are themselves potential causal channels that lead from inequality to reduced economic growth. And if economic growth is impacted negatively, the prospects for improving the material well-being of the poor and ordinary citizens are also very likely to be directly undermined. The causal logic at work is not hard to imagine. Political instability, for instance, can disrupt economic growth because (or if) it negatively affects the general business and investment climate. Heightened rent-seeking and corruption cause state-mediated resource misallocation and thus hurt economic growth through reduced economic efficiency. Lastly, inaccessible education is likely to lead to talent misallocation, which again constitutes economic inefficiency and leads to reduced economic output. Whatever the particular causal mechanism, it is highly theoretically plausible that increased inequality negatively impacts economic growth in some way.

What does the empirical literature tell us about this? In the 1990s, an empirical consensus was emerging in economics that high and rising inequality, indeed, significantly reduces economic growth.[104] As one team of researchers in 1999 summarized the evidence, 'The picture [recent studies] draw is impressively unambiguous, since they all suggest that greater inequality reduces the rate of growth.'[105] However, early dissenters started appearing already at the turn of the century.[106] After that, the consensus shrank considerably or even disappeared, with many new studies reporting non-existent, mixed, or inconclusive results, especially in advanced economies.[107] There are a few recent exceptions, but these are also disputed.[108] In the 2017 iconoclastic collection *Economic Ideas You Should Forget*, Clemens Feust pithily proclaims, taking note of the just-mentioned exceptions, that

> Recent studies published by the OECD and IMF … constitute a misin-
> terpretation of the existing data and research findings. … There is exten-
> sive academic literature on the nature of the link between inequality and
> growth. The consensus finding of this research is that there is no robust
> correlation – either negative or positive – between the two.[109]

To my knowledge, there exists only one contemporary meta-analysis (from
2008) pooling together the various existing studies and using them to estimate
the overall average effect of inequality on growth. Its main conclusion is twofold:
'In the empirical literature, the majority of cross-sectional studies have found a
negative relationship between income inequality and growth. However, the negative effect seems to disappear when the models are estimated using panel data
techniques.'[110] This means that, 'So far no clear conclusions has been reached
… it is simply misleading to simply speak of a positive or negative relationship
between income inequality and economic growth.'[111]

Nowadays, more complex studies that do not simply look at the relationship between inequality and growth, but also include interaction terms such
as intergenerational mobility, seem the most promising in shedding new light
on this controversy. For instance, a recent study again confirmed, in contrast
to the emerging consensus of the 1990s, that the simple (negative) relationship
between inequality and growth simply does not hold.[112] But the same study also
demonstrated that, *dependent on the presence of low intergenerational mobility*, rising
inequality can significantly affect growth. More precisely, the researchers found
that, if inequality increases by ten units of Gini (expressed in percentage points)
and if the starting intergenerational income elasticity (IGE) is not too high – as is
the case in France, which sits at the 40th percentile –, then the average economic
growth over the next five years is only 0.1 percentage points lower than it would
have been otherwise. However, the same increase in inequality in a country with
much higher IGE – say, Brazil, which is at the 75th percentile – results in a significant reduction of economic growth: 0.7 percentage points over the next five
years. Theoretically, this is also perfectly plausible, but further empirical research
on this topic is needed before concluding a robust negative relationship.

Aside from economic growth, there is almost an inexhaustible set of potential other important social outcomes inequality is regularly claimed to damage.
The provocative and highly publicized book *The Spirit Level* famously set out
to demonstrate in 2010 that rising and high inequality is not only tied to worse
economic outcomes, but that it also exacerbates crime, leads to obesity and drug
use, increases child mortality, mental illness, and teenage pregnancies, reduces
social trust, and so on.[113]

The book has been rightly criticized as several of the presented analyses failed
to replicate. For instance, the association between inequality and mental illness,
obesity, and life expectancy loses statistical significance when OECD data is used
instead of UN data. More importantly, it has been pointed out that some of the
demonstrated correlations are not likely to be causal.[114]

Nevertheless, some of the book's claims seem to be borne out in the research (including the research generated after its publication). For instance, there is a clear correlation between higher inequality and certain health problems.[115] To some researchers, the correlation lends itself to a causal interpretation, but others remain more sceptical of its causal status.[116] Moreover, recent research typically finds that both happiness and generalized trust are decreased by rising or high inequality, at least after a certain critical inflection point has been reached.[117] Further still, the idea that inequality and crime seem to be connected – even causally so – has generally stood up to detailed scrutiny. Multiple meta-analyses find inequality to be a strong and consistent predictor of crime, especially homicide, with more inequality being associated with more crime.[118] Interestingly, however, the first such meta-analytic study to cover *Europe specifically* goes somewhat against this emerging consensus. It does replicate the finding that income inequality is associated with an increase in inequality, but the effect is extremely small, accounting for only 3% of the variance. Moreover, the effect was statistically significant only in Eastern and Northern Europe but not Western and Southern Europe.[119]

It is not the intention of this section to go over the whole scholarly debate on inequality's social correlates. However, I hope that both the theoretical and empirical sampling I provided above gives one a taste for the complexities involved.

In the beginning of the section on inequality, we have seen McCloskey rightly point out that rising inequality almost never results in 'the rich getting richer and the poor getting poorer' scenario decried by the political slogans of many social activists. Nevertheless, we have also seen that inequality is not only a trivial aesthetic social issue having primarily to do with our uglier, superficial emotions such as envy, which we can and should ignore if we are rational, adult, virtuous people (as McCloskey also seems to suggest). To the contrary, it can potentially be a serious social phenomenon that does, in certain circumstances, lead not only to an erosion of social stability, trust, and order but can even affect people's basic material well-being in a negative fashion by, for instance, impinging on their health and by creating economic deadweight loss. Despite McCloskey's justified point about the rising tide lifting all boats, inequality as a contemporary social phenomenon should be taken seriously, not dismissed out of hand.

Conclusion

In 1996, the economics Nobel laureate James Buchanan wrote for the *Wall Street Journal* that,

> Just as no physicist would claim that 'water runs uphill,' no self-respecting economist would claim that increases in the minimum wage increase employment. Such a claim, if seriously advanced, becomes equivalent to a denial that there is even minimal scientific content in economics, and that, in consequence, economists can do nothing but write as advocates for ideological interests.[120]

He wrote this in the 1990s, when rigorous empirical research on the effects of minimum wage in real-world markets was basically in its infancy. We now possess, as Buchanan did not, decades of evidence to show that, at least in some markets, modest increases of the minimum wage decrease employment only scarcely, do not decrease it at all in others cases, and can even increase it sometimes. But even apart from this, Buchanan's insinuation that there is simply no theoretical possibility of a minimum wage resulting in increased employment is (and was) wrong.[121] As the monopsony model demonstrates, it definitely is at least a theoretical possibility.

In 2017, the economist Russ Roberts made the argument that economics as a science is quite empirically under- or even undetermined, primarily because economists cannot create robust experimental conditions and really examine the impact of a variable in total (or at least sufficient) isolation from other variables.[122] From this claim, he arrived at two conclusions. First, he laudably calls for less selective sharing of empirical findings. However, second, he also claims that 'Economics is primarily a way of organizing one's thinking in considering incentives and costs and the interactions between individuals that we call a market but is really emergent behavior with feedback loops.'[123] In a word, economics is for Roberts primarily a theoretical activity. With this, he is – perhaps unintentionally – intimating something similar to what Buchanan seems to have said in 1996. That is, *theoretically*, increases in the minimum wage simply cannot increase unemployment due to the fundamental theoretical law of supply and demand.

What Roberts overlooks, however, is that there is not only one theoretical model generated by the economic way of thinking but many. Assuming perfect competition, Roberts' basic economic analysis of incentives correctly suggests increases in minimum wage will increase unemployment. However, *assuming imperfect competition* – the presence of market power, search costs and frictions, market concentration – the same economic way of thinking theoretically suggests a different possibility (or even necessity, in certain cases). In short, economic theory itself is not unambiguous but instead points in two completely different directions. And to know which theoretical assumption (and, therefore, conclusion) is more appropriate for the real world – or, more precisely, for *a certain corner of* the real world – one cannot do anything else but rely on empirical investigation. Roberts' counterpoint that empirical research can be undertaken in a biased way, or reported selectively (knowingly or not), is well taken. However, the solution then cannot be to 'primarily' rely on economics as a body of theory, as Roberts in part suggests. It cannot be, simply because that body of theory produces many different predictions for different social environments.

The present chapter strove to demonstrate that fact, and to show how one can use a combination of rational choice analysis and both simple and more complex statistics to arrive at nuanced and tentative, not partisan and absolutist, conclusions about how the modern economy works.

Notes

1 Chibber (2018, 22–23).
2 Chibber (2018).
3 Roser (2013).
4 In Baumol (1983), one of the world's most influential economists (according to IDEAS/RePEc), the now-deceased William Baumol, reviews the relevant textual evidence and clearly demonstrates that Marx mostly argued *against* the naïve Lassalean 'iron law of wages,' according to which wages in capitalism should be driven to the bare subsistence minimum. As Baumol puts it,

> Both vulgar Marxists and vulgar opponents of Marx have propounded two associated myths: that he believed wages under capitalism are inevitably driven near some physical subsistence level and that he considered this to constitute robbery of the workers and a major evil of capitalism.
>
> Baumol (1983, 303)

5 Hickel (2019a).
6 Beer (2020).
7 Ibid.
8 Oxfam (2021).
9 Elkins (2018).
10 Alvaredo et al. (2018).
11 Hickel (2019a); Milanovic (2019a); Hasell and Roser (2019).
12 See, e.g., Hickel (2019b; 2021).
13 Hickel (2019a). All subsequent points come from this source.
14 See Roser (2013); Hasell and Roser (2019).
15 Ibid.
16 Allen (2017).
17 Moatsos (2021).
18 Ibid.
19 The following are all the countries used from each individual world region:

> Japan for East Asia; South Africa (and Ghana up to 1870) for sub-Saharan Africa; Jordan, Lebanon, Egypt, Iran, Morocco, Tunisia, Syria and Turkey for the Middle East and North Africa; Denmark, Norway, Austria, Ireland, Italy, the Netherlands, France, the United Kingdom, Finland, Sweden and Portugal for Western Europe; the United States, Canada and Australia for the Western Offshoots; Argentina, Brazil, Chile, Colombia, Jamaica, Mexico, Peru, Uruguay and Venezuela for Latin America and the Caribbean; Indonesia, Sri Lanka, Myanmar, Malaysia, Nepal, the Philippines, Thailand and India (up to 1821) for South and Southeast Asia; and Poland for Eastern Europe and the former Soviet Union. More countries are used for imputations later in the 19th century and in the 20th and 21st centuries.
>
> Ibid., n18

20 Ibid.
21 See, e.g. Acemoglu and Robinson (2012).
22 Brenner (2001; 2007). See also Brenner (2006). Compare Teschke and Lacher (2007).
23 Moatsos (2021).
24 Roser (2021).
25 Ibid. All subsequent data in this paragraph come from the same source.
26 Roser (2013).
27 Ibid.
28 Aguilar et al. (2021).
29 Ibid. All subsequent data in this paragraph come from this source.
30 See, e.g. Milanovic (2019b, chapter 3).

31 For a brief review and references, see Rutar (2022, 49–50).
32 Gwartney et al. (2020, 56).
33 Ibid.
34 Roser (2021). All subsequent data in this paragraph come from this source.
35 Ibid.
36 Moatsos (2021), figure 9.14.
37 Gwartney et al. (2020, 20). All subsequent data in this paragraph come from this source.
38 Kenworthy (2011, 6–8).
39 Ibid., 5.
40 Ibid., 10–13.
41 Ibid., 9. My emphasis.
42 Ibid., 15.
43 Marx (1983 [1867]).
44 Chibber (2018); Wright (2010, chapter 3).
45 Wright (2010, 28).
46 Chibber (2018, 25).
47 See, e.g. Cowen and Tabarrok (2015, 329–333).
48 Gintis (2018, 1–2).
49 The critical and heterodox-leaning economist Dani Rodrik makes the same point in Rodrik (2015).
50 Isen (2013); Naidu et al. (2018).
51 Acemoglu (2002). See also Lohr (2022).
52 Autor (2014).
53 Ibid.
54 Autor et al. (2016).
55 Chibber (2018, 22).
56 Cowen in Anderson (2019, 109).
57 Card and Krueger (2015). See Preface to the Twentieth-Anniversary Edition.
58 For example, Dube (2019) and Cengiz et al. (2019). But see, also, the contrary, more critical research by David Neumark that demonstrates a more classical empirical result, e.g. Neumark and Wascher (2006); Neumark and Shirley (2021).
59 Azar et al. (2019).
60 Sokolova and Sorensen (2020).
61 Ibid., 51.
62 Council of Economic Advisers (2016, 6).
63 Ibid., 5.
64 Ibid.
65 Azar et al. (2020).
66 Gutiérrez and Philippon (2017, 1).
67 Ibid., 1.
68 Ibid., 2.
69 De Loecker and Eeckhout (2018).
70 Stansbury and Summers (2020).
71 Roser and Ortiz-Ospina (2013).
72 Ibid.
73 OECD (2011).
74 Piketty (2014, 348).
75 Alfani (2021, table 5.5).
76 Piketty (2014, 349).
77 Alfani (2021, table 5.5).
78 FRED (2021a; 2021b).
79 McCloskey (2015, 7).
80 Milanovic (2019b, 7); see also Bourguignon (2015, 27).
81 Gradín (2021, Figure 14).

82 Liberati (2015); Gradín (2021).
83 Liberati (2015); Milanovic (2016, 166). See also Milanovic (2018) and Gradín (2021).
84 Roser Ortiz-Ospina (2013); Lustig et al. (2016).
85 Lustig et al. (2016).
86 Ibid.
87 OECD (2021).
88 OECD (2011), Figure 1.
89 Ibid.
90 Roser Ortiz-Ospina (2013).
91 Ibid.
92 Ibid.
93 Human Development Report (2019, 111).
94 Ibid.
95 Van Zanden et al. (2014, 285). See also Liberati (2015, 252).
96 Liberati (2015, 252).
97 Alfani (2021), table 5.5.
98 Piketty (2014, 349).
99 Ibid.
100 Zucman (2019).
101 Piketty (2014, 349).
102 See CORE Team (2017), Chapter 19.
103 Zucman (2019, 127).
104 Persson and Tabellini (1994); Aghion et al. (1999); Mo (2000); Keefer and Knack (2002).
105 Aghion et al. (1999, 1617).
106 Patridge (1997); Forbes (2000); Li and Zou (2002).
107 Barro (2008); Chambers and Krause (2010); Kraay (2015); Dollar et al. (2015); Aiyar and Ebeke (2020).
108 See Kraay (2015).
109 Fuest (2017, 63–64).
110 de Dominicis et al. (2008, 677).
111 Ibid., 677–678.
112 Aiyar and Ebeke (2020).
113 Pickett and Wilkinson (2010).
114 See, on both points, the careful report by Rowlingson (2011); see also, more controversially, the critique of *The Spirit Level* by Saunders (2010). Noble (2010) criticizes Saunders' critique.
115 Subramanian and Kawachi (2004); Babones (2008); Pickett and Wilkinson (2015); Matthew and Brodersen (2018).
116 Picket and Wilkinson (2015) explicitly affirm causality, while Babones (2008) remains sceptical. For scepticism see also Deaton (2003).
117 For instance, Oishi et al. (2011); Barone and Mocetti (2015); Yu and Wang (2017); Graafland and Lous (2018). See also the review by Nannestad (2008).
118 Nivette (2011); Trent and Pridemore (2011).
119 Kim et al. (2020).
120 Quoted by Perry (2013).
121 Although see Magness (2021) on how Buchanan's quote can be misread. Magness also points out that Buchanan's quote should not be construed as Buchanan denying the theoretical possibility of minimum wage increases leading to higher unemployment, because Buchanan himself discussed the positive employment effects of this legislation under conditions of monopsony in his and his colleagues' 1954 economics textbook.
122 Roberts (2017).
123 Ibid.

References

Acemoglu, Daron. 2002. 'Technical Change, Inequality, and the Labor Market,' *Journal of Economic Literature* 40, no. 1, 7–72.

Acemoglu, Daron, and James Robinson. 2012. *Why Nations Fail: The Origins of Power, Prosperity, and Poverty.* London: Profile Books.

Aghion, Philippe, Caroli, Eve, and Cecilia Garcia-Penalosa. 1999. 'Inequality and Economic Growth: The Perspective of the New Growth Theories,' *Journal of Economic Literature* 37, no. 4, 1615–1660.

Aguilar, R. Andres Castaneda, Fujs, Tony, Lakner, Christoph, Mahler, Daniel Gerszon, Nguyen, Minh Cong, Schoch, Marta, and Martha Viveros. 2021. 'March 2021 Global Poverty Update from the World Bank', World Bank, March 16. Accessible via: https://blogs.worldbank.org/opendata/march-2021-global-poverty-update-world-bank/.

Aiyar, Shekhar, and Christian Ebeke. 2020. 'Inequality of Opportunity, Inequality of Income and Economic Growth,' *World Development* 136, 1–10.

Alfani, Guido. 2021. 'Wealth Inequality in the Long Run,' in OECD, *How Was Life? Volume II: New Perspectives on Well-being and Global Inequality Since 1820*, 103–123. Paris: OECD Publishing.

Allen, Robert C. 2017. 'Absolute Poverty: When Necessity Displaces Desire,' *American Economic Review* 107, no. 12, 3690–3721.

Alvaredo, Facundo, Chancel, Lucas, Piketty, Thomas, Saez, Emmanuel, and Gabriel Zucman. 2018. 'The Elephant Curve of Global Inequality and Growth,' *AEA Paper and Proceedings* 108, 103–108.

Autor, David. 2014. 'Skills, Education, and the Rise of Earnings Inequality among the "Other" 99 Percent,' *Science* 344, no. 6186, 843–851.

Autor, David H., Dorn, David, and Gordon H. Hanson. 2016. 'The China Shock: Learning from Labor-Market Adjustment to Large Changes in Trade,' *Annual Review of Economics* 8, 205–240.

Azar, José, Huet-Vaughn, Emiliano, Marinescu, Ioana, Taska, Bledi, and Till von Wachter. 2019. 'Wage Employment Effects and Labor Market Concentration,' NBER Working Paper 26101. Accessible via: https://nber.org/papers/w26101/.

Azar, José, Marinescu, Ioana, and Marshall I. Steinbaum. 2020. 'Labor Market Concentration,' *The Journal of Human Resources*, May 12, Published online before print.

Babones, Salvatore J. 2008. 'Income Inequality and Population Health: Correlation and Causality,' *Social Science & Medicine* 66, no. 7, 1614–1626.

Barone, Guglielmo, and Sauro Mocetti. 2015. 'Inequality and Trust: New Evidence from Panel Data,' *Economic Inquiry* 54, no. 2, 794–809.

Barro, Robert J. 2008. 'Inequality and Growth Revisited,' Working Paper. Accessible via: https://www.econstor.eu/handle/10419/109529/.

Baumol, William J. 1983. 'Marx and the Iron Law of Wages,' *The American Economic Review* 73, no. 2, 303–308.

Beer, Tommy. 2020. 'Top 1% Of U.S. Households Hold 15 Times More Wealth Than Bottom 50% Combined,' *Forbes*, October 8. Accessible via: https://www.forbes.com/sites/tommybeer/2020/10/08/top-1-of-us-households-hold-15-times-more-wealth-than-bottom-50-combined/?sh=6ec464f65179/.

Bolt, Jutta, and Jan Luiten van Zanden. 2021. 'The Long View on Economic Growth: New Estimates of GDP,' in *OECD, How Was Life? Volume II: New Perspectives on Well-being and Global Inequality Since 1820*, 29–52. Paris: OCED Publishing.

Bourguignon, François. 2015. *The Globalization of Inequality.* Princeton: Princeton University Press.

Brenner, Robert. 2001. 'The Low Countries in the Transition to Capitalism,' *Journal of Agrarian Change* 1, no. 2, 169–241.

Brenner, Robert. 2006. 'What Is, and What Is Not, Imperialism?' *Historical Materialism* 14, no. 4, 79–105.

Brenner, Robert. 2007. 'Property and Progress: Where Adam Smith Went Wrong,' in Chris Wickham (ed.), *Marxist History-writing for the Twenty-first Century*, 49–111. Oxford: Oxford University Press.

Card, David, and Alan B. Krueger. 2015. *Myth and Measurement: The New Economics of the Minimum Wage – Twentieth-Anniversary Edition*. Princeton: Princeton University Press.

Cengiz, Doruk, Dube, Arindrajit, Lindner, Attila, and Ben Zipperer. 2019. 'The Effect of Minimum Wages on Low-Wage Jobs,' *The Quarterly Journal of Economics* 134, no. 3, 1405–1454.

Chambers, Dustin, and Alan Krause. 2010. 'Is the Relationship Between Inequality and Growth Affected by Physical and Human Capital Accumulation?' *The Journal of Economic Inequality* 8, no. 2, 153–172.

Chibber, Vivek. 2018. *The ABCs of Capitalism: Understanding Capitalism*. New York: Jacobin.

Council of Economic Advisers. 2016. 'Benefits of Competition and Indicators of Market Power,' Council of Economic Advisers Issue Brief, April 2016. Accessible via: https://obamawhitehouse.archives.gov/sites/default/files/page/files/20160414_cea_competition_issue_brief.pdf/.

Cowen, Tyler, and Alex Tabarrok. 2015. *Modern Principles of Economics: Third Edition*. New York: Worth Publishers.

de Dominicis, Laura, Florax, Raymond J. G. M., and Henri L. F. de Groot. 2008. 'A Meta-Analysis on the Relationship Between Income Inequality and Economic Growth,' *Scottish Journal of Political Economy* 55, no. 5, 654–682.

De Loecker, Jan, and Jan Eeckhout. 2018. 'Global Market Power,' NBER Working Paper 24768. Accessible via: https://nber.org/papers/w24768/.

Deaton, Angus. 2003. 'Health, Inequality, and Economic Development,' *Journal of Economic Literature* 41, no. 1, 113–158.

Dollar, David, Kleineberg, Tatjana, and Aart Kraay. 2015. 'Growth, Inequality, and Social Welfare: Cross-country Evidence,' *Economic Policy* 30, no. 82, 335–377.

Dube, Arindrajit. 2019. 'Impacts of Minimum Wages: Review of the International Evidence,' *Independent Report for the UK Government*. Accessible via: https://www.gov.uk/government/publications/impacts-of-minimum-wages-review-of-the-international-evidence/.

Elkins, Kathleen. 2018. 'How Much Money You Need to Be Part of the 1 Percent Worldwide,' CNBC, November 1. Accessible via: https://www.cnbc.com/2018/11/01/how-much-money-you-need-to-be-part-of-the-1-percent-worldwide.html/.

Forbes, Kristin J. 2000. 'A Reassessment of the Relationship Between Inequality and Growth,' *The American Economic Review* 90, no. 4, 869–887.

FRED. 2021b. 'Real Median Personal Income in the United States,' U.S. Census Bureau. Accessible via: https://fred.stlouisfed.org/series/MEPAINUSA672N.

Fuest, Clemens. 2017. 'Inequality Reduces Growth,' in B. Frey and D. Iselin (eds.), *Economic Ideas You Should Forget*, 63–64. Cham: Springer.

Graafland, Johan, and Bjorn Lous. 2018. 'Economic Freedom, Income Inequality and Life Satisfaction in OECD Countries,' *Journal of Happiness Studies* 19, 2071–2093.

Gradín, Carlos. 2021. 'Trends in Global Inequality Using a New Integrated Dataset,' WIDER Working Paper 2021/61. Accessible via: https://www.wider.unu.edu/

sites/default/files/Publications/Working-paper/PDF/wp2021-61-trends-global-inequality.pdf/.

Gutiérrez, Germán, and Thomas Philippon. 2017. 'Declining Competition and Investment in the U.S.,' NBER Working Paper 23583. Accessible via: https://nber.org/papers/w23583/.

Gwartney, James, Lawson, Robert, Hall, Joshua, and Ryan Murphy. 2020. Economic Freedom of the World: 2020 Annual Report. Fraser Institute.

Hasell, Joe, and Max Roser. 2019. 'How Do We Know the History of Extreme Poverty?' OurWorldInData.org. Accessible via: https://ourworldindata.org/extreme-history-methods/.

Hickel, Jason. 2019a. 'Bill Gates Says Poverty Is Decreasing. He Couldn't Be More Wrong,' The Guardian, January 29. Accessible via: https://www.theguardian.com/commentisfree/2019/jan/29/bill-gates-davos-global-poverty-infographic-neoliberal/.

Hickel, Jason. 2019b. 'A Letter to Steven Pinker (And Bill Gates, For That Matter) About Global Poverty,' Jason Hickel blog, February 4. Accessible via: https://www.jasonhickel.org/blog/2019/2/3/pinker-and-global-poverty/.

Hickel, Jason. 2021. 'Extreme Poverty Isn't Natural, It's Created,' Jason Hickel blog, March 28. Accessible via: https://www.jasonhickel.org/blog/2021/3/28/extreme-poverty-isnt-natural-it-is-created/.

Human Development Report. 2019. *Beyond Income, Beyond Averages, Beyond Today: Inequalities in Human Development in the 21st Century*. New York: United Nations Development Programme.

Isen, Adam. 2015. 'Dying to Know: Are Workers Paid Their Marginal Product,' Unpublished Manuscript. Summary accessible via: https://research.upjohn.org/cgi/viewcontent.cgi?article=1056&context=dissertation_awards/.

Jordahl, Henrik. 2007. 'Inequality and Trust,' IFN Working Paper No. 715. Accessible via: https://www.ifn.se/Wfiles/wp/wp715.pdf/.

Keefer, Philip, and Stephen Knack. 2002. 'Polarization, Politics and Property Rights: Links Between Inequality and Growth,' *Public Choice* 111, 127–154.

Kenworthy, Lane. 2011. *Progress for the Poor*. Oxford: Oxford University Press.

Kim, Bitna, Seo, Chunghyeon, and Young-Oh Hong. 2020. 'A Systematic Review and Meta-analysis of Income Inequality and Crime in Europe: Do Places Matter?' *European Journal of Criminal Policy and Research*, OnlineFirst.

Kraay, Aart. 2015. 'Weak Instruments in Growth Regressions: Implications for Recent Cross-country Evidence on Inequality and Growth,' World Bank Policy Research Working Paper. Accessible via: https://papers.ssrn.com/sol3/papers.cfm?abstract_id=2690633/.

Li, Hongyi, and Heng-fu Zou. 2002. 'Income Inequality is not Harmful for Growth: Theory and Evidence,' *Review of Development Economics* 2, no. 3, 318–334.

Liberati, Paolo. 2015. 'The World Distribution of Income and Its Inequality, 1970–2009,' *Review of Income and Wealth* 61, no. 2, 248–273.

Lohr, Steve. 2022. 'Economists Pin More Blame on Tech for Rising Inequality,' The New York Times, January 11. Accessible via: https://www.nytimes.com/2022/01/11/technology/income-inequality-technology.html/.

Lustig, Nora, Lopez-Calvan, Luis F., Ortiz-Juarez, Eduardo, and Célestin Monga. 2016. 'Deconstructing the Decline in Inequality in Latin America,' in Kaushik Basu and Joseph E. Stiglitz (eds.), *Inequality and Growth: Patterns and Policy. Volume II: Regions and Regularities*, 212–247. London: Palgrave Macmillan.

Magness, Phillip W. 2021. 'Eyes on the Politicized Prize,' American Institute for Economic Research, October 12. Accessible via: https://www.aier.org/article/eyes-on-the-politicized-prize/.

Matthew, Pravin, and Donka Mirtcheva Brodersen. 2018. 'Income Inequality and Health Outcomes in the United States: An Empirical Analysis,' *The Social Science Journal* 55, no. 4, 432–442.

McCloskey, Deirdre N. 2015. 'How Piketty Misses the Point,' *Cato Policy Report* 37, no. 4, 5–8.

Milanovic, Branko. 2016. *Global Inequality: A New Approach for the Age of Globalization.* Cambridge: The Belknap Press of Harvard University Press.

Milanovic, Branko. 2018. Tweet on 'Three concepts of inter-national income inequality, 1952–2017,' October 19. Accessible via: https://twitter.com/BrankoMilan/status/1053062464479334401/photo/1/.

Milanovic, Branko. 2019a. 'Global Poverty Over the Long-Term: Legitimate Issues,' Globalinequality Blog, February 6. Accessible via: https://glineq.blogspot.com/2019/02/global-poverty-over-long-term.html?spref=tw/.

Milanovic, Branko. 2019b. *Capitalism, Alone: The Future of the System That Rules the World.* London: The Belknap Press of Harvard University Press.

Moatsos, Michail. 2021. 'Global Extreme Poverty: Present and Past since 1820,' in *OECD, How Was Life? Volume II: New Perspectives on Well-being and Global Inequality since 1820*, 186–215. Paris: OECD Publishing.

Mo, Pak Hung. 2000. 'Income Inequality and Economic Growth,' *Kyklos* 53, no. 3, 293–315.

Naidu, Suresh, Posner, Eric A., Weyl, and E. Glen Weyl. 2018. 'Antitrust Remedies for Labor Market Power,' Working Paper. Accessible via: https://equitablegrowth.org/working-papers/antitrust-remedies-forlabor-market-power/.

Nannestad, Peter. 2008. 'What Have We Learned About Generalized Trust, If Anything?' *Annual Review of Political Science* 11, 413–436.

Neumark, David, and Peter Shirley. 2021. 'Myth or Measurement: What Does the New Minimum Wage Research Say about Minimum Wages and Job Loss in the United States?' NBER Working paper nr. 28388. Accessible via: https://www.nber.org/papers/w28388/.

Neumark, David, and William Wascher. 2006. 'Minimum Wages and Employment: A Review of Evidence from the New Minimum Wage Research,' *Foundations and Trends in Microeconomics* 3, no. 1–2, 1–182.

Nivette, Amy E. 2011. 'Cross-National Predictors of Crime: A Meta-Analysis,' *Homicide Studies* 15, no. 2, 103–131.

Noble, Hugh. 2010. 'The Spirit Level Revisited: Regression Lines, Correlation, Outliers and Multivariate Analysis,' Equality Trust. Accessible via: https://equalitytrust.org.uk/sites/default/files/hughnobletslrevisited.pdf/.

OECD. 2011. An Overview of Growing Income Inequalities in OECD Countries: Main Findings. Accessible via: https://www.oecd.org/social/soc/49499779.pdf/.

OECD. 2021. 'Income Inequality'. Accessible via: https://data.oecd.org/inequality/income-inequality.htm/.

Oishi, Shigehiro, Kesebir Selin, and Ed Diener. 'Income Inequality and Happiness,' *Psychological Science* 22, no. 9, 1095–1100.

Oxfam. 2021. '5 Shocking Facts About Extreme Global Inequality and How to Even It Up,' Oxfam International. Accessible via: https://www.oxfam.org/en/5-shocking-facts-about-extreme-global-inequality-and-how-even-it/.

Patridge, Mark D. 1997. 'Is Inequality Harmful for Growth? Comment,' *The American Economic Review* 87, no. 5, 1019–1032.

Perry, Mark J. 2013. 'Quotation of the Day: James Buchanan on the Minimum Wage,' AEI, January 11. Accessible via: https://www.aei.org/carpe-diem/quotation-of-the-day-james-buchanan-on-the-minimum-wage/.

Persson, Torsten, and Guido Tabellini. 1994. 'Is Inequality Harmful for Growth?' *The American Economic Review* 84, no. 3, 600–621.

Pickett, Kate, and Richard Wilkinson. 2010. *The Spirit Level: Why Equality Is Better for Everyone*. London: Penguin.

Pickett, Kate E., and Richard G. Wilkinson. 2015. 'Income Inequality and Health: A Causal Review,' *Social Science & Medicine* 128, 316–326.

Piketty, Thomas. 2014. *Capital in the Twenty-First Century*. London: The Belknap Press of Harvard University Press.

Roberts, Russ. 2017. 'What Do Economists Actually Know?' NewCo Shift. Accessible via: https://shift.newco.co/2017/03/02/what-do-economists-actually-know/.

Rodrik, Dani. 2015. *Economics Rules: Why Economics Works, When It Fails, and How to Tell the Difference*. Oxford: Oxford University Press.

Roser, Max. 2013. 'Economic Growth,' OurWorldInData.org. Accessible via: https://ourworldindata.org/economic-growth/.

Roser, Max. 2021. 'What Is Economic Growth? And Why Is It So Important?' OurWorldIn-Data.org. Accessible via: https://ourworldindata.org/what-is-economic-growth/.

Roser, Max, and Esteban Ortiz-Ospina. 2013. 'Income Inequality,' OurWorldInData.org. Accessible via: https://ourworldindata.org/income-inequality/.

Rowlingson, Karen. 2011. 'Does Income Inequality Cause Health and Social Problems?' Joseph Rowntree Foundation. Accessible via: https://www.jrf.org.uk/report/does-income-inequality-cause-health-and-social-problems/.

Rutar, Tibor. 2022. *Rational Choice and Democratic Government: A Sociological Approach*. London: Routledge.

Saunders, Peter. 2010. 'Beware False Prophets: Equality, the Good Society and The Spirit Level,' Policy Exchange. Accessible via: https://policyexchange.org.uk/wp-content/uploads/2016/09/beware-false-prophets-jul-10.pdf/.

Sokolova, Anna, and Todd Sorensen. 2020. 'Monopsony in Labor Markets: A Meta-Analysis,' *ILR Review* 74, no 1, 27–55.

Stansbury, Anna, and Lawrence Summers. 2020. 'Declining Worker Power and American Economic Performance,' Brookings Papers on Economic Activity, March 19. Accessible via.

Subramanian, Subu V., and Ichiro Kawachi. 2004. 'Income Inequality and Health: What Have We Learned So Far?' *Epidemiologic Reviews* 26, no. 1, 78–91.

Teschke, Benno, and Hannes Lacher. 2007. 'The Changing "Logics" of Capitalist Competition,' *Cambridge Review of International Affairs* 20, no. 4, 565–580.

Trent, Carol L. S., and William Alex Pridemore. 2011. 'A Review of the Cross-National Empirical Literature on Social Structure and Homicide,' in Marieke C. A. Liem and William Alex Pridemore (eds.), *Handbook of European Homicide Research*. New York: Springer, 111–136.

Van Zanden, Jan Luiten, Baten, Joerg, Foldvari, Peter, and Bas van Leeuwen. 2014. 'The Changing Shape of Global Inequality, 1820–2000; Exploring a New Dataset,' *Review of Income and Wealth* 60, no. 2, 279–297.

Yu, Zonghuo, and Fei Wang. 2017. 'Income Inequality and Happiness: An Inverted U-Shaped Curve,' *Frontiers of Psychology* 8, 1–6.

Zucman, Gabriel. 2019. 'Global Wealth Inequality,' *Annual Review of Economics* 11, 109–138.

4

CAPITALISM GLOBALIZED

The spectre of neoliberalism and the ambitions of industrial policy

Introduction: the visible costs and hidden benefits of globalization

Donald Trump's knowledge of economics is profoundly wrong and misguided. But like a broken clock, Trump is correct about one thing. Free international trade does not generate only benefits for every person in the two (or more) countries involved in international exchange. Instead, it also carries with it costs for some people.

For instance, even though most Americans (including, most importantly, low-income families) benefit greatly from being freely able to buy Chinese-made products, as the cheaper products increase their wage's purchasing power, and even though most Chinese benefit from being able to produce these goods and receive higher wages from their production, there are Americans who are hurt due to Chinese competition.[1] Offshoring causes some Americans to lose their jobs, which is a big hit for them and, when job losses accumulate, even for the larger community around them. Down the line, some of these workers, fortunately, get employed again – although not necessarily soon. But some do not. Some stay unemployed. Moreover, of those who get re-employed, some are paid significantly less now than when they worked in manufacturing. This has a devastating impact on their lives. The same holds, *mutatis mutandis*, for Europe and its trade with the world.[2]

In short, the benefits of liberalized trade (or, to use a few synonyms, of globalization or neoliberalism) are large but spread out over a lot of people. This makes them less noticeable and immediate, which then enables Trump to downplay the benefits of free trade in front of his crowds. The costs are much smaller in comparison, but they are highly concentrated among a vastly smaller population, which makes them highly visible and unbearable for those affected.

DOI: 10.4324/9781003305811-4

Trump railed against globalization by seizing on this latter fact and by amplifying and distorting it.

Trump is, of course, *Trump*. Not only did he ignore the (real) benefits and play up the (real) costs of free trade, but he also conveniently overlooked that the *majority* of American manufacturing job losses at the height of globalization, between 1990 and 2007, happened *regardless of the China shock*.[3] Even globalization's arch nemesis, the iconoclast economist Joseph Stiglitz, readily admits this. As he puts it in his book-length criticism of globalization, 'Most of the job loss in manufacturing is in fact due to technology.'[4] This does not make the 10–40% of manufacturing job losses that did, in fact, occur due to globalization irrelevant; far from it. But it highlights the fact that the primary solution to the problem cannot be to simply abandon globalization or highly constrict it, as Trump is wont to do.

What also underscores this conclusion, and what Trump also conveniently ignored, are two further important facts. First, the percentage of American workforce employed in manufacturing has been steadily declining year after year already since the early 1950s.[5] General economic development – or more precisely the well-nigh inevitable technological shift of production from industrialism to post-industrialism – is primarily responsible for the decline in manufacturing. Globalization adds to this dynamic but is not the originating, or most important, cause. Second, manufacturing job losses (as a percentage of total American employment) *stopped* after 2009.[6] The percentage in 2018 is the same as in 2009. The absolute number of manufacturing workers even increased in the last decade.[7]

All of this and more is why the very same economists who have empirically diagnosed the problem with globalization, and want something significant to be done about it, nevertheless strongly disagree with Trump's proposed remedy, namely protectionist policies which include tariff increases and the tearing up of free-trade agreements. Here is David Autor, one of the lead researchers of the China shock and its devastating effects on certain groups of workers:

> [Trump's trade vision] is extremely naïve and uninformed. I don't think it has any basis in economic reasoning about costs and benefits of trade. … I think the idea of slapping large tariffs, or border taxes, on imports is a very destructive idea on all kinds of fronts. I think tearing up the Trans-Pacific Partnership [TPP] was an incredibly shortsighted decision; the country that most benefited from us tearing up the TPP was China.[8]

What does Autor suggest instead as a fix for globalization woes?

> One would be to strengthen trade adjustment programs. You would offer more generous benefits that are easier to access or longer-lasting and help people transition to other sectors. … Maybe we should just give people a lump sum for a while to help ease the pain of switching sectors. … We should also think about how we have a strategic interest in some sectors that we should not ignore.[9]

These few introductory paragraphs have already, I think, given you a taste of the complexities, nuances, and controversies of – and types of political responses to – the capitalist economy in the global era. It is the purpose of this chapter to dig into them more, from even just defining the elusive term 'neoliberalism' that has dominated discussions about globalized capitalism in recent decades to examining whether the world today really is more neoliberal (and in what respects), how bad or good this is, and if one could realistically wield statist industrial policy to improve upon neoliberal free trade (or bypass its inevitable costs).

Is the world really becoming more neoliberal – and is that a bad thing?

Trump is a rich capitalist businessman who is also a protectionist right-wing populist. He is not a typical right-winger. The right, especially the American right, is typically associated not with protectionism but precisely with its opposite, namely free trade and neoliberalism. Neoliberalism, of course, is not said to be only the dominant ideology of the American right but has also been tied in America to left-of-centre Democrat politicians such as Bill and Hillary Clinton (the latter was the arch-nemesis of Trump in the 2016 presidential race) and Barack Obama, Trump's predecessor in office.

But what even is *neoliberalism*? Too often, it is a conversation-ending swearword that seems to be on everyone's tongues. In 2016 (and 2020), it was not only the right-wing populist Trump who railed against it – the left-wing populist presidential candidate Bernie Sanders also decried it. Before splitting up, both co-hosts of the popular YouTube talk-show *Rising with the Hill's Krystal Ball and Saagar Enjeti* regularly denounced neoliberalism, one from the left, the other from the right.

The dreaded neoliberal spectre is not only on the mind of duelling politicians and pundits. It also has a huge currency in the academe. Perhaps this speaks to my lack of imagination, but I actually cannot think of a single general term with a negative valence in the social sciences, especially the so-called critical social sciences, that has become more pervasive and entrenched in the past decades as 'neoliberalism.' Social power, surveillance, consumerism, post-colonial, exploitation, bourgeois, … nothing comes close to having the same conversational currency as neoliberalism.

A quick *Google Scholar* search corroborates my suspicion. The number of scholarly articles using the term neoliberalism hovered around 1,000 in the two decades leading up to 1990, it was just over 11,000 results between 1990 and 2000, and then a big jump happened to more than 90,000 results between 2000 and 2010, with the last decade garnering 180,00 hits. Since 2000, and especially since 2010, 'neoliberalism' has, indeed, figured more frequently in scholarly articles compared even to such staple sociological terms as 'social power.'

Regardless of how frequently neoliberalism is being written about, or perhaps because of this high frequency, a serious issue confronts the researcher who wants to examine whether the world is becoming more neoliberal and what to make of this hypothetical development. The key issue is that we are not sure what neoliberalism means, exactly.

One study from 2009 found that 'In present usage, neoliberalism conveys little common substantive meaning but serves as a clear indicator that one does not evaluate free markets positively.'[10] Another study from 2015 claims that, as the term proliferated, it 'has become a deeply problematic and incoherent term that has multiple and contradictory meanings, and thus has diminished analytical value.'[11] The lack of common substantive meaning stems primarily from at least two issues: (1) scholars tend not to define what the term means, even when they use it for purposes of empirical research as a key independent or dependent variable and (2) the term tends to be applied to very different, non-overlapping, sometimes even contradictory phenomena.[12] When scholars are more careful with their definitions, some clarity and even a certain amount of general substantive convergence does emerge. Drawing on several expansive literature reviews, I would propose that neoliberalism has been widely used as referring to (i) an economic system, (ii) a set of economic reforms policies, (iii) an all-encompassing ideology or worldview, and (iv) an economic theory or a paradigm.[13]

But even with these more coherent referents, certain smaller issues remain. For instance, in regards to point (i) above, neoliberalism is sometimes used simply as a *synonym for capitalism* in general, not a specific *subtype* of the capitalist system, say free-market capitalism (which is also one meaning of the term). If ambiguity is to be avoided, we have to decide which of the two meanings of neoliberalism as an economic system is the preferred one.

With respect to (ii), neoliberalism has been used interchangeably with the Washington consensus. This is a term coined by John Williamson in 1989 with which Williamson described a list of ten economic policies, such as the privatization of state enterprises, the provision of secure property rights, abolition of regulations that prevent potential new economic actors to enter the market, and so on.[14] This is quite clear and understandable. At the same time, however, one can use neoliberalism in this category more narrowly to simply mean (fiscal) *austerity*, which is a set of policies aiming to reduce government budget deficits by cutting state spending or increasing taxes. So the question again is: which meaning is to be used?

As (iii) an ideology, neoliberalism has traditionally been argued to mean a broad outlook characterized by a strong support for free markets, a hostility to the welfare state, and a strong distrust of (democratic) government and unions. Thus, oftentimes, neoliberalism and (the more radical forms of) libertarian ideology are elided and joined together. According to the *Stanford Encyclopedia of Philosophy*, however, a new evidence-based stream of historical research on the topic argues today that neoliberalism as an ideology actually meant (and means) something more mellow, namely a 'politico-economic doctrine that embraces robust liberal capitalism, constitutional democracy, and a modest welfare state.'[15] That this holds, it is argued, can be ascertained even – or precisely – by examining the works of the more infamous neoliberals, such as F. A. Hayek, Milton Friedman, and James Buchanan.[16]

Lastly, (iv) neoliberalism can be used as a synonym for a certain brand of economic thinking and theorizing originally associated with the University of Chicago's Economics Department. More confusingly, however, neoliberalism is sometimes also used to refer simply to the general enterprise of mainstream, neoclassical economics, even when this has nothing to do with the Chicago School. Moreover, it can be frustrating to hear Hayek and Friedman named as the two foremost neoliberals, as they usually are, while, at the same time, knowing that although Friedman infamously belonged to the Chicago School and relied on neoclassical economics, Hayek was actually an economist of the Austrian variety, which is a theoretical paradigm that sometimes clashes quite strongly (and foundationally) with some of the assumptions of neoclassical economics. Both economists were extremely fond of free markets, it is true, but their theorizing was not as paradigmatically unified as this ideological definition of neoliberalism would have it.

Given all of this, how should one proceed with investigating how neoliberal the world has become recently? I will not be interested in ascertaining how neoliberal the world is in (iii) ideological or (iv) theoretical terms, partly due to the difficulty of measuring such ephemeral phenomena. Instead, in what follows, I will employ various measures of neoliberalism as (i) an economic system and as (ii) a set of economic reforms.

To do so, I shall first (in the next subsection) operationalize neoliberalism as a set of economic institutions that structure economic behaviour in a society. This will be done empirically with the use of Fraser Institute's index of economic freedom, which ranks countries (and the world as an aggregate) on a scale from 0 to 10 by considering the performance of five key areas of a society's economic institutions; more on this below.

Second, the spread and influence of neoliberalism (as an economic system, structure, or reform) can also be measured more indirectly by looking at how various specific economic indicators and phenomena, such as rates of taxation, unionization, and social spending, have changed over the years in different societies, as the world presumably become more and more neoliberal. This latter exercise is intended to examine whether these and other economic phenomena have moved in the direction one would expect given the hypothesis of increasing neoliberalism.

The general idea, then, is to examine how neoliberal the world is, or has become over time, both in its economic institutions (say, secure property rights and trade openness) and effects (say, social spending and union strength).

Economic freedom of the world and its social correlates

The Fraser Institute publishes an annual survey of economic freedom, using third-party data, with detailed scores for each country along five dimensions: (1) size of government, (2) legal structure and property rights, (3) access to sound money, (4) freedom to trade internationally, and (5) regulation of credit, labour, and business.[17]

If a particular country spends a lot of money on social and similar government services, if it has a high taxation rate, and if it controls a large percentage of enterprises, then it receives a lower (or low) score on the first dimension, namely the (1) size of government. Sweden, for instance, typically gets quite a low score in this area (below 5.0), while Hong Kong (or Mexico) scores much higher (above 8.0). Along the government size dimension, Sweden could then rightly be said to be much less neoliberal (or much more socialist) than either Hong Kong or Mexico.

However, because Sweden also has a robust legal system with strong protection of property rights, it is typically scored very high along this second dimension (above 8.0) – comparable to or higher than Hong Kong (or, of course, Mexico, which scores below 5.0 in this area). So, when it comes to property rights, Sweden is highly capitalist/neoliberal, much more so than Mexico, which is less neoliberal (or more socialist) on this dimension.

Something similar can be said of Sweden's regulation, which is actually quite comparatively *modest*, and of Sweden's freedom to trade internationally, which is among the most robust in the world. These, then, are two other areas Sweden is scored quite high in, and so Sweden in these respects can be called quite neoliberal as well. (Overall, the mixed fact that Sweden scores as pretty neoliberal on a few dimensions, but also quite socialist on the government size dimension, makes it neither purely neoliberal nor purely socialist, but a *social democratic capitalist* country or a *free-market welfare state* society. The same holds for other Nordic countries, especially Denmark and Norway.)[18]

Most importantly for my present task, we can look at the changes in the overall – *world* – index of economic freedom to assess whether the world has become, on average, more economically free ('neoliberal') through the decades.

So, what do the data show? They show that economic freedom (as an aggregate of all five areas noted above) has increased substantially in the 1980s and 1990s.[19] Just as one would expect from the typical dating of the late 1970s and early 1980s as the era of 'neoliberal revolution' – most infamously personified by Margaret Thatcher's and Ronald Reagan's rise to power in Britain and the US – the world has, indeed, become more neoliberal since that time. What about the 21st century? Here, even more reliable and fine-grained data are available. Between the years 2000 and 2019, the average economic freedom rating has increased almost every year with the exception of 2008, 2009, 2012, and 2015. Over the whole 19-year period, the rating increased from 6.61 to 7.04.

On the whole, the world today is (significantly) more neoliberal than it had been in the past. But we also want to know how destructive (or not) this neoliberal transformation has been economically, politically, and socially. The easiest statistical way to go about doing so is to search for correlations between economic freedom and a variety of measures of economic development, political freedom, and general social well-being. If most correlations show up as negative, then the neoliberal restructuring of societies is, indeed, probably a worrying development.

It turns out, however, that economic freedom mostly correlates positively – not negatively – with the most common social and other indicators of interest. For instance, the most economically free societies (those in the first quartile) have, on average, high levels of GDP per capita, low rates of absolute poverty, high subjective happiness scores, high rates of political and civil freedoms, lower gender disparities, and so on. Moreover, compared to less economically free societies, the first quartile *outperforms* them on virtually every single one of those measure. The effect is almost linear: 1st quartile outperforms the 2nd, the latter outperforms the 3rd, and this one outperforms the last, 4th quartile. Figures 4.1–4.4 present this general pattern using two concrete measures: extreme poverty rates and aggregate democracy scores.

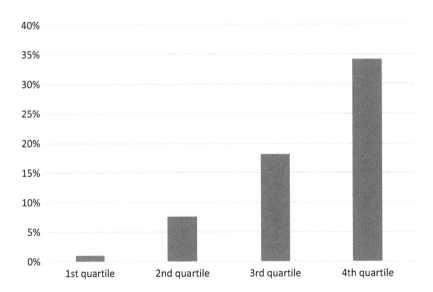

FIGURE 4.1 Share of population living in extreme poverty (int-$1.9 per day or less, adjusted for inflation) in countries classified by 4 quartiles of economic freedom (1 – most economically free; 4 – least economically free).

Sources: Fraser Institute (2022); PovcalNet World Bank via Our World in Data (Roser 2021).

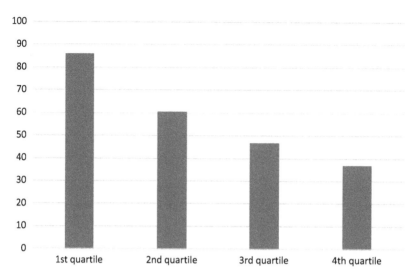

FIGURE 4.2 Average aggregate democracy score for countries classified by 4 quartiles of economic freedom (1 – most economically free; 4 – least economically free). Higher democracy score denotes more political and civil rights.

Sources: Fraser Institute (2022); Freedom House (2022).

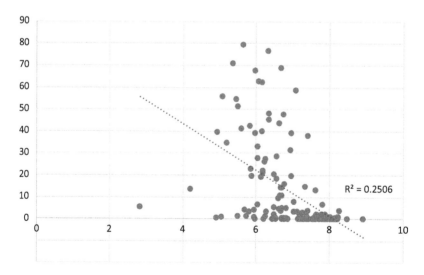

FIGURE 4.3 Scatter plot showing the correlation between economic freedom and extreme poverty. A quarter of all the variance in extreme poverty between countries is accounted for by how economically free they are; the freer, the less poverty.

Sources: Fraser Institute (2022); PovcalNet World Bank via Our World in Data (Roser 2021).

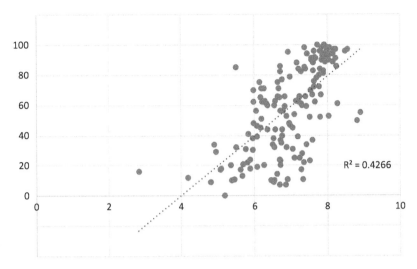

FIGURE 4.4 Scatter plot showing the correlation between economic freedom and level of democracy. More than 40% of all the variance between how democratic countries are is accounted for by how economically free they are; the freer, the more democratic.

Sources: Fraser Institute (2022); Freedom House (2022).

Also noteworthy is that if one looks at how GDP per capita, years of education, political rights, and life expectancy *changed over time*, it is clear that those countries that became much more economically free through the years registered significant improvements, while those which slid back economically also stagnated on measures of well-being.[20]

What, precisely, does this tell us about neoliberalism (as proxied by economic freedom)? Correlation is not causation, so it certainly does not mean (or even suggest) that neoliberalism is what is responsible for the improvement. A whole host of other variables should be considered (and statistically controlled for) if one wanted to advance such a claim. Still, even these simple correlations definitely do tell us that neoliberalism cannot be an *overwhelmingly negative* social force (as critics otherwise tend to postulate that it is). Why so? Because if it had been so overwhelmingly negative that its negative effects won out on net, this would have then weakened and even reversed the correlations.

In other words, it could perfectly well be that as the world started becoming more and more neoliberal since the 1980s, it also registered all sorts of improvements (described above) *due to completely non-neoliberal reasons*. This is completely possible. As said, simple correlation is not evidence of causation. Put differently, neoliberalism might have had negative (or neutral) effects on social welfare, but the correlation between increasing neoliberalism and social welfare still turned out positive in the end simply because of certain hidden non-neoliberal causes that have, at the same time, increased social well-being to such an extent that, on net, we saw a general increase. So, neoliberalism is not necessarily responsible for the discussed social improvements with which it correlates, but it also cannot be indicted as a phenomenon that destroys these improvements. The data show that neoliberalism is, on average, at least *consistent* with an overall increase in social well-being.

Researchers have, of course, gone beyond such simple statistics. There is a wealth of more complex and robust data that allows us, tentatively at least, to infer causal effects. Studies that control for confounding variables and, therefore, ostensibly look only at the relationship between economic freedom on the one hand and various socially relevant metrics on the other have found a mostly positive effect. The authors of a 2013 comprehensive literature review looked at the results of 198 published studies that used the Fraser Institute's economic freedom index as an independent variable.[21] This is what they concluded:

> Over two-thirds of the studies, 134 out of 198, found economic freedom corresponding to a 'good' outcome such as faster growth, better living standards, more happiness, etc. Only eight papers, less than 4% of the sample, found economic freedom to be associated with a 'bad' outcome such as increased income inequality. ... [T]he balance of evidence is overwhelming that economic freedom corresponds with a wide variety of positive outcomes with almost no negative tradeoffs.[22]

If we go over some of the positive findings from this vast pool of studies, we most clearly see the following:

i.   Economic freedom causally contributes to *economic development* (measured as GDP per capita).[23]
ii.   Through its contribution to economic development, it then (indirectly) contributes to the *reduction of poverty* and an *increase in material well-being* for individuals across the society.[24]
iii. Similarly, economic freedom indirectly contributes even to *subjective life satisfaction* through this same developmental, GDP channel, as there is plenty of robust evidence that increases in income lead to increases in life satisfaction (both across societies and within them).[25] Moreover, there is also evidence of a direct causal effect of economic freedom on life satisfaction, but this turns out to be more modest than the indirect (GDP) contribution of economic freedom on satisfaction.[26]

One recent study, however, goes against the latter literature and warns that in reality only one aspect of economic freedom, i.e. the quality of the legal system and protection of property rights, directly contributes to life satisfaction, and even this effect is strongly mediated by GDP per capita.[27] The study points out that, overall, the net effect of economic freedom does not seem to be directly positive – or negative – with regards to life satisfaction, because one of its other aspects, i.e. the (small) size of government, actually decreases it. As the researchers put it,

> [T]he golden straightjacket that neoliberals propose … is not optimal in all respects. We find robust evidence that countries with a high respect for private property rights indeed show more life satisfaction than other countries. But we also find strong indications that a small government size might jeopardize rather than increase life satisfaction.[28]

This is only one study, but it is useful as it disentangles the different effects that various aspects of economic freedom can have on life satisfaction. Further research along the same lines is needed to say anything more specific on the direct relation.

This much can be said for economic growth, poverty reduction, and life satisfaction as outcomes of economic freedom. What about income inequality? Currently, the evidence is surprisingly mixed. Certain samples, measures, and methods show increasing economic freedom to be associated with less inequality, while other study designs indicate that it is associated with more inequality, with the relationship also potentially changing based on current levels of economic freedom within country samples.[29] Moreover, some aspects of economic freedom (say, free trade) seem to increase it, while others (say, sound monetary policy) work protectively.[30] Right now, we cannot make a very confident general, pithy statement about whether the move towards a more neoliberal capitalist form of society increases or decreases inequality.

To conclude, neoliberalism (defined as increasing or high rates of economic freedom) tends to be directly or at least indirectly (via GDP) associated with many positive social outcomes, both correlationally and causally, though there are a few plausible negatives as well. Does this settle, at least in rough terms, neoliberalism's overall social performance?

Not necessarily. The problem with the assessment I have presented above could be that not everyone agrees with the proposed method of measuring neoliberalism. Writing for the popular Marxist journal *Jacobin*, Ben Burgis argues that one should not conflate Fraser Institute's economic freedom index with how capitalistic or, for our purposes, neoliberal a country is. For him, a big concern with the index is simply that some of the measured dimensions do not have much (or even anything at all) to do with how capitalistic a given country's set of economic institutions is. For instance, is the rate of inflation ('access to sound money') really an important indicator of the underlying economic structure of a society? In the index, it accounts for a whole 1/5 of the final score, so it better be as important as 'size of government.' But, says Burgis, this is plausibly not so.

Moreover, if we look at the subcategories which make up the index's 'legal structure and property rights' category, we see that of the eight subcategories, only a few have something direct to do with capitalism. Some of them, such as reliability of police, integrity of the legal system, impartial courts, and judicial independence could be said to be a spurious measurement of the extent of free markets, neoliberalism, or capitalism more generally. Burgis even goes so far as to claim that only *one* subcategory – protection of property rights – is plausibly a measurement of capitalism. Because of this, relying on the aggregate country score provided by the index is going to be misleading – at least for the purposes of our analysis.

There are conceptual problems with Burgis' critique. But let us, for the sake of the argument, grant it. It still does not necessarily follow from his critique that the economic freedom index becomes useless. Instead, we have to examine whether it, in fact, does so. For instance, we can look at how the relative standings of particular countries change *were we to recalculate the index* by eschewing the 'access to sound money' category and seven of the eight subcategories in the 'legal structure and property rights' area due to their alleged irrelevance to capitalism. If country scores change significantly after recalculation, i.e. if many countries from the first quartile trade places with countries from the second, third or even fourth quartile, then the alleged correlations of the original economic freedom ratings with measures of well-being should no longer hold true for our adjusted and ostensibly more accurate ratings. In short, the connection between how capitalist or neoliberal a country is and how well it is doing on measures of growth and poverty rates, and so on, would break down. In this case, Burgis' critique has bite. If, however, this does not happen and the relative standings stay largely the same, Burgis' critique would seem to be short-circuited.

I recalculated the ratings published in the 2021 *Economic Freedom of the World* annual report for each country according to Burgis' suggestion. The main outcome is that the vast majority of countries (around 75%) in the 1st quartile retain their original placing, and the same goes for countries in the 4th quartile (more than 80% remain where they were). There are more shifts in the 2nd and 3rd quartile, but even here, more than 50% of countries in both quartiles stay where they were. Furthermore, of those that get shifted, every single country only moves *one quartile* up or down. That means that no country that was originally in the 4th quartile moves to the 1st (or even 2nd), and no country from the 1st (or even 2nd) quartile moves to the 4th.

In short, the changes are nowhere near as drastic as intimated by Burgis' critique. In the large majority of cases, the original and the recalculated index of economic freedom both produce the same or similar picture of how capitalist (or neoliberal) a country is. That means that the original index of economic freedom cannot be such an inappropriate measure of capitalism as Burgis suggests. This, in turn, means that Burgis cannot sustain his speculation that the impressive association of economic freedom with positive social outcomes is just a definitional artefact, i.e. that if one uses a more correct definition of capitalism, the correlation will disappear.

To make this even more clear, I used the recalculated economic freedom ratings of individual countries and calculated the quartile averages for extreme poverty and democracy scores. The results of my exercise are displayed in Figures 4.5–4.8. They show the *same trend* as Figures 4.1–4.4, even though the second set of figures was created using the recalculated index of economic freedom, while the first set was drawn using the original index.

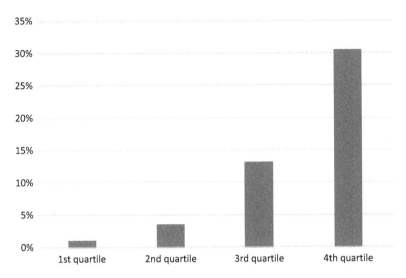

FIGURE 4.5 Share of population living in extreme poverty (int-$1.9 per day, adjusted for inflation) in countries classified by 4 quartiles of economic freedom (1 – most economically free; 4 – least economically free). Index of economic freedom recalculated to exclude the 'sound money' category and all subcategories of the 'legal system' category except for security of property rights.

Sources: Fraser Institute (2022); PovcalNet World Bank via Our World in Data (Roser 2021).

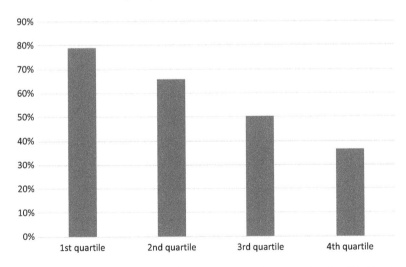

FIGURE 4.6 Average aggregate democracy score for countries classified by 4 quartiles of economic freedom (1 – most economically free; 4 – least economically free). Higher democracy score denotes more political and civil rights. Index of economic freedom recalculated to exclude the 'sound money' category and all subcategories of the 'legal system' category except for security of property rights.

Sources: Fraser Institute (2022); Freedom House (2022).

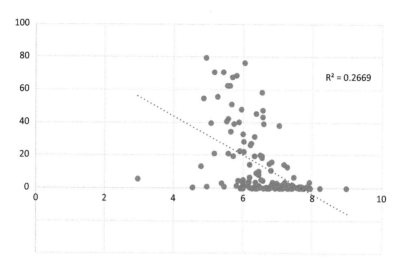

FIGURE 4.7 Scatter plot showing the correlation between economic freedom and extreme poverty. A quarter of all the variance in extreme poverty between
countries is accounted for by how economically free they are; the freer,
the less poverty. Index of economic freedom recalculated to exclude the
'sound money' category and all subcategories of the 'legal system' category except for security of property rights.

Sources: Fraser Institute (2022); PovcalNet World Bank via Our World in Data (Roser 2021).

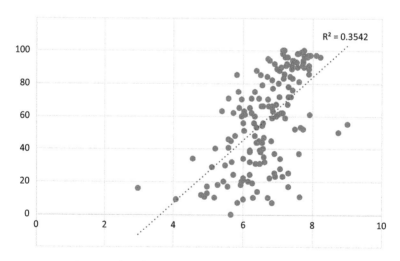

FIGURE 4.8 Scatter plot showing the correlation between economic freedom and
level of democracy. 35% of all the variance between how democratic
countries are is accounted for by how economically free they are; the
freer, the more democratic. Index of economic freedom recalculated to
exclude the 'sound money' category and all subcategories of the 'legal
system' category except for security of property rights.

Sources: Fraser Institute (2022); Freedom House (2022).

Of course, we cannot use these results to claim that had the complex, multivariate studies I mentioned above employed the recalculated index, they would have also come to the same set of positive findings as with the original index. This is impossible to know as things stand now. The studies would have to be redone using the recalculated index. But the simple association between economic freedom and positive social outcomes that Burgis speculates would dissolve (if we used the recalculated index) definitely survives his critique.

Measuring neoliberalism indirectly

Let us, now, turn to a different way in which we can measure and assess the ostensible growth of neoliberalism in the past 40 years. How have the welfare state, government spending, trade unions, and taxation fared under the alleged neoliberal onslaught? Have they moved in the expected, i.e. diminished, direction? Or have they not? And what does that tell us about neoliberalism's effects on societies?

The welfare state

Compared to the 'pre-neoliberal' era of the 1960s and 1970s, most Western countries (including the more neoliberal US, UK, New Zealand, Ireland, and Australia) have not actually seen their welfare states deteriorate throughout the neoliberal period of the last decades of the 20th century and the first decades of the 21st century.[31]

To take one measure of welfare state generosity, i.e. public transfer replacement rates, these have either remained stable or have increased in the past few decades, and so today remain comparable to, or are even higher than, in the 1960s and 1970s.[32] Today, as before the 'neoliberal revolution,' the US, UK, New Zealand, and Australia are expectedly at the bottom of the pack.[33] Compared to the top countries – Austria, Norway, Belgium, Finland, and Germany – their replacement rates are very modest. But they are no more modest today than they were in the past. An interesting development is that Sweden and Finland today have lower rates than at their peak in the 1980s – yet their rates still remain very high overall.[34] On the other hand, Norway and Denmark today have as high (or higher) rates than they had in the 1980s.[35] Overall, neoliberalism's ostensible quest of slashing the welfare state has not been successful.

The other obvious measure of welfare state robustness is the size of government social expenditures. Since the 1960s and 1970s, these have grown in virtually every Western country.[36] Today, the developed governments that spend *the least* on the public (as a share of their GDP) sit at the same percentage as the developed countries that spent *the most* back in the 1960s. So, it is not only that across the neoliberal Western world public expenditure increased in absolute terms (which is obviously the case as the economies expanded significantly) – rather, public expenditure also grew in relative terms. In other words, a developed Western country that today has a much bigger economy than in the 1960s also allots a *larger proportion* of its now *larger economy* to public social expenditure. A double whammy.

Now, a sceptic might say that the growth of the welfare state in recent decades is not as impressive when one confronts the fact of ageing populations. In other words, the idea is that the welfare state under neoliberalism has primarily grown on account of pensions and other services for the elderly, which does not help the young and the poor. But this rebuttal is misguided for two reasons.

First, even if the welfare state has grown mostly due to ageing population, this still means that the 'neoliberal revolution' thesis, which suggests the annihilation of welfare under neoliberalism, simply does not hold. Critics of neoliberalism do not say that the welfare state has been decimated only for the youth; rather they say that it has been decimated *tout court*, which is clearly not the case.

Second, we can look at the various elements that comprise total social expenditure and examine whether, say, the share going to pensions really is skyrocketing. It turns out that it is not. The average spending of 13 OECD countries showing up as pensions has remained constant between 1980 and 2010, as has the share of ('non-elderly') spending on family assistance, labour-market assistance, and public housing subsidies.[37] What has been increasing is the share of social expenditure going to public health (the increase started in the 1960s). It is true that this is primarily used up by the elderly, but then again the relative shifting of state welfare from the young and the poor to the elderly has happened primarily *before* the 'neoliberal revolution,' namely between 1910 and 1960, when pensions rose from a few percent of total social expenditure to more than 30%.

One of two conclusions follows from this. Either we maintain that (the developed) world has become more neoliberal but neoliberalism simply has not had the destructive social welfare state impact critics worry about. Or, if one insists on defining neoliberalism as 'that which diminishes the welfare state,' we could say that the world has not become noticeably more neoliberal as far as the welfare state is concerned. Whatever the case, critics who sounded the alarm about the imminent destruction of the welfare state in the post-1980s era seem to have been quite wrong.

Total government spending

How about government spending as a whole, not merely the welfare-state part of government spending? Did the size of governments radically shrink after neoliberalism, as folk wisdom has it? Not really. Across the Western world, government expenditure in the second decade of the 21st century remains broadly similar in size (as a share of GDP) to what it has been in the 1980s – roughly 50% – and is much higher than it had been in the 1950s or 1960s.[38]

It is true that the rapid increase in government size between World War II and the early 1980s has, thereafter, largely stopped. This halting – but not a reversal, let alone a radical reversal – of government expansion could perhaps be said to represent neoliberalism (or be a result of triumphant neoliberalism). But, at the same time, one could sensibly retort to this that if neoliberalism did not manage to noticeably reduce government spending, instead merely stalling it after it had reached a very high level, then the rumours of neoliberalism's success have been greatly exaggerated.

What about Latin America? If anywhere, surely there one will be able to find obvious traces of neoliberalism's destruction of the state? In reality, Brazil, Argentina, Venezuela, Bolivia, Nicaragua, Paraguay, Colombia, and Uruguay today (in 2011) spend *much more* of their GDP via the government – between 30% and 45% – than was the case in the 1980s. In the Dominican Republic, the share has also increased, but not as significantly and it remains low overall (18%). Peru today is about the same as Peru in the 1980s. Mexico, Chile, and Costa Rica have shrunk in recent decades although they are still above 20%. So, some data for Latin America go in the opposite direction of the 'neoliberal revolution' thesis, while other data points are consistent with it. Reality is again more complicated than opponents of neoliberalism present it.

The strength of trade unions

One would also predict that, since neoliberalism took hold, unions should be losing their strength. And, indeed, according to one measure of union strength, this is precisely what has been happening. The share of employees who are also union members is noticeably lower today in most Western countries than it has been in the 1980s.[39]

Interestingly, however, the long-term decline of unionization actually predates the neoliberal revolution. In the US, for instance, unions started losing their members already in the 1950s, a trend that has continued quite linearly through the 1960s, 1970s, 1980s, and so on to present day.[40] Ronald Reagan probably helped union decline, but he was clearly not its maker. More than 33% of American workers were union members after World War II, at American union's historical peak. Almost every year since, the number got lower. Today, only around 10% of all workers still carry their union cards, which is comparable to the first decades of the 20th century.

In Europe, the overall picture is largely the same (with a few important exceptions). As in the US, so too in Europe union decline originates from before the neoliberal era. However, as in the US, union density decline has then continued – and in some countries even accelerated – in the post-1980 neoliberal era. With the exception of Finland, Sweden, Denmark, Belgium, and Norway, which today still stand at a respectable 50–65% (and Iceland, which boast rates of above 90%), most Western countries today have unionization rates of below 20–25%.[41] The OECD average is 15.8% in 2019.[42] It stood at 20.9% in 2000.

Therefore, the data on union density are consistent with the neoliberalism hypothesis although given the partial mismatch in timing they can be seen as only partially supporting the hypothesis. There are other forces at work apart from neoliberalism that are responsible for the decline in union membership.

Tax rates and revenue

Tax revenues captured by governments have been remarkably stable as a percentage of the GDP since the 1980s in virtually all key Western countries.[43] The OECD average has actually *increased* in the last 40 years. It stood at exactly 30% in 1980, and in 2020 it was more than 3 percentage points *higher* (33.5%).[44] The average never dipped below 30% in any year since 1980, while before 1980s (i.e. before the neoliberal revolution) the average was *lower* than 30% (for example, it stood at 24.8% in 1965, 27.2% in 1971, 28.6% in 1975, steadily increasing to 30% in late 1970s and early 1980s).

But how about taxes on corporate profits? What I have discussed up till now is *aggregate* tax revenue generated by taxes on a whole host of things, including personal income and goods consumption. So, what if we instead focus only on the taxes that corporations have to pay on their profits? The result is the same. Since the early 1980s, when OECD countries received around 2.3% of GDP as taxes on corporate profits, the percentage has only increased, not decreased.[45] In 2019, the share stood at 3%. The same trend holds if we extend the period under investigation back in time to the pre-neoliberal era of the 1960s and 1970s. The average then was about 2.1%.

Where a significant decline has most definitely been happening in the second part of the 20th century – although this happened even before the neoliberal era – are top marginal tax rates. Marginal tax rates are taxes on every additional amount of income earned above a certain threshold, which means that *top* marginal taxes are paid only by those who achieve the highest threshold (say, the threshold of 300,000 $). These taxes have been set quite high in many OECD countries before the 1970s, while today they are much lower in many – not just a few – cases. In the early 1960s, for instance, the majority of OECD countries had a top marginal tax rate set at around or above 70%.[46] In the late 2000s, no country had the rate set at above 60%, but instead all were in the 40–60% range.[47] This could, at least in part, be plausibly blamed on neoliberalism.

In sum, neoliberalism's record on account of the welfare state, total government spending, trade union strength, and tax rates and revenues presents us with a mixed picture. Some evidence fits the 'neoliberal revolution' story well or is at least consistent with it. Other evidence not so much; some of it is even *spectacularly inconsistent* with the received wisdom. Any hyperbolic and absolutist claims about how neoliberals have been successfully destroying the West for decades now should crumble in face of what has been presented above. Critics of neoliberalism will need to develop a significantly more nuanced thesis than what they had been offering us in the past if they are to salvage their operation.

Lessons from the three waves of research on the Washington consensus

Another way of evaluating neoliberalism is to examine what the effects were on economic development around the world when a set of economic reforms known as the Washington Consensus (WC) was introduced. As I already pointed out in the beginning of the previous section, WC is the list of ten reforms Williamson codified in the 1980s as, to use his own words, 'practically agreed in Washington to be desirable in most Latin American countries as of 1989.' When critics use the word 'neoliberalism,' the various policy proposals on the WC list are, oftentimes, what they have in mind.[48] In *The Shock Doctrine*, for instance, Naomi Klein directly describes WC as 'nothing less than Friedman's neoliberal triumvirate of privatization, deregulation/free trade and drastic cuts to government spending.'[49] In *A Brief History of Neoliberalism*, David Harvey sees the late 1980s articulation of the WC in similar terms, namely as the event that inaugurated neoliberalism 'as a new orthodoxy.'[50]

As with neoliberalism more generally, there is a strong presumption (clearly on display, for instance, in Klein's and Harvey's book) that the practical implementation of the consensus has mostly been disastrous for the economies of the targeted countries. The thought is that, at the very least, the WC policies do not *economically* work as their proponents argue they should. They do not unleash economic growth and, thus, will not and cannot reduce poverty.

Extant systematic empirical research, however, presents a much more mixed picture on how well the WC performs. Perusing studies that have accumulated on the topic in the last three decades, one can discern three distinct waves of research.

The first wave of studies hit in the 1990s, with most researchers finding positive associations between the implementation of (some of the) reforms and economic development. One early and widely cited study uncovered that 'trade liberalization, devaluation of the real exchange rate, and maintenance of a stable real exchange rate could dramatically improve growth performance in many poor countries.'[51] This was so because, at least for the period between 1976 and 1985, a strong association was found between such outward orientation of countries and their per capita GDP growth. The most open countries had the highest growth rate (2.9%), while least open had a notably negative growth rate (−1.3%).[52] Another influential study followed which similarly demonstrated that trade liberalization was a growth success in the last third of the 20th century. Between 1970 and 1989, more economic openness was strongly associated with high growth rates both within developing countries (4.49% annual growth for open vs. 0.69% annual growth for closed) and the developed world (2.29% annual growth vs. 0.74% annual growth).[53] Other studies came to similar conclusions.[54] Organizations such as the International Monetary Fund (IMF) and the Organisation for Economic Co-operation and Development (OECD) were emboldened by these studies in their belief that various neoliberal reforms are good for the economy.

In the early 2000s, however, a second wave of research emerged, and it overturned the findings of the first. Provocatively subtitled 'A Skeptic's Guide to the Cross-National Evidence,' one widely cited paper uncovered serious methodological issues with the studies from the 1990s.[55] The paper claimed that previous positive findings were sometimes based on weak data and that the findings were not actually robust and largely disappeared once one used different controls (say, once one controlled for macroeconomic imbalances and bad institutions) or more appropriate measures of trade liberalization. Furthermore, the authors of the paper suggested that because trade restrictions do not theoretically necessarily lead to diminished growth, but can under conceivable conditions, i.e. the presence of market failure, even increase GDP, one should not expect to find 'an unambiguous, negative relationship between trade barriers and growth rates in the types of cross-national data sets typically analysed.'[56]

Another famous study from the second wave warned of an inconvenient fact that occurred during the 1980s and 1990s, the time that the WC reforms first ostensibly gained most steam in Africa and Latin America.[57] The fact is that the typical, i.e. median, growth rate of developing countries was much lower – stagnant, in fact – in the 1980s and 1990s as compared to the 1960s and 1970s. This finding was, as the paper concluded, 'a blow to the optimism surrounding the "Washington Consensus".'[58] A new critical, anti-neoliberal, anti-WC mind-set was forming in the first decade of the 21st century, emboldened by the popular movement against globalization most infamously on display in 1999 in Seattle and 2001 in Genoa.

But then the third, most recent wave of research hit. A fresh round of papers was generated and they came, yet again, to a different set of conclusions. In part, this is simply because a different time period is typically under examination in the latest wave of research. One paper, for instance, looks at the *post-2000* performance of the WC. It finds three 'stylized facts,' of which two are especially crucial for our purposes.[59]

First, since 2000, several of the recommended WC policies were implemented much more thoroughly throughout the world than before the mid-1990s. The share of countries with high or extremely high inflation, black markets, high or extremely high overvaluation, and bad trade to GDP ratios has declined significantly.[60] The share of countries with 'bad policies' (with respect to the WC standard) was around 60% between 1961 and 1991, while in the past two decades, this share has declined to around 20–25%. The biggest WC policy improvement has been in Latin America but also in Africa.

The second stylized fact is that improvements in policy implementation are, for the most part, correlated with growth across countries. This result holds even when controlling for various other factors such as civil wars and export price booms (or busts). Importantly, however, the most significant effect shows up primarily when looking at extremely bad policies. In other words, if we look only at countries with moderate levels of bad (i.e. non-WC) policies, most associations turn out not to be robust. So, WC reforms seem to have helped growth in countries where WC prescriptions were totally lacking, but not so much in countries where they were only somewhat absent.

Because they do not overlap temporally, these positive findings are consistent with the more negative ones from the previous wave. But what accounts for the difference in outcomes of the two different periods? Why did the WC not work in earlier decades but does seem to work now? As already intimated, it is possible that reforms in the late 20th century were not adopted as strongly as they should have been for the effect to show – an eventuality that cannot plausibly be argued for the 21st century as many countries nowadays clearly employ WC prescriptions to a significant extent. It is also possible that not enough time passed since the early 1990s, when reforms had only started to be adopted, for any significant effects to be registered before the 2000s. Indeed, as one researcher who originally contributed to the second wave of studies on the WC puts it, 'Earlier judgments on the reforms often happened before the reform process was complete and/or not enough post-reform growth data to evaluate reforms.'[61] Moreover, the number of liberalizers in the late 1980s and early 1990s was much smaller than in the late 1990s and early 2000s, which means that the more recent samples are larger and, thus, more reliable.

Other papers within the third wave of research on the WC, however, include earlier decades and still find that various WC reforms robustly correlate with growth even before the late 1990s or early 2000s, at least of course where these reforms were actually implemented to a significant degree. Douglas Irwin has performed an exhaustive review of this literature, examining the results of dozens of papers with various different statistical methodologies (not only cross-country regressions). His conclusion is that, 'The findings from recent research have been remarkably consistent. For developing countries that are behind the technological frontier and have significant import restrictions, there appears to be a measurable economic payoff from more liberal trade policies.'[62] Multiple studies claim a gain of up to 20% of income after a decade since the implementation of reforms.[63] One very recent 2021 study that looked at the period between 1970 and 2015, and used the Fraser Institute's index of economic freedom as proxy for WC reforms, is concordant with this assessment.[64] It finds that countries with sustained economic reforms seem to be 16% richer a decade later in comparison to a counterfactual without reforms.[65]

Note that the fact that the WC reforms mostly worked is important not because we care about increasing economic growth for its own sake or because economic growth is good for the rich, but instead because economic growth typically helps reduce poverty and raise ordinary people's material living standards, thus increasing social well-being.[66] I have already discussed the reasons for, and the empirical literature on, this fact in Chapter 3 (the section on poverty) and in the present chapter above (the section on economic freedom).

How industrial policy works, or does not work

Many who are doubtful, or outright critical, of the success of the neoliberal Washington consensus policies (WC) point to a set of countries which, they say, managed to spectacularly develop *in defiance* of the vaunted neoliberal nostrums. The so-called East Asian Tigers – Hong Kong, Singapore, South Korea, and Taiwan – are common cases trotted out by sceptics of neoliberalism, with the latter two being seen as especially crucial. Japan is sometimes also thrown in the mix, as are late 19th-century US, France, and Germany, to name a few more.

The alternative to the free-market neoliberal developmental program, an ostensibly highly successful alternative model these cases embodied, is known as industrial policy (IP), especially an intensive form of IP which – at least at first – shields domestic companies from (instead of exposing them to) world trade. IP can generally be defined simply as the 'effort by a government to alter the sectoral structure of production toward sectors it believes offer greater prospects for accelerated growth than would be generated by a typical process of industrial evolution.'[67] What the critics of neoliberalism argue in this regard is, for instance, that instead of opening up a developing economy, i.e. liberalizing its trade by reducing tariffs and non-tariff barriers, and instead of leaving it up to the free market to determine which companies will thrive and which ones will go bust, the government should step in and direct the economy by favouring certain industries and firms, while discouraging others. This is a form of protectionism which goes directly against neoliberalism.

It is true that in the second part of the 20th century the East Asian Tigers started becoming very economically successful in short order, even though they were economically very undeveloped not long before that. Given the extraordinary growth rates these countries achieved, it can be said that they went from poor to rich in a matter of mere decades, which is an incredible, unprecedented feat in human history.[68] It is also correct that they (with the notable exception of Hong Kong) employed a substantial degree of protectionist industrial policy in the early years of their path to success. A natural conclusion seems to flow from these facts, namely that industrial policy caused (or at least significantly contributed to) the rise of the Asian Tigers, and that without it, they would have been significantly worse off or even remained undeveloped.

The natural seeming conclusion, however, does not necessarily follow, as many other countries also employed industrial policy but did not reap any rewards, let alone the kind of rewards enjoyed by the Asian Tigers. Moreover, the mere fact that one event (industrial policy) was followed by another (development) in principle allows for the possibility that the two are not, in fact, related. Thinking otherwise would be committing the 'post hoc, ergo propter hoc' fallacy. It might even be that the economic success of South Korea and Taiwan could be greater still had they not been experimenting with industrial policy. In other words, maybe IP *inhibited* even higher levels of growth. If something like this turned out to be the case, IP should not be credited as a successful alternative to the Washington consensus. Even in this case, however, IP obviously could not have been an *overwhelmingly* negative force for growth since the East Asian Tigers grew so impressively – but it could have been *somewhat* negative (or neutral), not necessarily positive, and one would still witness the tremendous growth of these countries for other reasons not related to IP.

The infant industry protection argument

Before looking at what the evidence says on this matter, we should step back and examine why it is theoretically plausible that IP would either work or not work.

The most famous and persuasive argument for IP is known as the *infant indus-try protection argument*. The idea is as follows. It is true that under perfect market conditions, where no market failures are present, one would expect free market economic activity to be undertaken by the firms optimally, i.e. with perfect ef-ficiency. This means that, under the stipulated conditions, governments do not (and should not) have to make top-down, planned decisions on which firms and production lines to favour and nurture; instead, the economic actors themselves will spontaneously make the economically most sensible decisions, which will, in turn, lead over time to a robust development of the country's economy. In short, it will go from poor to rich as the free market is unleashed because free markets (in absence of market failures) provide the best economic incentives and information through the price mechanism. Put more concretely, firms will use the prices formed on the free market to make decisions on what to produce (i.e. what is actually demanded by buyers and will be bought once produced, instead of lying on the shelves), how to produce it (i.e. which inputs to use in produc-tion and in what way so as to minimize costs and not unnecessarily waste extra inputs), and how much of it to produce (i.e. how much of what is demanded is to be produced). The resulting optimal economic activity will lead to economic growth and development, as what is produced will actually be bought and it will be produced in an efficient (i.e. not wasteful) manner.

None of this is denied by the infant industry protection argument for IP. The rationale of the argument, however, is that market conditions are simply not per-fect or close to perfect in poor, developing countries. Had they been, IP would, indeed, be unnecessary. But they are not. There are many market failures present in poor countries.

To understand what that means, let us imagine that a certain undeveloped country's automobile industry would have been a great domestic and interna-tional success and had the domestic economic actors been presented with the opportunity and incentive to start investing into cars. Put simply, the country has a 'latent comparative advantage.' However, because at the present moment cars are already being produced by other developed countries in a highly effi-cient manner, it is doubtful whether the undeveloped country's automobile in-dustry will ever get off the ground (to later become highly successful, utilizing as it will the once latent and in the future actualized comparative advantage it possesses). Why will its industry not take off? Because the domestic producers of cars in the undeveloped country will at first produce cars at a comparatively lower quality and higher price than foreign producers do. They do not yet enjoy economies of scale that others do, as the infant automobile industry is by definition small-scale, so costs can be higher per unit of product. Moreover, the producers are not as of yet skilled enough in the production of cars, as the learning-by-doing process has only started for them while it has been going on for quite some time outside of the country. The result is that buyers at home and abroad will not be rushing to buy this worse product, and consequently, the industry will never take off.

Because the free market cannot foresee – that is, provide information and incentives for – production that will only become economically sensible 15 years later, but is economically not justified at the present, an otherwise net-beneficial development opportunity will have been foregone. Of course, it is in principle possible that would-be producers themselves know (or hope) that even though their endeavour will not be profitable at first, it will become profitable later, and so they are willing to undertake it anyway on the free market without government involvement. But the problem is that they might be hard-pressed to find private financiers and banks that will be willing to lend them investment funds for such a risky, long-term project, especially because the credit system is not as robust and dynamic in poor countries as it is in the developed world.

The infant industry protection argument therefore claims that sometimes the government should help and protect infant industries despite their inefficiencies and short-term economic infeasibility – at least if the government thinks that the presence of market failures prevents certain promising industries to spring up. The government can offer protection by, for instance, subsidizing the producers or by erecting tariff barriers for foreign competition. If it subsidizes the producers, cars (to continue with my example) can then be sold cheaply, the prices no longer reflecting higher per-unit costs of the new, inefficient industry. This, in turn, stimulates buyers to demand the cars and to generate profits for the firms, helping them develop further. Or if the government raises tariffs and stifles foreign trade, the foreign cars will be sold for a higher price in this country than they otherwise would have been, which makes the domestic inefficiently produced cars again relatively more attractive for the (domestic) buyer in the undeveloped country. The original demand problems are thus curtailed, and the firms can thrive and develop, overcoming their initial deficiencies and later reaping the benefits of economies of scale, learning-by-doing, etc.

This stifling of the free market principles, the infant industry protection argument admits, is not a perfect solution. After all, the government is protecting an inefficient industry and thus hurting the public interest – consumers are lead to buy lower quality cars that have been produced with (comparatively) higher costs, which means that they get a worse product and that the resources that went into the production of the car have been used wastefully (in comparison to efficient foreign producers), so less resources are available for other production needs of the country. Moreover, the protection enjoyed by the domestic industries removes one otherwise powerful incentive they would have to improve their productive efficiency – foreign competition. The protected industries do not have to work as hard because being shielded from competition they face a captured consumer base. However, the promise of the argument is that these social costs will be more than compensated for when the industry takes off. Then, the protection can be removed as the firms will have become efficient (through achieving economies of scale, learning, etc.) and can now withstand the international competitive pressure. So, the costs of protection can be done away with now, and at the same time, the country possesses a world-class, competitive automobile industry, which it otherwise would not have. This benefits everyone, and if the costs of protection have been lower than the (later) benefits generated by the once-infant, now-mature industry, this is a net-positive development.

The government failure rebuttal

Before turning to the empirical record, another set of theoretical arguments has to be confronted if one wants a full picture of the potential merits and pitfalls of IP. More specifically, although market failure is a plausible rationale for IP, government failure is a plausible rationale against it.

In the account given for IP above, I assumed governments to *know* which industries are worth protecting (due to market failure), to *want* to protect only those worth protecting (due to market failure), and to later stop protecting them when this is no longer necessary for their development. If all of this holds, the argument for IP goes through. If it does not hold, the argument does not work.

Public choice economics, the literature on rent-seeking, and basic rational choice considerations all suggest we should not be too quick to accept these crucial IP assumptions.

Take, first, the knowledge issue. Is it really plausible that governments – more specifically, people staffing them – will generally know which sectors of the economy the latent comparative advantage is hiding in? Will they know which enterprises to subsidize (and to what extent), or what particular goods their proposed tariffs should target (and how high, or low, these tariffs should optimally be)? If such knowledge is lacking, IP cannot be the quick fix it is touted to be. Put more concretely, without the appropriate knowledge, the wrong industries might be protected. That, in turn, would make a country's development prospects (and societal well-being) even more dire than they have been without IP, as economic costs of subsidies and tariffs mount in the present without a future payoff. Even if the right industries are targeted, the balance of present costs of protection and future benefits of the once-protected industries might not be net-positive as (due to the knowledge problem) the protection phase perhaps involved too much subsidizing and too high tariffs.

Moving on to the question of interests, or wants, it is not at all obvious that governments in the developing world are primarily interested in the welfare of their publics. Politicians and bureaucrats are, after all, not angels but people. And people tend to be quite a bit more self-interested than public-spirited. So, if the political decision-makers recognize an unpunished opportunity to enrich themselves, or to gain clout and powerful supporters without whom they cannot rule, by offering government protection to the wrong firms and industries (in exchange for money or support from their owners), they will do so more often than not. With this, we are not talking about lacking knowledge or stupidity with regards to which economic actors require shielding so as to improve the country's longer-term development chances. Instead, I am simply pointing out that rational, strategizing politicians tend to do what they have to in order to stay in power (right now). If this means *consciously, knowingly* abusing IP mechanisms to capture personal economic rents or, as said, to create powerful cronies who help them stay in office longer, so be it.

In short, even when the government knows which nascent industries should be protected so that the public interest is pursued, it can still *decide* to instead protect decrepit, 'sunset' industries the protection of which will only hurt the public interest through lower quality products, higher prices, and resources lost to rent-seeking. Government officials can decide to act that way because even though the public interest is hurt in doing so, the few private owners and government officials engaged in this corrupt deal benefit greatly. Of course, a mix of protection that is in the interest of the public and of protection that is in the interests of politicians and businessmen is also possible.

Lastly, and relatedly, even if the government mostly targets meritorious industries, it is still possible that (due to considerations from the last two paragraphs) the once-protected industries will never shake off the protection they have been enjoying so far. Protectionist measures might outstay their welcome (and so hurt the development of the country) again due to the mutually beneficial, private deals happening between the officials and owners. The owners will lobby for continuing protection as they personally benefit by receiving economically unjustified government funds and by being shielded from foreign competition, which would otherwise force them to lower prices and be more efficient. And the officials might assent to the pressure and offers made to them by the owners. The public, however, is burdened by the mounting costs of such protection.

So, if the original thought behind IP was that where markets fail in optimally satisfying the public interest, governments should step in and naturally succeed, it has now been demonstrated that governments – not only markets – can also fail in serving the public. Not only can failures occur, we should also not simply assume that cases of government failure will necessarily or even likely be fewer than cases of market failure.

A general case in point, the famous rare examples of ostensibly successful development through IP – South Korea, Taiwan, and a few others – are conspicuous precisely due to their rarity. And it is not that only a few countries in the last century tried IP at all – say, the Asian Tigers – which would then naturally mean we do not have many successful cases of IP, simply because IP itself is so rare in this hypothetical. No, IP in its various forms was tried in virtually all developing countries in the second half of the 20th century. And from dozens and dozens of trials, only a few victors emerged.

What the empirical record shows

General impressions aside, what does empirical research say on the success and failure of IP for development? There is a large quantitative economic literature that mostly comes to a negative conclusion.[69] The conclusion of one large review of existing evidence is clear, but judicious:

There are instances where infant-industry protection was successful–particularly in the late nineteenth and early twentieth centuries–and could work today in developing countries. Still, the conditions needed for infant-industry protection to succeed are generally not satisfied. ... The hundreds of studies on trade policies, trade shares, productivity, and growth show a strong correlation between increasing trade shares and country performance, and no significant correlation between tariffs on final goods and country outcomes.[70]

Even so, the authors of the review add that they would advocate for a certain modest form of IP:

We envision an important role for what we refer to as 'soft' industrial policy ... [I]nstead of tariffs, export subsidies, and tax breaks for foreign corporations, we think of programs and grants to, for example, help particular clusters by increasing the supply of skilled workers, encouraging technology adoption, and improving regulation and infrastructure.[71]

The most common type of ('hard') IP, called 'import substitution industrialization' (ISI), that has been pursued especially in the 1960s and 1970s (but also parts of the 1980s) has especially been associated with poor growth, underdevelopment, and failure. ISI is the type of IP that does not lead to the removal of protection down the line, does now allow for increasing exposure to foreign competition of the now-mature industries, or opening of trade and specialization. It is the direct opposite of the neoliberal Washington consensus. That ISI is a developmental failure is recognized today even by supporters of (a certain softer kind of) IP.[72] As the previously cited literature review puts it:

[T]wo general lessons ... may be drawn from the voluminous evidence. First, there was no significant relationship in the second half of the twentieth century between average protection levels and growth. Second, there is a positive association between trade volumes and growth.[73]

This should be taken to 'suggest that any successful IP strategy must ultimately increase the share of international trade in GDP.' But, because in the typical case IP had a strong antitrade bias, this was ultimately not achieved.[74] Hence, IP failure prevailed.

The successful Asian Tigers, however, did not pursue ISI *tout court*. They did not engage solely in the failing 'hard' IP. In their early years, they did employ a variety of interventionist and protectionist measures typical of ISI. But they then relatively soon started opening up in a sense, by forcing their firms to be export-oriented. Moreover, as one IP-friendly report on the Asian Tigers puts it, they pursued 'fierce competition both abroad and domestically with strict accountability.'[75] So, the argument could be that even though we can (and should) be sceptical of IP in general, *a particular type* of IP can work and does work. It should, of course, be recognized that this form of IP is *not* in direct opposition to neoliberalism. In fact, it is more a marriage of the two approaches. It says 'protection now, free trade and competition later.' As discussed before, the thought is that early protection generates latent economic benefits (that otherwise would not have been generated), which can then be reaped only by removing protection (and shedding its costs) and by liberalizing trade. The one does not work without the other (see more on this below).

Whatever we decide to call it, what does the evidence say about the type of IP specifically pursued by the Asian Tigers? Did it help? Was its effect neutral? Did it hurt development? One early comprehensive review concludes that 'on balance, the weight of the evidence derived from both econometric and input-output studies … indicates that industrial policy made a minor contribution to growth in Asia.'[76] So, a positive effect of IP on development, albeit a minor one. A recent report for the IMF also comes to a positive, but an even less modest conclusion about IP in Asian Tigers, saying 'the success of the Asian Miracles was not a matter of luck but the result of TIP.' By TIP, the authors of the report are referring to what they call 'true industrial policy,' i.e. early protection plus free trade and competition later on. As they describe it:

> [F]irst, TIP was based on the state intervention to facilitate the move of domestic firms into sophisticated sectors beyond the existing comparative advantage. Second, export orientation since the onset played a key role in sustaining competitive pressure and pushing firms to innovate. … Finally, the discipline of the market and accountability were enforced in a strict manner.

The authors are clear that they *do not think* that 'tools traditionally associated with industrial policy, such as subsidies, tariffs and the use of [state-owned enterprises] are necessarily effective ways to pursue TIP.' In fact, they say, these tools might explain why IP was such as failure in the typical case. TIP, the authors continue, 'favors more competition and autonomy of the private sector, not less.'

In a recent book-length treatment, Arvind Panagariya examined various purported cases of IP success, most notably South Korea and Taiwan, and the theoretical and empirical accounts put forward by famous champions of IP such as Robert Wade, Dani Rodrik, and Ha Joon-Chang. He is quite critical of these IP proponents and favours free trade policies, not protectionism. His case studies, for instance, reveal that,

> [I]n every case, low or declining barriers to trade were an integral part of the growth strategy. The case studies reveal that in no country was a growth strategy pursued in isolation. … I do not find a single case in which high or rising protection has accompanied sustained rapid growth.[77]

This conclusion, however, is consistent with the findings cited above, namely that at least a certain form of IP which also involves (at a certain period in time) free trade, exports, and competition, can work. In other words, we cannot argue IP did not work in the Asian Tigers based on Panagariya's (correct) conclusion that their IP was an extremely outward-oriented IP which was very different from the traditional ISI form of IP that resulted in failure when used in developing countries. His case studies are definitive only on one question: did IP work if it was not accompanied with an increasing exposure to world trade? The answer is: no, it did not work. But it could have worked (and arguably did work) when pursued in a much more open manner, like the one embodied by the Asian Tigers.

As I see it, the general conclusion from all this must be that IP in the second part of the 20th century overall hurt development more than helped it. However, this does not mean that unqualified neoliberalism is the right way to go.

First, neoliberalism as it is implemented in the real world does not necessarily reflect the abstract neoliberal principles as written on paper (just as one would expect IP to not necessarily be followed as prescribed), so caution is needed. For instance, studies show that if trade is liberalized in a country, but at the same time infrastructure remains lacklustre and economic actors are still facing barriers to free entry on the market, then 'trade liberalization will not generate faster growth unless accompanied by changes in other parts of the economy,' for example the two just mentioned.[78] Under certain imperfect conditions, neoliberalism does not work as advertised (the same, of course, goes for IP). Panagariya concurs.[79]

Second, at least a certain form of export-oriented IP, which admittedly is hard to pull off in the real world, seems to spur on development (even if not as spectacularly as claimed by some) or at the least not hinder it. This is an important and interesting finding.

The democratizing effects of capitalist economic development

Even if the existing evidence suggests that neoliberalism in its various economic guises actually works, i.e. that it is mostly positively, not negatively, associated with economic growth – which is itself positively associated with poverty reduction – it could still be charged against it that it does not work politically. The critique could be that even though neoliberalism might unleash economic development, this still comes with a significant, intolerable collateral cost, namely the destruction of political freedom – of democracy. In *The Shock Doctrine*, Naomi Klein does not quite make this claim although she gestures at it. She stops just short of it, claiming instead that various neoliberals, such as Milton Friedman, are anti-democratic (or, at least, prefer economic growth over democracy); that neoliberal reforms have infamously been introduced around the world in a non-democratic manner; and that neoliberalism has no problem coexisting with autocratic politics. As I said, this is not quite the claim that neoliberalism actively destroys, or significantly hurts, political freedom, but given Klein's disdain for neoliberals and neoliberalism, even such a serious claim does not seem to be a stretch for her.

Statistically, the anti-democratic charge against neoliberalism does not seem to pan out. (The same, incidentally, goes for the actual anti-democratic charge Klein makes against Friedman – it does not hold.)[80] As explained in the first section, economic freedom ('neoliberalism') is generally associated with *more*, not less, civil and political freedoms. And, as explained, although we cannot conclude from this simple correlation that neoliberalism *causes* democracy, it is still causally suggestive in an important way. It is causally suggestive in the sense that this correlation should not be able to exist if neoliberalism in actuality either destroys democracy or significantly reduces it. So, what the correlation implies is that neoliberalism is, on average, at the very least probably neutral with respect to democracy. This is an important, if more modest, causal finding. Studies looking at change over time go even a step further, suggesting a possible *positive* causal effect of neoliberal institutions on democratic durability.[81]

In this section, however, I take a step back from neoliberalism specifically. I do so because there is, in fact, much more one can say about what we know about the general relationship between economic development and political freedom. Taking, then, capitalism more broadly as my point of departure I begin with a fascinating discovery. At closer inspection, it turns that the two rhetorically highly antagonistic social-scientific paradigms, namely Marxism and the anti-Marxist Chicago School of economics, actually point in the same – positive – direction with respect to how capitalist economic development and democratic politics relate to each other.

The converging Marxist and anti-Marxist theoretical perspectives on the capitalism-democracy connection

Here are two similar quotes expressing a similar idea:

> [T]here has been a tendency [within Marxism] to perpetuate the rigid conceptual separation of the 'economic' and the 'political' ... In one form or another and in varying degrees, Marxists have generally adopted modes of analysis which, explicitly or implicitly, treat the economic 'base' and the legal, political, and ideological 'superstructures' that 'reflect' or 'correspond' to it as qualitatively different, more or less enclosed and 'regionally' separated spheres.[82]

> It is widely believed that politics and economics are separate and largely unconnected ... that any kind of political arrangements can be combined with any kind of economic arrangements. ... The thesis of this chapter is that such a view is a delusion, that there is an intimate connection between economics and politics, that only certain combinations of political and economic arrangements are possible ...[83]

Can you tell, without looking at the endnotes, whether the author of the quotes is a Marxist or an anti-Marxist? Can you tell which quote belongs to free-market economist Milton Friedman and which to the Marxist political theorist Ellen Meiksins Wood? What if both quotes are from the same author, either Friedman or Wood, can you tell who of the two authors has written both quotes? What if I help you further and tell you that the author of the first quote blames modern varieties of Marxism for the unfortunate tendency to completely sever the link between economics and politics? I can add that the author of the second quote identifies the idea of democratic socialism (more so than Marxism) as the unfortunate outgrowth of the naïve view that economics and politics are mostly separate phenomena. Still cannot quite tell?

Last try. Here are two more quotes from the same author(s):

> The kind of economic organization [that is capitalism] … promotes political freedom because it separates economic power from political power …[84]

> These conceptual devices [i.e. the separation of the 'economic' and the 'political'] do reflect, if only in a distorting mirror, a historical reality specific to capitalism, a real differentiation of the 'economy' … Capitalism is uniquely capable of maintaining private property … without the proprietor wielding direct political power in the conventional sense. The state – which stands apart from the economy though it *intervenes* in it – can ostensibly (notably, by means of universal suffrage) belong to everyone … [T]he capitalist has economic rather than extra-economic powers …[85]

Friedman, Wood, or both? The answer is that in the initial set of quotes, the first is Wood's and the second Friedman's, while in the second set the order is reversed. Friedman's quotes come from his famed book *Capitalism and Freedom*, Wood's quotes come from her book *Democracy Against Capitalism*. My point is, of course, not that Wood and Friedman would agree with each other – the titles of their respective books, if nothing else, prove the contrary. Rather, the point is that two scholars who have a very different opinion on capitalism, one a Marxist, the other a Chicago School free-market economist, are led by their different theoretical apparatuses to at least a few fundamentally similar conclusions.

The conclusions are, first, that politics and economics are generally deeply intertwined. Second, in capitalism specifically, politics and economics are to an important extent nevertheless separated. Third, this capitalist separation of the two spheres has a profound influence on the possibility and probability of a democratic order emerging in its midst.

Now, why would capitalism from both a Marxist and an anti-Marxist perspective be thought of as conducive to democratic development, and how does the mentioned separation of the two social spheres figure in?

On the anti-Marxist side, one argument is that when economic and political power are separated (as much as they can be), the state is less powerful – as it does not possess economic power over and above its own political power – and so can enact less coercion against the citizenry. With the separation, aggregate power in a society is more dispersed than it would have been without the separation. As a consequence, the fight of ordinary people for democracy in such a society is more likely to be carried out, to not be put down by the state, and to be successful.

On the Marxist side, the main argument is that, in capitalism, the elites can enrich themselves without relying on force. This is so because in a capitalist society the direct producers (i.e. workers) no longer possess plots of land and other types of capital with which they could sustain themselves, as they have in pre-capitalist times. Instead, the bulk of the population has to primarily rely on the regular sale of their own labour power to the capitalists in order to receive a pay-check that can then be used to sustain itself. Having no other realistic option, workers are willing to give their work effort to employers, and seek them out, *by their own accord* (knowing that otherwise they cannot lead a sustainable life in modern society). As a consequence, capitalist elites are not too bothered by giving their political power away – with the transition to democracy – as they know that this relinquishment of political power will not *ipso facto* lead to loss of economic resources and power. It would have done so only under pre-capitalist economic arrangements, where the elites were dependent on the use of political coercion for the extraction of wealth from the masses. This is why, Marxists argue, democracy was virtually impossible under feudalism. Pre-capitalist elites simply had too much to lose, economically, by giving their political power away, and so would never assent to such an arrangement.

None of this is to say that capitalism is a *sufficient* condition for democratization. It is not, and both Wood and Friedman say as much. Wood claims that, where the 'economic' and the 'political' are separated (i.e. in capitalism), the elites *can* – if they want to – extract surplus product from the exploited without having to rely on political power and domination to achieve that. In other words, capitalists are able to carry on exploiting workers even if the political system under which they operate is democratic. But the mere fact that they are *able* to do that (as they were once, under feudalism, not able) does not guarantee that they will, in fact, *want* to extract surplus from workers without also dominating them politically. The capitalism-democracy combination is only a structural possibility (as the feudalism-democracy combination was not), a possibility that has to be fought for by struggle from below if it is to be enacted, realized. So, capitalism is a necessary, but not by itself wholly sufficient, condition for democratization.

Friedman is also careful to note that,

> I know of no example in time or place of a society that has been marked by a large measure of political freedom, and that has not also used something comparable to a free market to organize the bulk of economic activity.[86]

This does not mean that wherever there is a robust capitalist system, there one will also necessarily find democracy. Rather, the reverse is true for Friedman: wherever there is democracy, one will also find capitalism. Capitalism is, for Friedman as for Wood, a necessary, but not by itself wholly sufficient, condition for democracy. Singapore, for instance, is a contemporary example of a highly capitalist, yet non-democratic, society.

Empirical evidence on the modernization thesis

But this is theory. What does the empirical record show on the connection between capitalism and democracy? Fortunately, there exists a large empirical literature exploring the so-called modernization thesis, i.e. the idea that economic development is in some important sense tied to democracy. The current conclusion is that the link mostly holds.[87] As the author of a large 2020 review article concludes:

> Over the last 200 years, as authoritarian states have grown richer they have transitioned to democracy more often. As democracies have grown richer they have reverted to authoritarianism less often. … For instance, the estimated probability that an authoritarian state will transition to a system with at least minimally competitive elections during the next two decades is 0.69 higher if the country's per capita income is $10,000 per year than if it is $1,000 per year. The estimated probability that the richer country will adopt competitive elections with universal male suffrage is 0.55 higher, and that it will transition to liberal democracy 0.23 higher. … In most years since 1850, income has correlated cross-nationally with democracy … From 1850 to 1972, correlations varied between a low of r = 0.39 in 1968 and a high of r = 0.74 in 1919. … From 1973, the cross-national correlation became much more variable, disappearing completely in some years. The main reason was the emergence of rich, authoritarian oil exporters. Excluding countries that annually produced more than $2,000 worth of oil or gas per capita, the correlations … remain high, ranging from r = 0.40 in 2014 to r = 0.68 in 1977.

A different team of researchers concurs.[88] They recently performed a large sensitivity analysis for the various determinants of democracy that are proposed in the literature, testing how robust they are to different measures and controls. Two of their main findings are the following. First, the link between economic development and democratization between 1960 and 1990 is positive and statistically significant. 'The coefficient' is 'also quite large; one standard deviation increase in GDP per capita, on average, increases the odds of democratization (in the Cold War period) by 1.39.'[89] This link, however, disappears after the Cold War. The other finding is that, once one controls for wealth accruing from oil and other natural resources, the link between economic development and democratization re-appears even in the post-Cold War period. 'The results indicate a clear relationship between GDP per capita and democratization, and the odds of democratization increases by 1.25 when GDP per capita increases by one standard deviation.'[90]

So, the evidence (still) suggests that, in accordance with modernization theory, the adoption and deepening of capitalist economic institutions in a country – which leads to constantly increasing, self-sustaining economic growth (typically measured in GDP per capita) – increases the structural possibility and probability of transition from a dictatorial to a democratic political regime.[91] The influence of economic growth on politics is not immediate and does not hold in all countries (especially not oil producers), as one would expect under the theory. But when a country has for some time – a few decades – been developing in a profound and sustained fashion, the odds of its democratic transition go up significantly.[92]

What is the underlying social logic at work here? Why does a country's growth of income increase its chances of democratization? And why is it not the case that *all* increases in GDP (in *all* periods) correlate with democracy?

There are many particular causal channels through which capitalism (or development, or growth) increases chances of democratization. Some – the separation of economics from politics – have already been mentioned above. Others involve the fact that, typically, capitalist development brings with it industrialization and urbanization, two processes which, in turn, inaugurate the appearance of a class of industrial (and later post-industrial) capitalists who replace the old landed elites. Industrialization and urbanization also breed an (increasingly large) middle class and a giant class of industrial workers (once peasants) with the capacity to organize economy-wide strikes. It is not the purpose of this section to detail how these social mechanisms work although I have written on this at length elsewhere.[93] The general idea is that long-run economic development makes ordinary collective action against the elite more likely and more successful, both because ordinary people are more motivated and able to demand political change in such circumstances and because elites are less fearful of giving away (some of) their political power in conditions of a sophisticated economy, and so are quicker to assent to popular pressure should it arise. If this is true, it would also make sense of the disappearing correlation between income and democracy when countries that got rich simply by siphoning wealth off of oil and other natural resources – instead of modernizing their economic structures – are introduced (or not controlled for) in the analysis.

Now, some research has challenged the modernization correlation. Two studies have been especially noteworthy.[94] Their findings, however, have not withstood the test of time; they have been overturned by several more recent studies.[95] The fact is that, once one properly controls for the impact of oil-wealth and country-fixed effects, and takes care of the time lag issue, economic development and democracy seem to quite robustly stand together. The correlation is so robust that we are able to say that economic development is causally related to democracy (not vice versa), especially over longer periods of time.[96]

Democracies can, of course, sometimes emerge even at lower (i.e. middling) levels of economic development.[97] We have been witnessing quite a few such cases in recent decades, as the post-1980s international environment has been so conducive for dictators to give in to outside pressure (or inducements) and allow for democracy. Some countries have become democracies even though, structurally and statistically, they 'should not' have yet been ready for democracy (according to the modernization thesis). This is true and seemingly anomalous, although less so when one keeps in mind that modernization is only probabilistically, not deterministically, tied to democratization.

However, three fundamental qualifications should be noted with respect to this. First, lower-development democracies are usually only semi-democratic, 'electoral democracies.' They are not typically the robust liberal democratic states one has in mind when thinking of the meaning of 'democracy.' Second, whatever their precise democratic quality, lower-development democracies are fragile, unstable, and typically only short-lived. They often revert back to dictatorship, while this almost never happens to the comparatively richer democracies, and has never happened to the richest, most developed ones.[98] Third, even when accounting for all the lower-development democratic exceptions seen in recent decades, it still turns out – even today – that odds of a democratic transition are higher the more GDP per capita a country has.[99]

So, as postulated by both Friedman and Wood, capitalism – or, more proximally, sustained economic growth unleashed by capitalism – does aid democracy. And if neoliberalism is seen as that set of economic reforms that infuses a higher degree of capitalism (and, thus, economic growth) in a country, one can come to the conclusion that neoliberal reforms probably indirectly contribute to democracy (not undermine it, as folk wisdom would have it). Admittedly, we have seen in a previous section that neoliberalism has not everywhere contributed to economic development (and, thus, indirectly to increasing chances of a democratic transition). Nevertheless, the theoretical considerations and empirical evidence presented in this section should make critics wary of breezily, and without question, maintaining that neoliberalism (or capitalism itself) strongly undermine democracy in the typical case. This is definitely not the case.

Conclusion

It has long ago become very fashionable in certain intellectual circles to bemoan and decry neoliberalism, the Washington consensus, or even globalization as a whole. Merely mentioning the word 'neoliberalism' in a deprecating manner is typically an instant crowd-pleaser, especially – this has to be said – if the crowd is made up of humanities professors and students.

This chapter has shown that, if we are to use the word, neoliberalism has to be defined more precisely. Once it is so defined, one can examine whether the world has actually been turning more and more towards neoliberalism. We have seen that, according to some definitions, this has, indeed, been the case. For instance, the overall level of economic freedom in the world has increased significantly since the 1980s. According to other definitions, however, the world has resisted the neoliberal pull. Since the 1980s, government spending remains very high in the developed world and even in many parts of Latin America, the alleged regional stronghold of neoliberal experimentation. Welfare states have also not been degraded by neoliberalism over the past half-century.

But the most important observation is that neoliberalism (understood as a broad array of institutional structures measured with the index of economic freedom) has mostly been a *success*. That is, the world has become more economically free over the past 40 years, and if one cares about poverty alleviation, increasing material standards of living, and heightened subjective life satisfaction, the neoliberal transformation of the world – and the economic development it unleashed – has to be judged as a good thing overall. It obviously has its downsides, and there are several good lessons to take from the East Asian experimentation with industrial policy, which at first *forestalls* free trade and increases government involvement in the economy, and only later allows for a more neoliberal type of development. However, industrial policy as it has typically been tried is not a successful developmental strategy, while neoliberalism – warts and all – has worked surprisingly well given how much intellectual abuse has been thrown its way over the years.

Notes

1 Autor et al. (2016).
2 Ibid.
3 Autor et al. (2013); Hicks et al. (2015); Bloom et al. (2019).
4 Stiglitz (2018, 21).
5 The Economist (2018).
6 Ibid.
7 Ibid.
8 Aleem (2017).
9 Ibid.
10 Boas and Gans-Morse (2009, 145).
11 Venugopal (2015, 165).
12 Boas and Gans-Morse (2009).
13 Similarly, the different uses of 'neoliberalism' in the particular articles studied by Boas and Gans-Morse can be classified as 'economic reform policies' (the most common use), a 'development model', an 'ideology', and an 'academic paradigm'. See Boas and Gans-Morse (2009, 143–145).
14 Williamson (2005).
15 Vallier (2021).
16 Ibid.
17 Gwartney et al. (2021b).
18 For more on what social democratic capitalism is, and how well it performs both economically and socially, see Kenworthy (2019).
19 Gwartney et al. (2021b, 16).
20 Leeson (2010).
21 Hall and Lawson (2013).
22 Ibid., 8.
23 Faria et al. (2016); Bennett et al. (2017). For an extensive review of the evidence see de Haan et al. (2006).
24 See the almost perfect correlation between real wage growth (even for unskilled workers) and growth of GDP per capita between 1870 and 2000 in de Zwart et al. (2014, 84).

25 Stevenson and Wolfers (2008); Diener et al. (2010).
26 Gropper et al. (2011); Belasen and Hafer (2013); Nikolaev (2014); Spruk and Kešelje-vić (2016). See also Ovaska and Takashima (2010), although they do not control for GDP.
27 Graafland and Compen (2014).
28 Ibid., 806. There is another sense in which economic freedom has a mixed effect on life satisfaction. Although it is generally associated with an overall increase in life sat-isfaction, higher economic freedom can cause higher income inequality and, to that extent, reduce life satisfaction somewhat. The net result can still be positive in the end, although this singular negative dimension also has to be noted. See Graafland and Lous (2018).
29 See Apergis et al. (2013); Pérez-Moreno and Angulo-Guerrero (2016); Bennett and Nikolaev (2017); de Soysa and Vadlamannati (2021).
30 Graafland and Lous (2018).
31 Kenworthy (2019, 67–68).
32 Ibid., 67.
33 Ibid.
34 Ibid.
35 Ibid.
36 Ibid., 68.
37 OECD (2021a,) Figure 4.2.
38 Ortiz-Ospina and Roser (2016).
39 Kenworthy (2019, 87).
40 Ibid., 186.
41 OECD (2022b).
42 Ibid.
43 Kenworthy (2019, 85).
44 OECD (2022a).
45 Ibid.
46 Piketty et al. (2014, 253).
47 Ibid.
48 Williamson (2005, 195).
49 Klein (2007, 163).
50 Harvey (2005, 13).
51 Dollar (1992, 540).
52 Ibid.
53 Sachs and Warner (1995, 36).
54 For instance, Edwards (1998); Frankel and Romer (1999).
55 Rodríguez and Rodrik (2011).
56 Ibid., 268.
57 Easterly (2001).
58 Ibid., 154.
59 Easterly (2019).
60 Ibid.
61 Easterly (2019).
62 Irwin (2019).
63 Ibid.
64 Grier and Grier (2021).
65 Ibid.
66 For more empirical evidence on the connection between the growth of the economy and income growth among both poor and rich citizens see Kraay (2006); Dollar et al. (2016).
67 Noland and Pack (2003, 10).
68 Panagariya (2019, 1–2).

69 Cherif and Hasanov, who view a certain type of IP very positively, report that 'Perhaps the consensus view among many economists is that industrial policy usually fails'. Cherif and Hasanov (2019, 9).
70 Harrison and Rodríguez-Clare (2010, 4110–4112). For scepticism over the notion that these older cross-country and industry-level regression studies can be used to evaluate the success of IP, see Lane (2020).
71 Harrison and Rodríguez-Clare (2010, 4110–4112).
72 Cherif and Hasanov (2019).
73 Harrison and Rodríguez-Clare (2010, 4042).
74 Ibid.
75 Cherif and Hasanov (2019).
76 Noland and Pack (2003, 93).
77 Panagariya (2019, 324–325).
78 Harrison and Rodríguez-Clare (2010, 4042).
79 Panagariya (2019, 325).
80 Norberg (2008, 3–5). See also Edwards and Montes (2020).
81 Boudreaux and Holcombe (2017).
82 Wood (1995, 19, 21).
83 Friedman (2002, 7–8).
84 Ibid., 9.
85 Wood (1995, 19, 40).
86 Friedman (2002, 9).
87 Treisman (2020).
88 Rød et al. (2020).
89 Ibid., 97.
90 Ibid., 99.
91 Rutar (2021), chapter 2.
92 Clark et al. (2013), Figure 6.7; Paldam and Gundlach (2012); Treisman (2020).
93 Rutar (2021, 2). See also Boix (2011); Treisman (2020, 251–254).
94 Acemoglu et al. (2008; 2009). See also Przeworski et al. (2000).
95 For example, Benhabib et al. (2013); Faria et al. (2014); Moral-Benito and Bartolucci (2012).
96 On short- and long-run causality see especially Paldam and Gundlach (2012); Treisman (2020).
97 See Boix (2011) and Figure 1 in Treisman (2020).
98 Przeworski and Limongi (1997); Brownlee (2017).
99 See already the long Treisman (2020) quote above; see also Paldam and Gundlach (2012).

References

Acemoglu, Daron, Johnson, Simon, Robinson, James A., and Pierre Yared. 2008. 'Income and Democracy,' *American Economic Review* 98, no. 3, 808–842.
Acemoglu, Daron, Johnson, Simon, Robinson, James A., and Pierre Yared. 2009. 'Reevaluating the Modernization Hypothesis,' *Journal of Monetary Economics* 56, 1043–1058.
Aleem, Zeeshan. 2017. '"Another Kick in the Teeth": A Top Economist on How Trade with China Helped Elect Trade,' *Vox*, March 29th 2017. Accessible via: https://www.vox.com/new-money/2017/3/29/15035498/autor-trump-china-trade-election/.
Apergis, Nicholas, Dincer, Oguzhan, and James E. Payne. 2013. 'Economic Freedom and Income Inequality Revisited: Evidence from a Panel Error Correction Model,' *Contemporary Economic Policy* 32, no. 1, 67–75.

Autor, David H., Dorn, David, and Gordon H. Hanson. 2013. 'The China Syndrome: Local Labor Market Effects of Import Competition in the United States,' *American Economic Review* 103, no. 6, 2121–2168.

Autor, David H., Dorn, David, and Gordon H. Hanson. 2016. 'The China Shock: Learning form Labor-Market Adjustment to Large Changes in Trade,' *Annual Review of Economics* 8, 205–240.

Belasen, Ariel R., and R. W. Hafer. 2013. 'Do Changes in Economic Freedom Affect Well-Being?' *The Journal of Regional Analysis & Policy* 43, no. 1, 56–64.

Benhabib, Jess, Corvalan, Alejandro, and Mark M. Spiegel. 2013. 'Income and Democracy: Evidence from Nonlinear Estimations,' *Economics Letters* 118, 489–492.

Bennett, Daniel L., and Boris Nikolaev. 2016. 'On the Ambiguous Economic Freedom-Inequality Relationship,' *Empirical Economics* 53, 717–754.

Bennett, Daniel L., Faria, Hugo J., Gwartney, James D., and Daniel R. Morales. 2017. 'Economic Institutions and Comparative Economic Development: A Post-Colonial Perspective,' *World Development* 96, 503–519.

Bloom, Nicholas, Handley, Kyle, Kurman, Andre, and Phillip Luck. 2019. 'The Impact of Chinese Trade on U.S. Employment: The Good, The Bad, and the Debatable,' *Working Paper*. Accessible via: https://nbloom.people.stanford.edu/sites/g/files/sbiybj4746/f/bhkl_posted_draft.pdf/.

Boas, Taylor C., and Jordan Gans-Morse. 2009. 'Neoliberalism: From New Liberal Philosophy to Anti-Liberal Slogan,' *Studies in Comparative International Development* 44, 137–161.

Boix, Carles. 2011. 'Democracy, Development, and the International System,' *American Political Science Review* 105, no. 4, 809–828.

Boudreaux, Christopher J., and Randall G. Holcombe. 2017. 'Economic Institutions and the Durability of Democracy,' *Atlantic Economic Journal* 45, 17–28.

Brownlee, Jason. 2017. 'The Limited Reach of Authoritarian Powers,' *Democratization* 24, no. 7, 1326–1344.

Cherif, Reda, and Fuad Hasanov. 2019. 'The Return of Policy That Shall Not Be Named: Principles of Industrial Policy,' *IMF Working Paper No. 19/74*. Accessible via: https://www.imf.org/en/Publications/WP/Issues/2019/03/26/The-Return-of-the-Policy-That-Shall-Not-Be-Named-Principles-of-Industrial-Policy-46710/.

Clark, William Robers, Golder, Matt, and Sona Nadenichek Golder. 2013. *Principles of Comparative Politics*. Los Angeles: Sage.

de Haan, Jakob, Lundström, Susanna, and Jan-Egbert Sturm. 2006. 'Market-Oriented Institutions and Policies and Economic Growth: A Critical Survey,' *Journal of Economic Surveys* 20, no. 2, 157–191.

de Soysa, Indra, and Krishna Chaitanya Vadlamannati. 2021. 'Free Market Capitalism and Societal Inequities: Assessing the Effects of Economic Freedom on Income Inequality and the Equity of Access to Opportunity, 1990–2017,' *International Political Science Review* (OnlineFirst).

de Zwart, Pim, van Leeuwen, Bas, and Jieli van Leeuwen-Li. 2014. 'Real Wages Since 1820,' in Jan Luiten van Zanden et al. (eds.), *How Was Life? Global Well-Being Since 1820*, 74–86. Paris: OECD Publishing.

Diener, Ed, Ng, Weiting, Harter, James, and Raksha Arora. 2010. 'Wealth and Happiness Across the World: Material Prosperity Predicts Life Evaluation, Whereas Psychosocial Prosperity Predicts Positive Feeling,' *Journal of Personality and Social Psychology* 99, no. 1, 52–61.

Dollar, David. 1992. 'Outward-oriented Developing Economics Really Do Grow More Rapidly: Evidence from 95 LDCs, 1976–1985,' *Economic Development and Cultural Change* 40, no. 3, 523–544.

Dollar, David, Kleineberg, Tatjana, and Aart Kraay. 2016. 'Growth Still is Good for the Poor,' *European Economic Review* 81, 68–85.

Easterly, William. 2001. 'The Lost Decades: Developing Countries' Stagnation in Spite of Policy Reform 1980–1998,' *Journal of Economic Growth* 6, no. 2, 135–157.

Easterly, William. 2019. 'In Search of Reforms for Growth: New Stylized Facts on Policy and Growth Outcomes,' *NBER Working Paper 26318*. Accessible via: https://www.nber.org/papers/w26318/.

Edwards, Sebastian. 1998. 'Openness, Productivity and Growth: What do We Really Know?' *The Economic Journal* 108, no. 447, 383–398.

Edwards, Sebastian, and Leonidas Montes. 2020. 'Milton Friedman in Chile: Shock Therapy, Economic Freedom, and Exchange Rates,' *Journal of the History of Economic Thought* 42, no. 1, 105–132.

Faria, Hugo, Montesinos, Hugo M., and Daniel Morales. 2014. 'Should the Modernization Hypothesis Survive Acemoglu, Johnson, Robinson, and Yared? Some More Evidence,' *Econ Journal Watch* 11, no. 1, 17–36.

Faria, Hugo J., Montesinos-Yufa, Hugo M., Morales, Daniel R., and Carlos E. Navarro. 2016. 'Unbundling the Roles of Human Capital and Institutions in Economic Development,' *European Journal of Political Economy* 45, 108–128.

Frankel, Jeffrey A., and David H. Romer. 1999. 'Does Trade Cause Growth?' *American Economic Review* 89, no. 3, 379–399.

Fraser Institute. 2022. 'Economic Freedom of the World Dataset.' Accessible via: https://www.fraserinstitute.org/economic-freedom/dataset/.

Freedom House. 2022. 'All Data, FIW 2013–2022.' Accessible via: https://freedomhouse.org/report/freedom-world/.

Friedman, Milton. 2002. *Capitalism and Freedom: 40th Anniversary Edition*. Chicago: The University of Chicago Press.

Graafland, Johan J., and Bart Compen. 2014. 'Economic Freedom and Life Satisfaction: Mediation by Income per Capita and Generalized Trust,' *Journal of Happiness Studies* 16, no. 3, 789–810.

Grier, Kevin B., and Robin M. Grier. 2021. 'The Washington Consensus Works: Causal Effects of Reform, 1970–2015,' *Journal of Comparative Economics* 49, no. 1, 59–72.

Gropper, Daniel M., Lawson, Robert A., and Jere T. Thorne Jr. 2011. 'Economic Freedom and Happiness,' *Cato Journal* 31, no. 2, 237–255.

Gwartney, James, Lawson, Robert, Hall, Joshua, and Ryan Murphy. 2021a. Economic Freedom Dataset, published in *Economic Freedom of the World: 2021 Annual Report*. Fraser Institute. Accessible via: https://www.fraserinstitute.org/economic-freedom/dataset/.

Gwartney, James, Lawson, Robert, Hall, Joshua, and Ryan Murphy. 2021b. *Economic Freedom of the World: 2021 Annual Report*. Fraser Institute.

Hall, Joshua C., and Robert A. Lawson. 2013. 'Economic Freedom of the World: An Accounting of the Literature,' *Contemporary Economic Policy* 32, no. 1, 1–19.

Harrison, Ann, and Andrés Rodríguez-Clare. 2010. 'Trade, Foreign Investment, and Industrial Policy for Developing Countries,' in Dani Rodrik and Mark Rosenzweig (eds.), *Handbook of Development Economics, Volume 5*, 4039–4214. Amsterdam: Elsevier.

Harvey, David. 2005. *A Brief History of Neoliberalism*. Oxford: Oxford University Press.

Hicks, Michael J., and Srikant Devaraj. 2015. 'The Myth and the Reality of Manufacturing in America,' *Center of Business and Economic Research, Ball State University*. Accessible via: https://conexus.cberdata.org/files/MfgReality.pdf/.

Irwin, Douglas A. 2019. 'Does Trade Reform Promote Economic Growth? A Review of Recent Evidence,' *NBER Working Paper 25927*. Accessible via: https://www.nber.org/papers/w25927/.

Kenworthy, Lane. 2019. *Social Democratic Capitalism*. Oxford: Oxford University Press.

Klein, Naomi. 2007. *The Shock Doctrine: The Rise of Disaster Capitalism*. New York: Metropolitan Books.

Kraay, Aart. 2006. 'When is Growth Pro-Poor? Evidence from a Panel of Countries,' *Journal of Development Economics* 80, 198–227.

Lane, Nathaniel. 2020. 'The New Empirics of Industrial Policy,' *Journal of Industry, Competition and Trade* 20, 209–234.

Leeson, Peter T. 2010. 'Two Cheers for Capitalism?' *Society* 47, no. 3, 227–233.

Moral-Benito, Enrique, and Cristian Bartolucci. 2012. 'Income and Democracy: Revisiting the Evidence,' *Economics Letters* 117, 844–847.

Nikolaev, Boris. 2014. 'Economic Freedom and Quality of Life: Evidence from the OECD's Your Better Life Index,' *The Journal of Private Enterprise* 29, no. 3, 61–96.

Noland, Marcus, and Howard Pack. 2003. *Industrial Policy in an Era of Globalization: Lessons from Asia*. Washington DC: Institute for International Economics.

Norberg, Johan. 2008. 'The Klein Doctrine: The Rise of Disaster Polemics,' *Cato Briefing Paper No. 102*. Accessible via: https://www.cato.org/briefing-paper/klein-doctrine-rise-disaster-polemics/.

OECD. 2022a. Tax Revenue (indicator). Accessible via: https://data.oecd.org/tax/tax-revenue.htm/.

OECD. 2022b. Trade Union Dataset. Accessible via: https://stats.oecd.org/Index.aspx?DataSetCode=TUD/.

Ortiz-Ospina, Esteban, and Max Roser. 2016. 'Government Spending,' *Our World in Data*. Accessible via: https://ourworldindata.org/government-spending/.

Ovaska, Tomi, and Ryo Takashima. 2010. 'Does a Rising Tide Lift All the Boats? Explaining National Inequality of Happiness,' *Journal of Economic Issues* 44, no. 1, 205–224.

Paldam, Martin, and Erich Gundlach. 2012. 'The Democratic Transition: Short-run and Long-run Causality between Income and the Gastil Index,' *European Journal of Development Research* 24, 144–168

Panagariya, Arvind. 2019. *Free Trade and Prosperity: How Openness Helps Developing Countries Grow Richer*. Oxford: Oxford University Press.

Pérez-Moreno, Salvador, and María J. Angulo-Guerrero. 2016. 'Does Economic Freedom Increase Income Inequality? Evidence from the EU countries,' *Journal of Economic Policy Reform* 19, no. 4, 327–347.

Piketty, Thomas, Saez, Emmanuel, and Stefanie Stantcheva. 2014. 'Optimal Taxation of Top LAbor Incomes: A Tale of Three Elasticities,' *American Economic Journal: Economic Policy* 6, no. 1, 230–271.

Przeworski, Adam, Alvarez, Michael R., Alvarez, Michael E., Cheibub, Jose Antonio, and Fernando Limongi. 2000. *Democracy and Development: Political Institutions and Well-Being in the World, 1950–1990*. Cambridge: Cambridge University Press.

Przeworski, Adam, and Fernando Limongi. 1997. 'Modernization: Theories and Facts,' *World Politics* 49, no. 2, 155–183.

Rød, Espen Geelmuyden, Knutsen, Carl Henrik, and Håvard Hegre. 2020. 'The Determinants of Democracy: A Sensitivity Analysis,' *Public Choice* 185, 87–111.

Rodríguez, Francisco, and Dani Rodrik. 2001. 'Trade Policy and Economic Growth: A Skeptic's Guide to the Cross-National Evidence,' *NBER Macroeconomics Annual* 15, 261–325.

Roser, Max. 2021. 'What Is Economic Growth? And Why Is It So Important?' *Our World in Data*. Accessible via: https://ourworldindata.org/what-is-economic-growth/.

Rutar, Tibor. 2021. *Rational Choice and Democratic Government: A Sociological Approach.* London: Routledge.

Sachs, Jeffrey D., and Andrew Warner. 1995. 'Economic Reform and the Process of Global Integration,' *Brookings Papers on Economic Activity* 1, 1–118.

Spruk, Rok, and Aleksandar Kešeljević. 2016. 'Institutional Origins of Subjective Well-Being: Estimating the Effects of Economic Freedom on National Happiness,' *Journal of Happiness Studies* 17, 659–712.

Stevenson, Betsey, and Justin Wolfers. 2008. 'Economic Growth and Subjective Well-Being: Reassessing the Easterlin Paradox,' *Brookings Papers on Economic Activity* 2008, 1–87.

Stiglitz, Joseph E. 2018. *Globalization and Its Discontents Revisited. Anti-Globalization in the Era of Trump.* New York: W. W. Norton & Company.

The Economist. 2018. 'Manufacturing Jobs are Defying Expectations,' *The Economist,* October 18th 2018. Accessible via: https://www.economist.com/united-states/2018/10/20/manufacturing-jobs-are-defying-expectations/.

Treisman, Daniel. 2020. 'Economic Development and Democracy: Predispositions and Triggers,' *Annual Review of Political Science* 23, 241–257.

Vallier, Kevin. 2021. https://plato.stanford.edu/entries/neoliberalism/notes.html#note-11.

Venugopal, Rajesh. 2015. 'Neoliberalism as a Concept,' *Economy and Society* 44, no. 2, 165–187.

Williamson, John. 2005. 'The Strange History of the Washington Consensus,' *Journal of Post Keynesian Economics* 27, no. 2, 195–206.

Wood, Ellen Meiksins. 1995. *Democracy Against Capitalism: Renewing Historical Materialism.* Cambridge: Cambridge University Press.

5

BUT CAPITALISM CORRUPTS OUR MORALS, DOES IT NOT?

Introduction: markets as gentle, markets as monstrous

Anti-capitalist critics no longer question the immense productive capacity and material superiority of capitalist market societies. If capitalism is anything, they agree, it is a wealth-generating machine. Not only that, even the more specific allegations about capitalism creating poverty and material hardship among working-class people (as distinct from the middle and upper classes, for which capitalism was never claimed to be calamitous) are nowadays less commonly upheld by the critics.

However, there exists a daring Enlightenment-era philosophical endorsement of the market society against which capitalism's critics would most definitely still scoff and towards which even most proponents of capitalism might be somewhat sceptical at first. The Enlightenment-era claim I have in mind is that competitive markets are not only economically efficient but that they also inadvertently cultivate pro-social, and even morally virtuous, behaviour such as (peaceful) cooperation, trust and trustworthiness, sharing and fairness, tolerance, and cosmopolitanism.

At first glance, this probably seem preposterous. How could such lowly and seemingly brutish processes as the commercialization of social life, the spread of money, an ever-present competitive struggle of seller against seller, and the expansion of private property result in *more* pro-sociality, more cooperation, more trust? Alas, this was precisely the view of ostensibly sober, intelligent, reasonable Enlightenment thinkers, such as Montesquieu, who claimed that '[c]ommerce ... polishes and softens barbaric ways as we can see every day.'[1] Condorcet agreed with him, saying that '[m]anners have become more gentle ... through the influence of the spirit of commerce and industry.'[2] So, too, did Thomas Paine.[3] They were all proponents of the so-called *doux commerce* – or 'gentle commerce' – thesis.

DOI: 10.4324/9781003305811-5

Those critical of capitalism would reject such a thesis most fervently. Capitalism might be productive, they would aver, but it certainly does not soothe the soul and make us virtuous. In fact, critics would point out the inherent trade-off one is arguably forced to make when choosing capitalism, namely trading material well-being for psychological well-being. Here are a few plausible-sounding arguments one can make to that effect.

First, markets cultivate an instrumental attitude towards others. Sellers on the market want to interact with buyers only insofar as the latter generate revenue for the former. Buyers come into contact with sellers only insofar as the latter give them a good deal. The real goal is profit, human interaction (and the satisfaction of a buyer's wants) is just a means to achieve that lowly economic goal. The greater the extent of markets in a society, the more human interaction becomes instrumentalized, hollowed-out.

Second, competition is the core of capitalist markets, and competition is simply the opposite of cooperation. Competition is a zero-sum struggle of many against many so that in the end only one prevails while others lose. Cooperation, instead, is a positive-sum act which does not entail losers (or struggle). The more capitalism, the more competition, and the less cooperation.

Third, on the market, both sellers and buyers are primarily looking out for their own selfish gain. Sellers want to profit as much as possible, and buyers want to get the best deal as cheaply as possible. Why would they trust one another? It seems that markets will breed mistrust and mutual suspicion, based as they are on selfish gain (and competition), not family ties, friendship, or pure altruism. Moreover, because markets fan the flames of our individual selfishness, an encroaching market society will make it less and less possible for people to secure collective goals and the general social interest. The latter can only be established on the basis of selflessness, not selfishness. Social cooperation will start breaking down, or it will at least be heavily corroded.

There are many other similar arguments one could make against the thesis that markets make us more virtuous, or at least not less virtuous. The general idea is that there is something selfish, impersonal, and zero-sum about markets which, if true, does not bode well for human pro-sociality in a market society. As Marx and Engels wrote in the *Communist Manifesto*, the bourgeoisie established its capitalist system and by doing so,

> [it] has left remaining no other nexus between man and man than naked self-interest, than callous 'cash payment'. It has drowned the most heavenly ecstasies of religious fervour, of chivalrous enthusiasm, of philistine sentimentalism, in the icy water of egotistical calculation. It has resolved personal worth into exchange value ....[4]

However, if one digs a bit deeper, a different set of intuitions about the market starts bubbling up – intuitions that are the basis for the Enlightenment-era *doux commerce* thesis. For instance, markets simply cannot exist if there is not also already present a certain (relatively high) amount of trust between prospective buyers and sellers who then decide (partially based on sheer trust) to trade with each other. How can a seller be sure that the buyer has not bought the seller's goods with unusable, forged money? How can a buyer be sure that the seller will hand over the bought goods after money is exchanged? They cannot be sure, and so they have to trust. As a consequence, the presence of markets implies the presence, not absence, of trust.

Moreover, if people are constantly meeting new strangers with whom they exchange words, goods, and money on the market, one would think that a certain more trusting, tolerant, and even cosmopolitan outlook might start forming among them. A person who has regular (and personally beneficial) contact with strangers – a diverse set of people who look, talk, and act differently than oneself – could start accumulating positive experiences which teach him or her that 'different' and 'strange' is not necessarily dangerous and bad but can be beneficial and good. A small, isolated, self-subsistent group of people whose members only interact with each other is much less likely to be trusting (of strangers), tolerant, or cosmopolitan than a large, interdependent, market-going group of people whose members are constant encountering strangers (with whom they have beneficial, if fleeting, relationships).

Lastly, competition can indeed be a zero-sum affair, as the typical intuitive sports examples quite vividly illustrate. In sports, one cannot win in any other way but by beating someone else who is, therefore, a loser. Alas, the sports analogy, however vivid, is, in fact, misleading when we are talking about most markets. That is because *market* competition – in contrast to *sports* competition – can be, and usually is, positive-sum. Free market exchange happens only if two (or more) people think they personally stand to benefit from it. Yes, the buyer wants to profit, i.e. win; but so does the customer. If both feel the offer is beneficial for them, they will make the trade. The result is that both are better-off, both have won.

Of course, economic actors can be manipulated into making a trade which is really only beneficial for one party. But, first, there are mechanisms (including government mechanisms) that try to prevent trade manipulation in developed capitalist societies. Moreover, second, it is precisely the *competitive* aspect of a capitalist market that itself tends to reduces the likelihood of being taken advantage of, at least in certain circumstances. For instance, if seller A is successfully manipulating his customers and profiting off of them, his competitors, i.e. seller B, C, or D, can have a strong interest to demonstrate this fact to the A's customers and then make them a better, more genuine offer which will actually benefit them (and these sellers themselves, of course, as A's customers will switch from A to B, C, or D).

So, seeing as how theoretical considerations are plausibly nudging us in one or the other direction with respect to capitalism and pro-social behaviour, how are we to solve this conundrum? Is capitalism making people less trusting, less cooperative, more selfish, more intolerant, more aggressive, as the standard anti-capitalist critique would have it? Or is capitalism actually pacifying us, bringing out and reinforcing our nicer, kinder, gentler behavioural dispositions towards others, as the Enlightenment-era *doux commerce* thesis suggests? Or, further still, is capitalism's record somewhere in-between?

As always, we should turn to the empirical literature to settle the dispute. What does the evidence show? Some scholars, such as Walker Wright, are convinced that the evidence is wholly clear and unambiguous. Capitalism is causally related – in a positive way – to virtually any measure of moral virtue. In a broad review article from 2018, Wright surveyed more than 60 pieces of contemporary empirical literature on the connection between capitalism and pro-social behaviour (and moral behaviour and attitudes in general).[5] His conclusion was strikingly univocal: 'commerce shapes these moral norms for the better. As the outreach of markets continues to cross borders, it is reasonable to assume that the world will continue to become a more liberal, fair, cooperative, trustworthy, tolerant, and peaceful place.'[6] And indeed, as I demonstrate below, the standard anti-capitalist critique – which Wright unequivocally rejects – truly does not withstand a thorough empirical test. Empirical research really does show that the *doux commerce* thesis is closer to the truth than the anti-capitalist critique.

Nevertheless, as I also demonstrate below, Wright's seamless, pro-capitalist assessment of the literature is not completely fair, even though it points in the right direction. For instance, one is struck by the complete absence of negative, or even just mixed, findings in Wright's otherwise broad review. It seems to me quite unlikely that he did not include negative findings in his paper solely because there were no negative (or mixed) findings to pull from the research. I do not want to speculate too much, but it seems to me instead that he might have been (wittingly or not) selective in the research he decided to include in his review, which is a bad scientific practice.

In this chapter, as before, I have tried hard to be more even-handed than Wright. And so even though in the end my general conclusions turn out to be quite in line with his pro-capitalist message, this was not the intention I set myself up with at the beginning, instead letting the evidence guide me to an impartial conclusion as much as possible. Therefore, the reader of this chapter will also encounter several strong pieces of evidence with negative (or at least mixed) findings which should reduce our confidence in how tightly and straightforwardly capitalism ties in to pro-social behaviour. The connection is there, but it is not as unambiguous as Wright claims.

Generalized trust

Does wealth make us more or less trusting?

Even a mere superficial glance at the data quite conclusively suggests that capitalism, and the economic development it brings, cannot be destructive of generalized trust overall. This so because the more developed, richer, capitalistic societies tend to also have significantly higher levels of trust than less developed, poorer, less capitalistic societies. In short, there is a quite strong correlation between GDP per capita and the share of population that trusts strangers.[7] Slightly more than 20% of all the variance in trust across nations is explained precisely by how wealthy or poor they are.[8]

However, as already discussed previously, this does not mean that wealth or, by proxy, capitalism *cause* trust. It could be that trust causes economic development, and there is also a possibility of both trust and economic development being mutually caused by a third, unknown factor.[9] All of these causal possibilities are consistent with the observed correlation, so none can be ruled out (or in). Nevertheless, the strong correlation clearly implies that, whatever the precise causal interactions, wealth and capitalism are evidently not destructive of trust to the extent that the rich and highly capitalist societies would be faring worse off than poorer and less capitalist societies (as is sometimes said by critics blissfully unaware of the data). Instead, the former societies are (significantly) better off than the latter as far as trust goes.

As before, we should and can go beyond simple correlational data if we want to know more. What do the studies that control for various confounding factors, such as Protestantism or education, that might cause higher trust apart from GDP (and thus, if they are common enough among wealthier societies, make us falsely think that it is wealth that causes trust) tell us about the association between wealth and trust? Does the connection survive statistical controls?

The current evidence is somewhat mixed. Multiple studies find that the correlation generally remains positive even after non-wealth controls are put in place.[10] As one paper summarizes the results, 'Simmel, rather than Tönnies, was correct to argue that modern money economics with greater individual freedom and personal independence have ways of maintaining social trust.'[11] Other studies, however, initially uncover a large and significant positive association, but when confounding variables are controlled for, GDP then turns out not to be statistically significant anymore. To take just two examples, one paper found increased levels of GDP per capita to increase generalized trust in a large and highly statistically significant way, but this finding later evaporates when a variable capturing the scientific contribution of a country is introduced.[12] The other paper similarly found that 'the relationship between GDP and generalized trust is statistically significant and positive,' but this turns out not to be robust to the introduction of fixed effects.[13]

So, what are we to make of this? I believe the mixed findings can be plausibly accounted for. The simple fact that economic development not only generates more *wealth* in a society but also tends, in many cases, to at least somewhat increase the country's *income inequality* could be an important reason for why increased wealth is not consistently associated with increased trust. This is so because, as I have discussed in Chapter 3, income inequality itself has been found to cause a reduction in trust. Therefore, if higher inequality (one consequence of economic development) reduces trust while more wealth (another consequence of economic development) increases it, the combined effect could very well be neutral.

A recent paper empirically tests this potentially dual trust-character of economic development. The findings are that,

> Economic development has a positive impact on trust, but this depends on the level of inequality. Income inequality mitigates the positive impact of GDP per capita on generalized trust. Our results show that for values of the Gini index larger than 40, a greater GDP per capita does not have a statistically significant impact on generalized trust.[14]

It is definitely not the case that – as the anti-capitalist critics otherwise falsely charge – capitalism has a net-negative impact on trust. At least going by the wealth of a country (which is to a significant degree a function of how capitalist the country is), capitalism does not erode trust. But does it perhaps increase it? To the extent that capitalism generates wealth without causing higher rates of inequality, it almost certainly does contribute to increased trust (through the prosperity channel). However, since in many (though, importantly, not all) countries economic development also goes hand in hand with an increase in inequality, the overall causal effect of capitalism's wealth generation on trust is likely to be more or less neutral, not largely positive.

Do capitalist institutions make us more or less trusting?

Up until now, I have only discussed how capitalism relates to trust *indirectly*, i.e. through increased prosperity (or increased inequality). But what about its potential *direct* influence? One can statistically control for wealth (and other relevant factors, as before) and look at how *capitalist economic institutions* themselves tie-in to trust, wholly separately from their indirect contribution to trust via economic growth. Perhaps it is not only the (increased) level of economic development – material prosperity – that is the crucial, or the only crucial, economic factor which makes people more willing to trust strangers. Rather, it could be their (increased) participation in market exchange, or their escape from the shackles of burdensome taxation or government regulation, that also matter. These eventualities have less to do with material prosperity than simply with the presence (and an increase in) capitalist institutions within a given society.

The overall findings from the past 15 years of research on this very possibility are broadly consistent: capitalist institutions (measured by the economic freedom index) are themselves directly related to, and seem to cause, higher levels of trust, independently of the economic development they also engender.[15] Going beyond this simple summary, one encounters several important nuances and complexities.

First, the largest and most robust effect on trust comes from the legal and property institutions of a society. Across studies and methods, trust is revealed to be consistently higher in countries with stronger protection of property rights, reliable rule of law, and an independent judiciary – even after controlling for a plethora of plausible confounding factors, including wealth, inequality, and religion. The effect seems to be causal and the arrow of causality goes from these institutions to trust. And seeing as how secure property rights are a central aspect of capitalism, it is not hard to conclude that capitalism deserves some of the credit for increasing trust. But given that the rule of law and an independent judiciary – not necessarily obvious capitalist phenomena – are also included in the set of institutions driving this same increase in trust, capitalism does not get *all* of the credit for the increase.

Second, other aspects of capitalist institutions (proxied by the economic freedom index) have a more modest effect, and some even have no effect at all. Regulation of business and credit, for instance, seems to matter quite a bit, but less so than legal and property institutions. That is, most studies find more government regulation to lead to somewhat lower trust, and less government regulation – a clearly capitalist phenomenon – to increase trust.[16] That said, one sociological paper with particularly stringent methods is sceptical of this finding:

> [W]e show that market deregulations are positively related to generalized trust. The finding supports the argument that economics, business, and credit markets regulated by government appointed bodies weakens community building, civil society, and generalized trust. … *[However,] the relationship between market deregulations and generalized trust found in the present study and prior research is likely a statistical artefact [because it] appears to be fuelled by Scandinavian cultural legacies, welfare state typologies, legal origins, and internal strife, and is also sensitive to the restructuring of data and resampling techniques.*[17]

Sound monetary policy – i.e. low inflation, which is arguably a capitalist phenomenon – is also important.[18] The institution of free international trade, on the other hand, has a more mixed record. Some studies find a large and statistically significant result.[19] Others point to no effect.[20] Lastly, the size of government does not seem to matter at all. That is to say, when countries start spending more through the government, when they have higher taxes, and when the government partly intervenes in the market (through allocation of resources or firm ownership) – at least up to a non-extreme point – generalized trust does not evince decline. In other words, when in this one aspect of how capitalist a country is (i.e. how big its government is) there is movement in the negative direction, this does not negatively affect trust.[21]

Third, at least some studies find that an additional increase in economic freedom has a positive effect on trust only in Western or economically developed countries, where economic freedom is already high compared to the world average.[22] Elsewhere, the effect is even somewhat negative at first, that is at very low levels of economic development and economic freedom. As one paper reports the finding, increases in legal property rights undermine generalized trust at low levels of property rights protection. This negative effect, however, attenuates as the robustness of legal property rights increases. ... But note how the increasing effect of legal property rights on generalized trust is relatively much greater than the decreasing effect. ... [T]he [negative] effect is relatively minor.[23]

In sum, capitalist institutions encourage trust although the strongest effect is by a set of institutions that is arguably the least distinctively capitalist – the legal system and property rights. Strong property rights are obviously a capitalist institution, but it is less clear if the same can be said for the rule of law and an independent judiciary.

Whatever one decides on this last matter, the evidence reviewed in this section clearly demonstrates the following. Richer, more economically developed, and more capitalist societies do not lack trust and, therefore, simply cannot be said to have an overwhelmingly negative effect on it. The anti-capitalist critique is wrong. How do we know this? Because, first, trust is on average both relatively and absolutely high (or higher) in these kinds of societies compared to the rest of the world. This much is obvious from even the simplest correlations. Furthermore, although it is not clear whether economic development is *causally responsible* for increased trust in wealthy societies, it is definitely clear that it does not have a net negative causal effect on it. Lastly, it is clear that at least certain – though not all – aspects of the institutional makeup of capitalist societies directly contribute to more trust.

More evidence on market competition and trust

That aspects of the capitalist economy impact generalized trust positively, not neutrally or negatively, is further buttressed by research demonstrating that as people are exposed to more market competition (a central feature of capitalism) they also become more trusting.

One wide-ranging 2018 study presents multiple types of evidence (cross-sectional, panel, and experimental), and all point in the same direction.[24] First, and most simplistically, there is cross-sectional data from the US that reveals higher shares of workers who report generalized trust tend to work in more competitive industries.[25] The authors of the study statistically controlled for various confounding variables to try to get at a causal interpretation of the data, and they find the positive relationship between competition and trust remains robust.

Second, because these data alone do not allow for a firm conclusion on whether competitiveness actually generates trust, the researchers turned to more suggestive evidence. They exploit the fact that, from the early 1980s, multiple US states deregulated their banking sectors, and did so at different times, which lead to an increase in the amount of market competition faced by the firms in the relevant states. Market competition increased because credit – which one can use to open a firm, enter the market, and thus contest existing firms – was much easier to obtain after banking deregulation. The authors found that, indeed, market competition (measured as the number of firm entry and closure per capita) showed no obvious trend in the ten years before banking deregulation started.[26] Furthermore, market competition suddenly started increasing after banks were deregulated (and credit was more available). The effect is positive for every year since deregulation except for the last one (year ten).

Now, the most relevant two findings are the following. The share of population that expressed generalized trust remained constant in the ten years before the state engaged in banking deregulation.[27] In subsequent years – after banks were deregulated – the share of trusting population started increasing significantly (with a lag of a few years, as one would expect). After nine years, the share of trusting individuals was around 15 percentage points higher than at the start of deregulation (or in the typical year before deregulation). As the researchers report, 'a state enacting an interstate banking reform experienced a 1.4 percentage point increase in the share of its population reporting that they "can trust" every year after the reform.'[28] The correlation between banking deregulation and increased trust is positive, large, and robust to a host of statistical controls for confounding variables. Moreover, additional analyses reveal that it is likely that deregulation increased trust precisely via increased market competition, as hypothesized, and not via a different channel, say income growth or changed migration patterns.

Third, perhaps the most compelling piece of evidence regarding competition and trust comes from longitudinal or panel data.[29] In one case, researchers looked at the changes in trust among German workers who moved (or did not move) to a more competitive (or less competitive) industry between the years 2003, 2008, and 2013. Crucially, the authors looked at how *the same workers* moved between industries and how their reported trust changed. What they found was that those who moved to a more competitive industry also became more trusting. Those who moved to a less competitive industry saw a decline in how they themselves were trusting. Workers who stayed in the same industry and experienced the same level of competition as before remained as trusting as they were at the start (so no change). Workers who switched industries but faced the same level of competition after the switch also remained as trusting as at the start (no change).

This is striking data that strongly suggest a positive causal relationship between competition and trust. It is not just that workers in more competitive industries happen to report more trust, while workers in less competitive industries happen to report less trust, which is what was demonstrated through cross-sectional data – a correlation that could plausibly be argued not to reflect a causal connection (even with all the controls). Instead, it is that when the same person *moves* to a more competitive industry they also *become* more trusting (and vice versa). As far as observational data goes, this is as good as it gets when one wants to infer causality.

Not to be outdone by panel data, we can further investigate whether the connection between competition and trust is a causal phenomenon by turning from observational data to laboratory experiments. With experiments, one could hardly challenge a causal interpretation of the results, although the methodological trade-off is that the lab environment does not necessarily reflect real-world environment, thus findings might be challenged not as spuriously causal (which is the standard charge against observational data) but simply as non-applicable outside the lab. Still, if findings from experiments demonstrate the same positive connection between competition and trust one sees in various observational studies, our confidence that competition fosters trust should grow stronger. And, indeed, the authors of the same 2018 study I have been discussing so far present experimental findings that reveal a very large positive outcome with regards to trust in a lab setting under competitive conditions. In a Public Goods Game, the share of participants reporting trust increased substantially – from slightly more than 50% of participants to almost 70% – once competition was introduced to the game.[30]

A different experimental study from 2008 looked at how willing individuals are to trade with each other online when they are partnered with someone for the whole duration of the game (15 rounds) and when they get a different trader each round.[31] Importantly, the study varied the competition condition, i.e. whether individuals can choose to buy from a single seller or multiple ones. Some could choose, while others could not. In all cases, buyers were also given information regarding sellers' past behaviour, namely whether sellers honoured the buyer's request for a sale and actually shipped them what they bought, or not. The most important finding of the experiment is that trust among non-partnered pairs or 'strangers,' i.e. pairs of traders who got shifted each round, increased significantly when competition was enabled.

Yet another study examined the evolution of trust among laboratory participants involved in a trust game with trustors and trustees, where the former have an opportunity to trust or not to trust, and the latter have an opportunity to honour the former's trust for mutual gain or exploit it for personal gain.[32] The researchers varied the conditions of the experiment such that trustors had more or less information about the past actions of trustees with whom they interacted. Apart from varying the level of information, researchers also presented trustors with the opportunity to pick a trustee (this was the competition treatment) or assigned them one at random (the no-competition treatment). What they found is that although increasing the amount of information raises the frequency of trustors trusting trustees, the increase is not very high. What increases the willingness of trustors to trust the most is the introduction of competition. With competition, levels of trust in the game increase to between 80% and 90%, while without competition they remain at 50%. Competition definitely fosters trust.

The researchers argue that it 'does so through two channels: creating sharper incentives for trustees who compete for being selected by trustors and selection itself.'[33] So, the prospect of competition (i.e. of not being chosen by the trustor if seen as untrustworthy) motivates trustees to honour trustors because the trustees know that this is the only way to build a good reputation for being trustworthy and, thus, for being selected by trustors (which is beneficial for the trustee). Moreover, even if some trustees are not moved to change their behaviour in such a way, trustors can then – due to the presence of competition – simply not choose them and instead choose to trust only those trustees who are actually trustworthy. These are the two channels through which competition works to increase trust: by *motivating* trustworthy behaviour on the part of trustees and by enabling the *elimination* or *selection* of the remaining recalcitrant trustees who were simply not moved to behave differently. Markets work similarly.

Cooperation and fairness

We have seen that (aspects of) capitalism and trust mix surprisingly well. But trust is not everything we care about. So, how about the relation between markets and other important human virtues we place a high value on aside from trust? Does the market not corrode the human altruistic impulse to share one's resources with others, instead selfishly motivating us to make others buy stuff from us and to rely on others simply through the impersonal act of commercial transaction? Capitalism and generalized – *impersonal* – trust might mix well, but what good does this do if at the same time markets (the lifeblood of capitalism) make us more selfish and less fair in our basic dispositions towards others?

There are multiple sources of data one can consult in trying to answer these questions. One very suggestive piece of evidence comes from a 2010 study carried out by a large team of researchers who played economic games, such as the Ultimatum and Dictator Game (UG, DG), with more than 2000 individuals from diverse societies in Africa, North and South America, Oceania, New Guinea, and Asia. The studied societies were diverse not only in a geographic and cultural sense, but also economically. Some of them relied on nomadic or semi-nomadic foraging and horticulture to survive, others on wage work and farming. The researcher's goal was to find out what the main differences are between individuals from different societies in their willingness to cooperate with a stranger and to (fairly) share money with him or her. In the aforementioned economic games, a player can split the money an experimenter endows him with in any way he chooses. A player can try to keep all the money for himself, he can give it away to the second player, or he can divide it more equally between the two.

The central initial finding was that offers one player makes to another differed substantially between populations. In some societies, offers were fair and egalitarian; here, players on average gave away around half of what they got from the experimenter to the other (unknown) players. In other societies, players were much stingier; they shared, but they shared only around 30% of what they were endowed with and kept most of the money for themselves.

What was the main variable responsible for this difference in fair or unfair sharing? After controlling for various factors that might influence how fairly a person is likely to behave – say, age, sex, education, income, or the size of one's community – it was market integration that explained more than half of the variance. (With one unusual outlier removed, market integration explained more than 70% of the difference between offers.) That is to say, individuals from households that got more of their total caloric intake from food bought on the market (as opposed to hunting or cultivating food at home) were *more likely* to share the money they got with a stranger in a fair 50-50 split.

Put more specifically, 'A 20-percentage point increase in MI [i.e. market integration] is associated with an increase in percentage offered ranging from roughly 2 to 3.4.'[34] So, a four-fold increase in market integration from, say, 20% market integration to 80% market integration results in around 10 percentage points increase of an offer, say from 35% (which is pretty unfair) to 45% (which is close to the perfectly fair 50-50 split). The data also show that belonging to a world religion (instead of a local religion) is tied to more fair giving. In sum,

> going from a fully subsistence-based society (MI = 0) with a local religion to a fully market-incorporated society (MI = 100%) with a world religion predicts an increase in percentage offered of roughly 23, 20 … in the DG, UG … respectively.[35]

As the researchers concluded,

> These findings indicate that people living in small communities lacking market integration or world religions—absences that likely characterized all societies until the Holocene—display relatively little concern with fairness or punishing unfairness in transactions involving strangers or anonymous others.[36]

The findings of other experiments further buttress the idea that aspects of capitalism – such as market integration I just discussed – increase, not reduce, fairness. For instance, the above 2010 study did not really discover something earth-shatteringly new. It just replicated the findings of an earlier famous study (which used a different sample of 15 small-scale societies), the main one being that market integration explains the bulk of variation in how giving people are, with more market integration associated with a higher (more fair) amount of money shared.[37]

Furthermore, the 2018 study already discussed in the previous section uncovered that *competition* (an integral part of capitalism, and one that is partially distinct from market integration) also seems to positively influence fair giving.[38] Participants in the Public Goods Game that were exposed to competition in that study not only trusted more (as already discussed) but were also willing to part their way with a much higher share of the money they personally received from the experimenter, i.e. they were behaving more fairly, more cooperatively.

That experiencing competitiveness and competition does *not* damage fairness at all – or at least behaviour related to fairness, such as altruism and honesty – is also the surprising finding of a 2015 study with the very appropriate title 'Who's Naughty? Who's Nice?'[39] The researchers found that, 'Compared to student population, internet business people lie less, and are more altruistic, more trusting, and more trustworthy.'[40] They placed students on the one hand and businesspeople from industries with 'cutthroat' competitive attitudes on the other in a laboratory setting to test who exhibits higher levels of altruism and lying (and trust). The businesspeople under scrutiny were said to come from cutthroat competitive industries because they were internet domain traders ('cybersquatters' who profit from an unrelated firm's recognizable brand) and online adult entertainers, two industries notorious for their ostensible lack of moral scruples and dog-eat-dog outlook. The exact results are worth quoting in full,

> We were surprised by what we found. Across dimensions of trust, trustworthiness, altruism, and lying, internet businesspeople were more prosocial than students. Moreover, the differences were not small. Compared to students in the lab, internet business people were twice as likely to be trustworthy and over 50% more likely to trust in a trust game. Internet business people contributed over 250% more in dictator games. They lie one-third less often than students.[41]

Importantly, however, the data also show that when the experiment was repeated in a field setting, the differences in pro-sociality between students and businesspeople were smaller. Still, 'even here, internet business people were, on the whole, "nicer" than students.'[42]

In the end, markets and competition seem to *boost* – not hurt – cooperating behaviour and fairness in giving. This is a very interesting finding, and it is especially important to emphasize and popularize it given the pervasiveness and surface plausibility of the anti-capitalist critique which supposes otherwise. Nevertheless, this finding is not wholly surprising when we remind ourselves of the prior result (discussed above) that markets increase trust. Trust is, after all, a crucial *precondition* for cooperation and sharing.

Tolerance and discrimination

In his 2011 bestseller *The Better Angels of Our Nature*, Steven Pinker uses a host of measures to demonstrate that the past five decades of human history (or more) have very clearly been 'decades of progress for racial minorities, women, children, gay people, and animals' both with respect to historical and contemporary moral standards. To illustrate this, here are just a few examples from the book. Between 1950 and 2003, the share of countries across the world that have official policies of discrimination against ethnic minorities decreased from 44% to 19% (the dataset includes 337 ethnic minorities in 124 countries). Likewise, aside from official governmental discrimination, polls measuring personal subjective responses by US citizens show an enormous decline in racist attitudes between mid-20th century and early 21st century – from the majority of the population espousing racism 70 years ago to only a (tiny) minority still doing so today. Discrimination, of course, persists. But there is less of it today than 70, or even just 30, years ago. Societies – especially economically developed, democratic societies – have been becoming more tolerant.

There are many plausible short- and long-term social causes of the various 'Rights Revolutions' documented by Pinker, and he goes over them in great detail in his book. But what concerns us here is how *capitalism*, in particular, might be contributing to increasing societal tolerance. Given that the world today is more tolerant than a century ago, and given that it has become much more capitalist since then, it seems impossible to claim – as critics perhaps are tempted to – that capitalism *worsens* discrimination. Going by the previously cited figures, it obviously has not done so. At the same time, however, one would be hopelessly naïve if one were to claim that since both capitalism and tolerance increased in the world, the former is a *cause* of the latter.

Unfortunately, there is not a lot of sophisticated evidence one can turn to in order to discern how exactly capitalism relates to tolerance and discrimination. It is interesting to note that one comes across theoretical arguments from both neoclassical economics *and* Marxist sociology in favour of the proposition that capitalism (or 'capital') is gender- or colour-blind. The main idea is that, under capitalism, personal discriminatory tastes of individuals can quickly become costly for them when engaging in market exchange, so profit-seeking individuals will tone down their racism (or sexism) if their primary goal is monetary benefit. An employer, for instance, has a strong economic incentive to hire the most productive individuals. If he foregoes hiring highly productive workers from the discriminated group due to his race prejudice, and instead hires less productive workers of his own race, he is losing economic value. Two consequences follow. First, most employers will be motivated by the prospect of higher profits and will increase their amount of tolerance in exchange for extra profit. Second, those employers who are nonetheless reluctant and hold out will be, in time, overtaken by their less discriminatory competitors and filtered out of the market.

The trouble with these theoretical considerations, however, is at least twofold.

First, the assumptions of the theoretical model can easily be tweaked and changed such that the outcome becomes 'sustained discrimination' or even 'increased discrimination' instead of 'reduced discrimination.' Imagine, for example, that markets are not perfectly competitive. If they are not, inefficient racist employers will not necessarily (or even likely) be driven out of business. Or, to take a different example, assume that the discriminated group contains – perhaps for reasons having to do with the history of discrimination itself – many members who are less productive. The economic logic of hiring them in order to reap higher profits will, then, not kick into gear and will not generate tolerance. There are other examples involving *consumers'* racist preferences, which can motivate even non- or anti-racist entrepreneurs to pragmatically tolerate racism in order not to lose customers. In short, as is usually the case, theory does not produce only one plausible conclusion but many.

Second, any theoretical analysis has to be tested against reality, no matter how unambiguous or convincing it is on paper. One large literature review from 2008 finds that, although racial discrimination in the US still afflicts employment, housing, credit, and consumer markets, 'great progress has been made since the early 1960s.'[43] An older review from the late 1990s agrees; in the US today, discrimination in employment persists, but there is less of it both in terms of gender and race than in the past.[44] A different, much more narrowly focused review of the empirical literature from the 1990s is less optimistic. It finds that 'discriminatory barriers to consumption show no signs of diminishing over the last 20 years ... Black and Hispanic households still face a significant chance of encountering discrimination when they inquire about housing or visit a car dealer.'[45] This more negative finding seems to be reconcilable with the other two studies' findings: the difference flows, partly, from the different time period under examination, and partly from the different industries examined. Overall, then, one can claim that progress in diminishing discrimination on the market has been real over the past 60 years, but it has definitely not been perfect (as discrimination today persists, albeit at a lower level than before), and in certain decades within certain sectors it has been very slow (or even non-existent).

The main question, however, remains. Did the fact that the US is *capitalist* and has *competitive markets* contribute to this decrease, or not? Did the market, specifically, have something to do with why discrimination has been reduced?

A pioneering sociological study from 2016 tried to directly empirically examine whether businesses that discriminate are also more likely to flop. It examined how discriminatory 170 New York businesses were in 2004, and which ones – the less or more discriminatory – were more likely to survive six years later, i.e. after the 2008 financial crash that weeded out many firms across the economy. The results of the study are striking:

> we see that 17 percent of non-discriminatory establishments had failed by 2010, relative to 36 percent of those that did discriminate. The likelihood of going out of business for an employer who discriminated thus appears more than twice that of its nondiscriminating counterpart ($p < 0.05$).[46]

Several relevant characteristics, such as business size and assets (as smaller business are more likely to fail than larger ones), as well as industry origin (as some industries are more likely to fail than others), were controlled for in the analysis. The correlation between discrimination and business failure remains robust to these controls.

This is suggestive evidence, but because it is a single (pioneering) study it is not much to go on. Moreover, one should note that the study does not offer conclusive evidence that discriminatory firms were more likely to flop *due to discrimination.* Instead, as the author cautions, 'It is possible, for example, that the kinds of employers who discriminate against racial minorities are also those who make poor choices in other areas of business management.'[47] In other words, although the study's findings are consistent with the theoretical proposition that markets eliminate discriminatory firms because of their inefficiency, there could also be other, non-discrimination factors that caused the discriminatory business to fail more regularly than the non-discriminatory ones. Therefore, what one can say with confidence based on this study is that 'the kinds of employers who discriminate are those more likely to go out of business. Discrimination may or may not be a direct cause of business failure, but it seems to be a reliable indicator of failure to come.'

As before, here too one way to assess this question is to turn to the economic freedom index. One 2013 study controlled for a variety of plausible determinants of tolerance, such as education, GDP per capita, the share of young people in a country, and religious fractionalization, and then looked solely at the relationship between economic freedom and tolerance (holding all else constant).[48] In a large sample of 70 countries across the world, it found a statistically significant and quite large connection between higher rates of economic freedom and tolerance towards homosexual people. As the researchers report, 'A one-unit increase in economic freedom is associated with the share of people being more tolerant towards homosexuals being about 7 percentage points higher.'[49] Additional analyses revealed that the 'legal system and secure property rights' and 'sound money' categories within the overall economic freedom index turned out to be most robustly important for tolerance. Importantly, the study also demonstrated that tolerance toward people of a different race is generally unrelated to economic freedom. There is neither a positive nor a negative relationship between the two variables.

A different study from 2016 investigated the same relationship in a sample of 41 US states between 1982 and 2008.[50] A similar battery of control variables was used in the analysis, and the main finding was that increases in economic freedom through time lead to subsequent increases in tolerance towards atheists, communists, and homosexuals. As the researchers conclude,

> a one-unit change in economic freedom on average corresponds to a six-percentage point change in tolerance. To get a feeling for these magnitudes we can give an illustrative example focusing on Tennessee and Texas. These two states had the very same level of tolerance (0.51) in 1982, but took somewhat different paths regarding economic freedom in the following decades. If Texas had increased its overall [economic freedom] score to the same extent as Tennessee over the time period (1.1 for Tennessee compared to 0.4 for Texas), this would have resulted in a further eight-percent increase of tolerance.[51]

Studies looking at the relationship between economic freedom and tolerance are, admittedly, few in numbers, and we should not rely on only a handful of studies to come to a definite conclusion in regards to this question. However, as things currently stand, it is quite clear that capitalism is definitely *consistent* with a reduction in discrimination (i.e. it allows for an increase in tolerance), and there are even some signs that it might itself be partly *causally responsible* for this reduction.

Conflict, violence, and war

We can hardly imagine a more important test of the *doux commerce* thesis than to investigate the connection between various forms of conflict and violence, on the one hand, and capitalism and economic development, on the other. If, as the Enlightenment thinkers proposed, markets and trade truly pacify, then one would surely expect to see the most capitalist countries in the world to be the least afflicted by violence. With this in mind, I will in this section run through many measures of conflict and violence, such as homicides (and non-violent crime), human rights abuses, coups, civil wars, and interstate wars to see how well or badly capitalism holds up.

Homicide

In 2017, parts of Latin America were one of the most violent regions in the world as far as homicide goes.[52] Since at least the mid-1990s on, in fact, Honduras, Guatemala, El Salvador, Colombia, Venezuela, and Brazil have consistently seen their rates of homicide exceed 30/100,000, with El Salvador and Honduras typically at around 50/100,000, even reaching 100/100,000 on certain years, and Venezuela and Colombia close behind. Mexico has also been a quite interpersonally lethal place, especially in the recent decade, though not to the same extent. Elsewhere in the world, only Russia and South Africa in the 1990s and early 2000s have been comparably as violent.

The least violent regions in terms of homicide are and have been Western Europe, parts of East and South Europe, Japan, Indonesia, Australia, New Zealand, Canada, and certain Muslim-majority countries such as Egypt, Tunisia, Morocco, Saudi Arabia, and Oman, with their rates typically below 1/100,000 or 1–2/100,000.

The US is quite a bit more homicidal, with its rate fluctuating around 7/100,000 in the past three decades. The same goes for most Sub-Saharan countries, for those other Latin American countries I have not mentioned in the previous paragraph, and for many parts of Asia. All of them are far removed from the most lethally violent places in the world, yet they themselves are also not very close to the least homicidal regions, instead typically hovering around a homicide rate of 5–10/100,000.

This rough overview demonstrates that, with some important exceptions, the richest countries in the world tend to have the lowest rates of homicide, while the poorer places see more, or much more, lethal interpersonal violence. A simple plot of homicides against GDP per capita confirms the trend.[53] As before, this general statistical observation does not allow us to make any causal inferences about how capitalist institutions, or the economic development they unleash, potentially reduce homicide. It is, however, causally suggestive in the sense that a highly capitalist and rich economy clearly cannot and does not turn people into *comparatively more violent murderers*, as, with the exception of the US, the most capitalist and richest societies in the world are simply among the *least homicidal*.

But let us yet again move beyond the simple correlation between economic development and homicide. What does a more sophisticated analysis tell us? Studies employing careful control variables and looking directly at the impact of *economic freedom* – not just GDP per capita – on homicide show that, in general, a more capitalist society does not evince any higher or lower rates of homicide compared to a less capitalist society.[54] The proverbial devil, however, lies in the details.

To see what I mean, let us take a closer look at one pioneering 2019 sociological study that pored over 142 countries to find how capitalism (or neoliberalism, as they termed it) and homicide did, or did not, mix. At first, the study found that the more capitalist a country is – namely the higher its economic freedom – the less homicidal crime it encounters.[55] The effect is statistically significant and quite large. However, researchers then controlled for a country's GDP per capita, inequality, democracy, and so on, so as to have a clear insight into how *the level of economic freedom itself* impacts lethal crime. The thought was that since a more economically free country is typically also more economically developed, more democratic, and so on, the correlation between economic freedom and lower rates of homicide could be spurious or indirect – namely it could be present due to the other factors that appear together with, or because of, economic freedom (i.e. high GDP per capita or democracy). And, indeed, once controls are implemented the evidence shows that economic freedom does not correlate either positively or negatively with homicide.[56] This suggests that how capitalist a country is by itself neither increases nor decreases lethal violence. (Remember, though, that here we are talking only about *direct* effects of capitalism – see endnote for more on this distinction.)[57]

Crucially, however, evidence was also uncovered that one particular element of economic freedom, i.e. the size of government, does go hand in hand with an increase in homicide. The data show that lower levels of government spending and lower marginal tax rates correlate with more lethal violence (even after controls).[58] Put simply, smaller welfare states seem to be tied to a higher rate of homicide.[59]

Tying all of this together, capitalist institutions, such as secure property rights, strong rule of law, only modest economic regulation, and robust free international trade do not, by themselves, increase or decrease lethal crime. In these aspects, then, capitalism cannot be said to directly pacify the populace or make it more bellicose (but note also the possible positive and negative *indirect* effects of capitalism discussed in endnote 57). However, insofar a highly capitalist economy also means a reduction in the welfare state – which it usually does not in the highly capitalist nations of Europe, but it does, say, in the US – this seems to contribute to lethal violence in a society. Social democratic capitalism, which is high on all aspects of capitalist economic freedom *except for the size of government*, then seems to be the safest bet as far as homicides are concerned.

Human rights abuses

Human rights abuses, such as torture, extrajudicial killings, and political imprisonment, are rife in the less economically developed parts of the world, while the wealthiest countries tend to have greater respect for all kinds of human rights, especially once oil producers are excluded from the tally. As per the usual pattern, a high level of GDP correlates positively with human rights protections.[60] Nevertheless, capitalism's critics charge that economic development and big corporations can (and usually do) tread all over human rights, especially when the developed world tells the less developed countries to adopt pro-market, neoliberal economic reforms, and when multilateral organizations, such as the IMF and World Bank, are involved in the liberalizing process.

In her bestseller *The Shock Doctrine*, Naomi Klein does not make a particularly intellectually persuasive, systematic, or rigorous case against capitalism and pro-market reforms, but she does present certain evocative episodes, such as the one in Chile in time of Augusto Pinochet, which cannot be dismissed away. More importantly, there exists a plethora of quantitative studies which aim to test the anti-capitalist (or anti-neoliberal) charge that globalization leads to human rights abuses.

One 2009 study discovered that the longer a developing country has been exposed to IMF lending programs (between 1981 and 2003), the more extrajudicial killings and torture it registered. The researchers were careful to control for the selection effect, i.e. the possibility that countries targeted for help by the IMF were chosen by the organization because they are the hardest cases. Not controlling for this eventuality is highly problematic as the analysis can yield spurious results, namely IMF-targeted countries faring badly on their human rights record not because IMF harmed them but because of their own intrinsic social problems which were the reason that IMF picked them in the first place. Many studies from the 1990s and early 2000s are unreliable for this reason, but the present study is not. It clearly suggests IMF lending to be associated with human rights abuses.

Others have persuasively challenged this finding, so currently the results are mixed. For instance, one study looked at the impact of actual flows of money from IMF, World Bank, and other multilateral organizations on human rights instead of just correlating the length of time under an IMF program and human rights abuses. The findings are as follows.

First, when a developing country is more indebted (to whomever, not just multilateral organizations), its respect for human rights significantly decreases – holding all else constant. Second, when a developing country receives net inflows of loans from the IMF and similar organizations, there is actually a *lower* level of human rights violations. Third, when countries have to pay the loans back and are unable to do so, human rights abuses increase. Importantly, 'This does not mean these payments cause violations, but it may very well mean that it is crisis countries that face dissent – those that generally have large arrears and do not get fresh infusions of loans.'

A crucial additional finding is that, fourth, the countries that got the laxest, least austere loans – and are now unable to pay back – engage in most human rights abuses. What this suggests is that it is not the lenders themselves who cause human rights violations because of the stringent conditions they put on the country taking out a loan. In other words, it is not true that had the conditions of the loan been much kinder – say, less neoliberal –, abuses would not have happened.

The researchers sum up by noting,

> receiving loans from the IFIs has positive effects on government respect for physical integrity rights. However, when loan payback exceeds fresh new loans, repression is more likely, possibly because of political problems emanating from the crisis and the attendant distributional struggles. Thus, at the point of receiving loans, the level of respect for human rights is positive, but it becomes negative if and when payback exceeds new disbursements.

These studies looked at the impact of multilateral organizations on human rights abuses in the developing world. But how about pro-market reforms, and globalization, in general? How does increasing economic freedom relate to human rights? When developing countries start globalizing, becoming more capitalist, more free-market oriented, do they also ramp up the abuse? The research is much less mixed on this matter: increases in economic freedom in the past few decades of so-called hyper-globalization have very likely contributed to government's *respect for human rights*.[61]

Here is just one representative example (for others see endnote 61). A study looked at a panel of 117 countries (95 of which are classified as 'least developing countries') between 1981 and 2006. The result is nothing less than striking:

> [There is] a strong positive association between reforms towards more free markets with regard to governments' respect for human rights, controlling for a host of relevant factors, including the possibility of endogeneity. The results are robust in relation to sample size, alternative data and methods, and a sample of only developing countries; and they are substantively quite large.[62]

So, even if a country does not become richer or more democratic, the mere fact that its economic freedom has increased seems to lead to more respect for human rights. Economic freedom directly impacts respect for human rights (in a positive way). But because the move towards more economic freedom usually also leads to more *economic development* and a higher chance of *democratization* – two variables that the study found are also positively tied to the respect for human rights –, capitalism can be said to also indirectly help with human rights respect through these latter two channels. All of this holds even if we exclude the 22 developed OECD countries from the sample and consider only developing countries.

Now, we should also reverse the arrow of causality and look at how human rights abuses influence the pace of pro-market reforms in developing countries. Do abuses help with liberalization or hurt it? If Klein's critique of neoliberalism and globalization is correct, one would expect that in countries where human rights abuses are already happening, Western pro-market reformers would jump up and seize the opportunity for their devious plans, as they ostensibly did in Chile. Never let a crisis go to waste, as the saying goes.

Thus, one study looking at the period between 1985 and 2005 asked, '[A]re countries where human rights are abused and where people are tortured, disappear, or are denied rights to movement, speech, and religion likely to see increases or decreases in economic freedom?'[63] It found that the flaunting of human rights is not a good conduit for economic reform. In fact, the reverse is true: human rights abuses *hurt* liberalization. As the researchers put it, 'The impact is very small, representing less than one tenth of one standard deviation, but it suggests that torture impedes rather than facilitates economic liberalization.'[64]

In conclusion, while there is some credible evidence for the thesis that both the forces behind market liberalization as well as those driving torture can co-exist, there is also strong and mounting evidence for the claim that globalized pro-market reforms and torture repel each other. Further research is definitely needed, as the existing literature remains mixed, but Klein's extravagant and overgeneralized anti-capitalist critique which characterizes liberalizing, pro-market reforms as inexorably tied to human rights abuses is, going by the available evidence, vastly overblown.

Coups

Since 1950, there were over 450 *coups d'état* in the world.[65] The vast majority of them happened in autocratic societies although a whole quarter of all coup attempts (about 100 in total) targeted democratic states. Put another way, coups 'arise at a rate of about 5.4% in autocratic years compared with 2.1% in democratic years.'[66] So, overall, autocracies are more prone to coups than democracies. This reasonably leads us to think that democracy, much more so than capitalism, protects against coups.

On closer inspection, however, capitalism and its typical consequent – economic development – nevertheless turn out to be very important if one wants to see less coups in the world. This is so for two reasons.

First, capitalism and economic development increase the chances of an autocracy turning into a democracy, and of a democracy turning into a stable, consolidated democratic regime (as per the modernization thesis research), which then offers the society a better protection against coups (as per the presently cited research). Capitalism helps with coups in an indirect, ultimate way via the political system it typically incubates.

Second, and more proximately, capitalism helps with coups through the typical wealth channel. Research shows that wealth itself – a primary consequent of capitalism – helps protect societies against coups, independently of the nature of the political regime. Wealthy democracies *and wealthy autocracies* are much better protected against coups than poor democracies and poor autocracies alike.[67] Put more specifically, '[w]ealthy democracies suffer coup attempts in about .008% of country years, compared with poor democracies in about .06% Poor autocracies suffer coups in .07% of country years compared with wealthy autocracies, at about .02%.'[68] So, wealth offers a much higher protection against coup-risk than democracy itself (seeing as how poor democracies remain quite vulnerable to coups, and to a similar degree as poor autocracies). But the absolute highest protection is offered by a combination of wealth and democracy, seeing as how wealthy democracies are the least vulnerable to coups, even much less than wealthy autocracies. In other words, 'As democracies move from below the mean of economic development to above it, their rate of coups decreases by more than 86% compared with autocracies at approximately 71%.'[69] (These trends remain robust under a more demanding statistical treatment.)[70]

All this quite clearly suggests that wealth (and, by proxy, capitalism as the thing that generates wealth) is an incredibly strong predictor of low coup frequency everywhere on its own, but especially so in democratic societies.[71]

There is further recent evidence corroborating capitalism's protective effect against coups. A 2019 study, for instance, first replicated the well-known finding that higher GDP per capita insulates against violent political instability, but then also found that when one statistically controls for economic complexity (i.e. specialized division of labour), GDP per capita loses its predictive strength and economic complexity instead emerges as a strong correlate of political stability.[72] In other words, it seems that – causally speaking – just any old form of wealth will not do. A wealthy society with low economic complexity (i.e. low level of specifically *capitalist* economic development), which got its wealth not through capitalist modernization but simply by extracting and selling oil or similar natural resources, will not be particularly well insulated against coups. At the same time, a highly economically complex society which currently perhaps possesses only middling amounts of wealth (as it is still developing) should be well protected simply on account of its capitalist economic structures. Of course, since high GDP is typically strongly correlated with high economic complexity, this finding is not earth-shattering. Nevertheless, it is important and it suggests that the capitalist nature of an economy itself, not just the wealth generated, has something to do with political stability.

Civil war

One would be perfectly sensible in conjecturing that religious and ethnic fragmentation is the strongest overall cause (or at least correlate) of civil war onset. What else would motivate citizens of the same state to turn their guns on each other than age-old religious and ethnic differences and hatreds? This is a sad fact about humankind, but one that seems irrefutable.

This conjecture, however, turns out not to be wholly accurate. In fact, one of the strongest and most robustly confirmed correlates of civil war is, once again, societal wealth or GDP per capita.[73] Its predictive power is even stronger – much stronger – than that of democracy, income inequality, or even religious and ethnic heterogeneity.[74] Robust datasets do demonstrate that, since 1945, most civil wars have – unsurprisingly – happened in societies with mountainous terrain and otherwise uncompromising geography.[75] Quite surprisingly, however, these same data also reveal that, between 1945 and 1999, the bottom fifth of societies (by wealth) have had an almost 10-fold higher probability of experiencing civil war in the next 5 years compared to the upper fifth of societies.[76] This is how one exhaustive literature review from 2010 puts it:

> The most robust empirical finding in the existing literature is that economic conditions – both low income levels and slow growth rates – contribute to the outbreak of civil wars and conflicts in less developed countries. This finding has found support at both the cross-country and micro levels, although the correct interpretation of these patterns in terms of underlying theoretical mechanisms remains contested. ... In contrast, the empirical evidence that social divisions, political grievances, and resource abundance are drivers of violence remains weaker and more controversial.[77]

So, as before, taking GDP per capita as a proxy for capitalist development, one can reasonably credit capitalism as an indirect contributor to the reduction of civil wars.

But what about capitalism as a possible *direct* pacifier of civil war? Controlling for the level of economic development and various other plausible independent variables that influence civil war, one study found impressive evidence in favour of this idea. The researchers looked at more than 120 countries across the world between 1970 and 2005 and found that the more capitalist countries (i.e. the ones classified higher on the economic freedom scale) turn out to be much less likely to undergo civil conflict.[78] The effect of economic freedom (net of economic development) on internal peace is substantively very large. As the researchers report,

> For a poor country at the lowest 25th percentile of the income distribution emerging from civil conflict, an improvement in the level of economic freedom from the 25th percentile to the 75th percentile reduces the annual predicted risk of civil conflict from 4.7% to 2.7%. In real-world terms, this is analogous to comparing the level of economic freedom in Botswana (since 1998) with that of Sierra Leone (1983–2000), which means that if Sierra Leone were to adopt Botswana's level of economic freedom then it would roughly halve its risk of reverting to conflict.[79]

Strikingly, the evidence shows not only that economic freedom reduces civil war risk (even net of economic development) but also that the reduction effect is similar in size as it is for economic development, a factor which existing research emphasizes as the most important correlate of civil peace. So, in one way or the other, a robust capitalist economy seems to play an important role in the reduction of civil war incidence.

A much narrower sample of 54 African countries (between 1985 and 2017), presented by authors of a 2021 study bluntly titled 'Does a free market system reduce conflict in Africa?,' points in the same direction but with one important caveat.[80] The main finding of the study is that, in the whole African sample, an increase in economic freedom (net of all controls) is a strong predictor of reduced internal conflict. This also holds for the sub-sample of the 'least economically free' African countries, which means that when an African country with low economic freedom experiences an increase in its level of capitalism, the chances of internal conflict afflicting the country decrease. Surprisingly, however, the second main finding of the study is that this same dynamic *does not hold* for the 'moderately free' and 'most free' sub-samples.[81] Countries which are already quite capitalist actually see a worsening of conflict with further increases in economic freedom. It is not clear why the effect from the complete African sample is preserved in one sub-sample and reversed in the other two, but this is a finding definitely worth noting. However, also important is the fact that the sub-sample of 'least economically free' is comprised of a healthy $n = 45$, while the 'moderately' and 'most free' sub-samples have a combined $n = 9$.

The authors' general conclusion in the study is that 'an improved level of economic freedom reduces conflict in Africa.'[82] Nevertheless, given the complications just discussed, I would emphasize that further research of capitalism's direct effects on conflict in Africa is needed before we can celebrate the authors' happy conclusion.

Interstate war

One of the most robust, tested, and empirically documented findings in political science and sociology is the fact that democracies never, or almost never, fight each other in an interstate war.[83] Researchers have systematically tried to overturn this 'democratic peace' finding for over three decades now, and they continually come up short. It is not just that virtually all scholars agree that interstate war is exceedingly rare among pairs of democratic states ('democratic dyads') but also that there is mounting statistical evidence which shows that there seems to be something about the *democratic nature* of states that defuses state-on-state war.[84] The theoretical mechanisms that underpin the connection between democracy and peace are many, and both their plausibility and empirical grounding remain debated.[85] But, to the best of our knowledge, at the macro-level, democratic peace is a non-spurious, causal relation that holds even when myriad other plausible independent variables are controlled for.

The most impressive and biggest challenge to the democratic peace finding comes from data showing that the wealth of nation and the level of trade between nations actually account for all, or some, of the correlation between democracy and interstate peace.[86] As already said, virtually no study manages to overturn the democratic peace correlation, but some do find that various (capitalist) economic factors help explain at least *some non-negligible part* of the variance. It seems that how economically developed states are, how pervasive markets are within them, and how much states trade with each other does influence somewhat their willingness to be peaceful or aggressive even independently of how democratic they are.[87]

For instance, several studies uncovered that trade alone – i.e. how economically interdependent countries are – stimulates peace.[88] The effect size is not negligible. As one team of researchers reports,

> a one-standard deviation increase in interdependence results in a net reduction of 29 percent in the probability of a fatal dispute. More importantly … this pacifying impact of interdependence appears to hold regardless of a dyad's level of democracy or development.[89]

Moreover, the level of economic development – although not a significant force for peace on its own, contrary to what we have just seen is the case for trade – at least boosts the otherwise independent probability of peace between two democracies. In other words, the wealthier democracies have an even lower chance to fight each other than poor democracies.[90] Admittedly, the threshold of economic development that a democracy needs to reach so as to receive the additional positive effect of development is quite low, so in this sense economic development is not a particularly interesting determinant of peace. As the paper puts it,

> If at least one democratic state in a dyad has a GDP per capita of 1400 USD or less, joint democracy is not a significant force for peace. Fortunately, this level of income is low enough that most democratic dyads in our sample [spanning the period between 1885 and 1992], 91 percent, are in the zone of peace at usual thresholds of statistical significance; and all democratic dyads exceed this threshold in 1992. Nevertheless, the strength of democracy's pacifying effect varies with the level of development. Peace is most secure among the economically advanced democracies.

If one takes economic development, marketization, and international trade as proxies for capitalism, as one should, then it seems that capitalism helps, in part, with interstate peace. It does so independently of democratic peace (this effect holds for trade and markets) and by boosting the already existing, independent effect of democratic peace (this effect holds for development).

To be sure, capitalism's positive effect on international peace is a much less robust finding than democracy's positive effect, and it thus (rightly) commands less of a consensus in the literature.[91] I do not want to overstate its importance (or reality). Furthermore, it cannot be emphasized enough that democracy alone, even apart from economic factors, seems to be the most important cause of peace (among democratic dyads). Put differently, capitalism should not get the credit that democracy is actually deserving of. Still, some credit could be due, and especially so when one thinks of the indirect contribution of capitalism – or, more specifically, economic development – to interstate peace through capitalism's modernizing contribution to democratization itself. For the most part, autocratic states transitioned to democracy, and then from democracy to consolidated democracy, because of all the economic development they experienced. So, even though democracy is the most important cause of peace, it was historically capitalism that was the most important structural cause of democracy.

However, the debate over capitalist peace will be resolved in the future; the existing evidence does not allow critics of capitalism to condemn it as *breeding* interstate war. If anything, capitalism is neutral towards war, or even seems to pacify states on the international stage.

Conclusion

In their book-length theoretical and empirical study of the relationship between markets and morality, Virgil Storr and Ginny Choi conclude that one does not have to choose between the material enrichment generated by (capitalist) markets and the moral corruption flowing from this same institution. As they say,

> [l]uckily, we do not appear to have this problem. Rather than being incompatible with morality, markets are not only consistent with morality but seem to promote morality. People in market societies exhibit the seven bourgeois virtues (i.e. prudence, justice, courage, temperance, faith, hope, and love). They also tend to be more altruistic, more cosmopolitan, less materialistic, and less corrupt, as well as more likely to be trusting and trustworthy.[92]

They support this conclusion throughout the book with their own analysis of wide-ranging data and indicators, and they also support the conclusion with a review of an enormous existing literature on the same topic. Now, their original analysis does not really allow them to make the causal statement that markets *generate* morality, only that they correlate with it. Nevertheless, even this is a significant finding since even such simple correlations can at least rule out certain causal statements, such as the anti-capitalist critique that markets turn us into much more terrible people in comparison with people in less marketized (or non-market) societies. If markets really worked that way, this would clearly show up in even the simplest cross-country comparisons employed by Storr and Choi.

Still, Storr and Choi's happy and univocal conclusion that markets seem to *causally promote* moral or pro-social behaviour (and that they do so *in all cases?*) does not sit completely comfortably with me. This is partly so due to the various mixed, or even negative, findings one can glean from the more statistically complex studies I have reviewed in this chapter. To be sure, there exists a wealth of data and positive results which attest to the fact that markets are consistent with pro-social behaviour and in several cases even promote it. However, not all good things go together. Moreover, it has to be admitted that Storr and Choi use only a very simple measure of markets. They divide countries into two categories: market societies (for instance, Canada, Chile, Oman, and Germany) and non-market societies (for instance, Italy, Portugal, India, and Egypt). I do not have to spell out all the issues with such a binary distinction for you to understand that their analysis is not wholly satisfactory.

What, then, can be said with confidence is that capitalism's critics are much too rash when they sweepingly condemn capitalism as corrupting our morals and pro-sociality. Capitalism's core – robust and pervasive markets, secure property rights, market competition, free international trade, modest regulation – is surprisingly consistent with, and sometimes even causally generative of, most of the crucial non-material goods people desire to populate their societies. There is only one aspect of capitalism that time and again seems not to point in the right direction as far as morality and pro-sociality are concerned: small government. In this one aspect, a higher degree of capitalism (i.e. lower government spending) seems to work against us.

So, is capitalism desirable if we want to keep (or even boost) our morals and pro-sociality? It is. But the form of capitalism which seems to be most desirable in this respect is *social democratic* capitalism. This form of capitalism maximizes everything in the capitalist core (markets, free international trade, modest regulation, strong property rights), save for the one element just mentioned – government size, which remains quite large in social democratic societies.

Notes

1 Hirschman (1982, 1464–1465).
2 Ibid., 1465.
3 Ibid.
4 Marx (2008, 37).
5 Wright (2018).
6 Ibid., 430.

7 Ortiz-Ospina and Roser (2016). See also Paldam (2011), Figure 12.1.
8 Algan and Cahuc (2013, 535).
9 Indeed, the possibility that trust causes development is quite plausible. As a major 2013 review paper concludes, 'Several recent papers find a strong impact of trust on GDP per capita.' Ibid., 544. See also the recent study by Berggren and Bjørnskov (2017), which suggests trust also positively influences economic freedom; that is, it both promotes and entrenches a higher level of capitalist institutions in a society.
10 Delhey and Newton (2005); de Soysa et al. (2017); Saravia (2016). See also Alesina and La Ferrara (2002).
11 Delhey and Newton (2005, 322).
12 Polillo (2012).
13 Robbins (2012).
14 Kyriacou and Trivin (2018).
15 Berggren and Jordahl (2006); Aghion et al. (2010); Robbins (2012); Saravia (2016); de Soysa et al. (2017). As before with GDP, here too merely looking at a simple correlation between economic freedom and trust is enough to demonstrate that a high degree of capitalist institutions in a society is, overall, at least consistent with – if not causally related to – high trust. See Saravia (2016).
16 Berggren and Jordahl (2006); Aghion et al. (2010); Robbins (2012); Saravia (2016).
17 Robbins (2012, 12). Emphasis added.
18 Berggren and Jordahl (2006); Saravia (2016).
19 Saravia (2016).
20 Berggren and Jordahl (2006).
21 Ibid.; Saravia (2016).
22 Robbins (2012); de Soysa et al. (2017).
23 Robbins (2012, 5–6).
24 Francois et al. (2018).
25 Although compare with Fischer (2008), who uses a large cross-country sample (with about 60 countries in total) and finds that competition increases trust only for individuals with more market interactions, i.e. individuals with higher rates of market integration.
26 Francois et al. (2018).
27 Ibid.
28 Ibid.
29 Ibid.
30 Ibid.
31 Bolton et al. (2008).
32 Huck et al. (2012).
33 Ibid., 205.
34 Henrich et al. (2010, 1482). Note the appended Erratum posted online on the 17th of June, 2011, although the Erratum does not (negatively) affect the findings I discussed.
35 Ibid.
36 Ibid., 1483–1484.
37 Henrich et al. (2001).
38 Francois et al. (2018).
39 Hoffman and Morgan (2015).
40 Ibid., 174.
41 Ibid., 185.
42 Ibid.
43 Pager and Shepherd (2008).
44 Darity and Mason (1998).
45 Yinger (1998, 38).
46 Pager (2016, 852).
47 Ibid., 855.

48 Berggren and Nilsson (2013).
49 Ibid., 190.
50 Berggren and Nilsson (2016).
51 Ibid., 61.
52 Roser and Ritchie (2013/2019).
53 Kenworthy (2019), Figure 1.14.
54 Bjørnskov (2015); McLean et al. (2019).
55 McLean et al. (2019).
56 Ibid.
57 Since countries that become more capitalist also become more economically developed, democratic, etc., it could still be argued that capitalism *indirectly* (through the channels just mentioned) contributes to lower rates of homicide. But because capitalism also tends to increase inequality, which has canonically been related to higher rates of homicide, there is also the possibility of capitalism indirectly contributing to higher rates of homicide. It is hard to say whether the net indirect effect is positive, negative, or zero.
58 McLean et al. (2019).
59 See also Bjørnskov (2015).
60 See, for one measure of human rights, Kenworthy (2019), Figure 1.18.
61 Eriksen and de Soysa (2009); de Soysa and Vadlamannati (2011; 2013).
62 de Soysa and Vadlammanati (2013).
63 Carden and Lawson (2010).
64 Ibid.
65 Schiel (2019).
66 Ibid., 1446.
67 Schiel (2019).
68 Ibid., 1446.
69 Ibid.
70 Ibid.
71 Moreover, with the exception of Hungary, no high income democracy has ever broken down (via coup attempts or otherwise) in the period between 1950 and 2021, while low income democracies fail regularly. See Przeworski and Limongi (1997); Brownlee (2017).
72 Cox et al. (2019).
73 Fearon (2008, 293); Blattman and Miguel (2010, 45).
74 Fearon (2008, 293).
75 Ibid., 292.
76 Ibid., 293.
77 Blattman and Miguel (2010, 45).
78 de Soysa and Fjelde (2010).
79 Ibid., 293.
80 Okunlola et al. (2021).
81 Ibid.
82 Ibid.
83 For a review of the literature, see Hegre (2014) and Reiter (2017). See also, on both empirical evidence and theory underpinning the democratic peace, my discussion in Rutar (2021), chapter 5.
84 Hegre (2014); Reiter (2017).
85 See my extended discussion in Rutar (2021), chapter 5.
86 For a review of the evidence, see Hegre (2014). Aside from economic development (or international trade), Gartzke (2007) forcefully argues that it is the extent to which markets prevail within a country that explains democratic interstate peace. Dafoe (2011) and Choi (2011) found serious and uncontroversial, easily confirmed flaws with his data and analysis, and demonstrated that democratic peace actually survives

Gartzke's controls with proper implementation and data. Interestingly, however, Choi also managed to replicate Gartzke's finding that the extent of society's marketization has a statistically significant pacifying effect. See Choi (2011, 764–767).
87 Mousseau et al. (2003); Gartzke (2007); Hegre et al. (2010); Choi (2011).
88 Mousseau et al. (2003); Hegre et al. (2010). For more, see the reviewed literature in Hegre (2014).
89 Mousseau et al. (2003, 297).
90 Ibid.
91 See Dafoe (2011); Choi (2011); Hegre (2014).
92 Storr and Choi (2019, 243).

References

Aghion, Philippe, Algan, Yann, Cahuc, Pierre, and Andrei Shleifer. 2010. 'Regulation and Distrust,' *Quarterly Journal of Economics* 125, no. 3, 1015–1049.

Alesina, Alberto, and Eliana La Ferrara. 2002. 'Who Trusts Others?' *Journal of Public Economics* 85, no. 2, 207–234.

Algan, Yann, and Pierre Cahuc. 2013. 'Trust and Growth,' *Annual Review of Economics* 5, 521–549.

Berggren, Niclas, and Christian Bjørnskov. 2017. 'The Market-Promoting and Market-Preserving Role of Social Trust in Reforms of Policies and Institutions,' *Southern Economic Journal* 84, no. 1, 3–25.

Berggren, Niclas, and Henrik Jordahl. 2006. 'Free to Trust: Economic Freedom and Social Capital,' *Kyklos* 59, no. 2, 141–169.

Berggren, Niclas, and Therese Nilsson. 2013. 'Does Economic Freedom Foster Tolerance?' *Kyklos* 60, no. 2, 177–207.

Berggren, Niclas, and Therese Nilsson. 2016. 'Tolerance in the United States: Does Economic Freedom Transform Racial, Religious, Political and Sexual Attitudes?' *European Journal of Political Economy* 45, Supplement, 53–70.

Bjørnskov, Christian. 2015. 'Does Economic Freedom Really Kill? On the Association Between "Neoliberal" Policies and Homicide Rates,' *European Journal of Political Economy* 37, 207–219.

Blattman, Christopher, and Edward Miguel. 2010. 'Civil War,' *Journal of Economic Literature* 48, no. 1, 3–57.

Bolton, Gary, Loebbecke, Claudia, and Axel Ockenfels. 2008. 'Does Competition Promote Trust and Trustworthiness in Online Trading? An Experimental Study,' *Journal of Management Information Systems* 25, no. 2, 145–170.

Carden, Art, and Robert A. Lawson. 2010. 'Human Rights and Economic Liberalization,' *Business and Politics* 12, no. 2., no pagination.

Choi, Seung-Whan. 2011. 'Re-Evaluating Capitalist and Democratic Peace Models,' *International Studies Quarterly* 55, 759–769.

Cox, Gary W., North, Douglass C., and Barry R. Weingast. 2019. 'The Violence Trap: A Political-Economic Approach to the Problems of Development,' *Journal of Public Finance and Public Choice* 34, no. 1, 3–19.

Dafoe, Allan. 2011. 'Statistical Critiques of the Democratic Peace: Caveat Emptor,' *American Journal of Political Science* 55, no. 2, 247–262.

Darity, William A. Jr., and Patrick L. Mason. 1998. 'Evidence on Discrimination in Employment: Codes of Color, Codes of Gender,' *Journal of Economic Perspectives* 12, no. 2, 63–90.

de Soysa, Indra, and Hanne Fjelde. 2010. 'Is the Hidden Hand an Iron Fist? Capitalism and Civil Peace, 1970–2005,' *Journal of Peace Research* 47, no. 3, 287–298.

de Soysa, Indra, and Krishna Chaitanya Vadlamannati. 2011. 'Does Being Bound Together Suffocate, or Liberate? The Effects of Economic, Social, and Political Globalization on Human Right, 1981–2005,' *Kyklos* 64, no. 1, 20–53.

de Soysa, Indra, and Krishna Chaitanya Vadlammanati. 2013. 'Do Pro-market Economic Reforms Drive Human Rights Violations? An Empirical Assessment, 1981–2006,' *Public Choice* 155, 163–187.

de Soysa, Indra, Jakobsen, Tor Georg, and Marthe Holum. 2017. 'Free-Market Capitalism, Interpersonal Trust, and Trust in Political Institutions: A Multilevel Empirical Analysis, 1994–2014,' *Journal of Globalization Studies* 8, no. 2, 3–13.

Delhey, Jan, and Kenneth Newton. 2005. 'Predicting Cross-National Levels of Social Trust: Global Pattern or Nordic Exceptionalism?' *European Sociological Review* 21, no. 4, 311–327.

Eriksen, Silja, and Indra de Soysa. 2009. 'A Fate Worse Than Debt? International Financial Institutions and Human Rights, 1981–2003,' *Journal of Peace Research* 46, no. 4, 485–503.

Fearon, James D. 2008. 'Economic Development, Insurgency, and Civil War,' in E. Helpman (ed.), *Institutions and Economic Performance*, 292–328. Cambridge: Harvard University Press.

Fischer, Justina A. V. 2008. 'Is Competition Good for Trust? Cross-Country Evidence Using Micro-Data,' *Economics Letters* 100, no. 1, 56–59.

Francois, Patrick, Fujiwara, Thomas, and Tanguy van Ypersele. 2018. 'The Origins of Human Prosociality: Cultural Group Selection in the Workplace and the Laboratory,' *Science Advances* 4, no. 9. DOI: 10.1126/sciadv.aat2201/.

Gartzke, Erik. 2007. 'The Capitalist Peace,' *American Journal of Political Science* 51, no. 1, 166–191.

Hegre, Håvard. 2014. 'Democracy and Armed Conflict,' *Journal of Peace Research* 51, no. 2, 159–172.

Hegre, Håvard, Oneal, John R., and Bruce Russett. 2010. 'Trade Does Promote Peace: New Simultaneous Estimates of the Reciprocal Effects of Trade and Conflict,' *Journal of Peace Research* 47, no. 6, 763–774.

Henrich, Joseph, Boyd, Robert, Bowles, Samuel, Camerer, Colin, Fehr, Ernst, Gintis, Herbert, and Richard McElreath. 2001. 'In Search of Homo Economicus: Behavioral Experiments in 15 Small-Scale Societies,' *AEA Papers and Proceedings* 91, no. 2, 73–78.

Henrich, Joseph, Ensminger, Jean, McElreath, Richard, Barr, Abigail, Barrett, Clark, Bolyanatz, Alexander, Cardenas, Juan Camilo, Gurven, Michael, Gwako, Edwins, Henrich, Natalie, Lesorogol, Carolyn, Marlowe, Frank, Tracer, David, and John Ziker. 2010. 'Markets, Religion, Community Size, and the Evolution of Fairness and Punishment,' *Science* 327, no. 1480, 1480–1484.

Hirschman, Albert O. 1982. 'Rival Interpretations of Market Society: Civilizing, Destructive, or Feeble?' *Journal of Economic Literature* 20, no. 4, 1463–1484.

Hoffman, Mitchell, and John Morgan. 2015. 'Who's Naughty? Who's Nice? Experiments on Whether Pro-social Workers are Selected Out of Cutthroat Business Environments,' *Journal of Economic Behavior & Organization* 109, 173–187.

Huck, Steffen, Lünser, Gabriele K., and Jean-Robert Tyran. 2012. 'Competition Fosters Trust,' *Games and Economic Behavior* 76, no. 1, 195–209.

Kyriacou, Andreas, and Pedro Trivin. 2018. 'Economic Development, Inequality and Generalized Trust,' *MPRA Paper No. 91651.* Accessible via: https://mpra.ub.uni-muenchen.de/91651/.

McLean, Craig, Long, Michael A., Stretesky, Paul B., Lynch, Michael J., and Steve Hall. 2019. 'Exploring the Relationship between Neoliberalism and Homicide: A Cross-National Perspective,' *International Journal of Sociology* 49, no. 1, 53–76.

Mousseau, Michael, Hegre, Håvard, and John R. Oneal. 2003. 'How the Wealth of Nations Conditions the Liberal Peace,' *European Journal of International Relations* 9, no. 2, 277–314.

Okunlola, Olalekan C., Ayetigbo, Olumide A., and Sam O. Ajiye. 2021. 'Does a Free Market System Reduce Conflict in Africa?' *Journal of Social and Economic Development*. OnlineFirst. Accessible via: https://link.springer.com/article/10.1007/s40847-021-00167-9/.

Ortiz-Ospina, Esteban, and Max Roser. 2016. 'Trust,' *Our World in Data*. Accessible via: https://ourworldindata.org/trust/.

Pager, Devah. 2016. 'Are Firms That Discriminate More Likely to Go Out of Business?' *Sociological Science* 3, no. 36, 849–859.

Pager, Devah, and Hana Shepherd. 2008. 'The Sociology of Discrimination: Racial Discrimination in Employment, Housing, Credit, and Consumer Markets,' *Annual Review of Sociology* 34, 181–209.

Paldam, Martin. 2011. 'Generalized Trust,' in L. Sacconi and G. D. Antoni (eds), *Social Capital, Corporate Social Responsibility, Economic Behaviour and Performance*, 331–357. London: Palgrave Macmillan.

Polillo, Simone. 2012. 'Globalization: Civilizing or Destructive? An Empirical Test of the International Determinants of Generalized Trust,' *International Journal of Comparative Sociology* 53, no. 1, 45–65.

Reiter, Dan. 2017. 'Is Democracy a Cause of Peace?' in *Oxford Research Encyclopedia of Politics*. Accessible via: https://oxfordre.com/politics/view/10.1093/acrefore/9780190228637.001.0001/acrefore-9780190228637-e-287/.

Robbins, Blaine G. 2012. 'A Blessing and a Curse? Political Institutions in the Growth and Decay of Generalized Trust: A Cross-National Panel Analysis, 1980–2009,' *PLoS One* 7, no. 4.

Roser, Max, and Hannah Ritchie. 2013/2019. 'Homicides,' *Our World in Data*. Accessible via: https://ourworldindata.org/homicides/.

Rutar, Tibor. 2021. *Rational Choice and Democratic Government: A Sociological Approach*. London: Routledge.

Saravia, Antonio. 2016. 'Institutions of Economic Freedom and Generalized Trust: Evidence from the Eurobarometer Surveys,' *European Societies* 18, no. 1, 5–24.

Schiel, Rebecca E. 2019. 'An Assessment of Democratic Vulnerability: Regime Type, Economic Development, and Coups d'Etat,' *Democratization* 26, no. 8, 1439–1457.

Storr, Virgil Henry, and Ginny Seung Choi. 2019. *Do Markets Corrupt Our Morals?* Cham: Palgrave.

Yinger, John. 1998. 'Evidence on Discrimination in Consumer Markets,' *Journal of Economic Perspectives* 12, no. 2, 23–40.

6

CONCLUSION

What about the environment?

We have seen throughout the book that the modern capitalist economy is a much more nuanced and complex phenomenon than it gets credit for by either its detractors or defenders. It has many virtues that are ignored, denied, or downplayed by its critics, and it embodies quite a few vices one would not know about if one only listened to the most passionate proponents of capitalism. Perhaps there is no single aspect of the modern economy that demonstrates this polarized tension better than, of course, its environmental aspect.

The topic is so heated that even those who broadly share the *same political convictions* do not see eye to eye. One recent example is the furore raised by the otherwise left-wing economist Branko Milanović over the claims and aims of the 'degrowth' movement. In a critique of degrowthers posted on his blog *Global Inequality*, Milanović was blunt right out of the gate:

> The difficulty of discussion with degrowthers comes from the fact that they and the rest of us live in two different ideological worlds. Degrowers live in a world of magic, where merely by listing the names of desirable ends they are supposed to somehow happen. In that world, one does not need to bother with numbers or facts, trade-off, first or second bests; one merely needs to conjure up what he/she desires and it will be there.[1]

The left-wing economist-blogger Noah Smith also chimed in, sharing Milanović's misgivings. As he put it contemptuously, 'The mad schemes degrowthers advocate are a fantasy that distracts us from real efforts to save the planet ... There are crusades out there worth fighting for; this not one of them.'[2] Unsurprisingly, proponents of degrowth fired back and dismissed Milanović's and Smith's vitriolic jabs.[3]

DOI: 10.4324/9781003305811-6

But even leaving this specific intra-left political controversy aside, there is plenty of heat to go around when it comes to the topic of capitalism and the environment. Left-wing magazines, from the fringe Trotskyist *Left Voice* to the established *Guardian*, regularly feature articles with bombastic titles such as 'Capitalism is killing the planet – it's time to stop buying into our own destruction' and 'Capitalism is destroying the planet – let's destroy capitalism!'[4] Naomi Klein's best-selling book on climate change is succinctly subtitled 'Capitalism vs. The Climate.'[5] The simple, yet radical, point these and many other authors are trying to make is that it is one or the other. Either we stick to capitalism and catastrophically wreck the environment, or we abandon capitalism and save the environment. Anthropogenic climate change is primarily, if not wholly, caused by some inherent feature of the capitalist economy we live in. The solution, then, is to abandon the current mode of production and to move towards a certain – usually quite unspecified – socialist form of production and exchange, which will bring a stop to environmental destruction.

In the concluding chapter of the book, I will demonstrate both empirically and theoretically that this radical position is untenable or at least much too hyperbolic. To be clear, there is absolutely no doubt that climate change is happening and that it is man-made.[6] It is also obvious that climate change is an extremely serious social and ecological phenomenon that is already impacting human civilization and will continue to do so in an exacerbated manner in the future, especially if nothing more is done about it. Furthermore, it cannot be doubted that capitalism has something important to do with climate change. Those libertarian defenders of capitalism who downplay, or even deny, these facts are quite misguided. But one cannot be politically serious about mitigating climate change if one is at the same time calling for the destruction of the only practicable economic system the world has right now, and one is not intellectually honest if one thinks capitalism is inherently and solely responsible for the potential environmental crisis we are facing.

Is there room for capitalism in a green future?

How much does capitalism have to do with climate change? In *what way* exactly are the two related? Is it simply the profit motive, or 'corporate greed,' that is to blame? What about the so-called capitalist mantra of endless growth, which critics say is in tension with our resource-limited and spatially finite planet? Moreover, is capitalism really the only, or the single most important, cause of climate change? Did non-capitalist but heavily industrialized alternatives such as the Soviet Union avoid pollution, or at least engage in it to a much lesser extent than today's capitalist societies do? Is climate change perhaps inherent to the very process of industrial economic development (be it capitalist or socialist), such that only reducing humanity's material standard of living is the 'true' – politically hopelessly unviable – solution, as the proponents of the degrowth movement would have it? Is climate change inherent in capitalism to such an extent that even a post-industrial capitalist economy with a strong regulatory state will inevitably lead to it, or not do enough in fighting against it? These issues have to be navigated carefully.

The profit-motive objection

Take, first, the set of issues that are said to be related specifically to capitalism. Let us start with the profit motive. To some, the fact that in capitalism producers produce not in order to help people (or society more general) but to take home a personal profit is one key reason for pollution and environmental degradation. They claim that capitalism makes people so selfish that they stop caring about the environment and other people around themselves. Remove capitalism, and this selfish profit-seeking orientation is gone, thus the environment is saved.

This charge, as it stands, is quite unconvincing. Within or outside capitalism, people who have produced for the market have always primarily done so in order to help themselves. Market participants today, 500 years ago, or 3,000 years ago have been buying, selling, and producing goods and services *in exchange for something that benefits them*, not out of the goodness of their hearts. The profit motive – i.e. seeking gains in exchange – has been a staple of markets and trade throughout history; it is not unique to capitalism. Therefore, removing the profit motive does not only get rid of capitalism but of trade in general, which is ostensibly not something we want to do. (As an aside, we have seen in Chapter 5 that high levels of market integration and the presence of market competition seem to make people *less selfish* and *more trusting* of others, a point missed by the critics.)

But the problem with the above anti-capitalist argument is deeper than that. If we follow the critics' advice and get rid either of capitalism or trade more generally, then some other system of production and exchange will have to take over in their stead. What is that system going to look like? It presumably will not be Soviet-style central planning, which both defenders and critics of capitalism despise. But if not that, what then? It is wholly unconvincing to simply state something like 'Well, people should just produce for the good of society and they should consume with the general welfare in mind.'

There are at least three kinds of problems with such a statement. First, we do not know what exactly the 'good of society' is. Are cars part of the 'good society?' Is full-fat chocolate part of the 'good society?' What exactly is – production-wise – a 'good society,' apart from the easy to enumerate generalities like having adequate sustenance, basic freedoms, overall happiness, and so on?

Second, if we do not know what exactly a 'good society' is, a mechanism will have to exist so that people can decide for themselves and aggregate their decisions on what shall be produced. But, we do not know what the decision mechanism would (or should) be like in a modern non-market economic system. Should people just vote every day on what they would like to see produced? Vote how and where? In the stores themselves, each day? But then how will people's unlimited desires be rationed and curtailed? Currently, markets, prices, and money are one of the main decision mechanisms that take care both of the voting and of the rationing problem. What is the alternative to such market mechanisms, apart from central planning and state rationing?

Lastly, we do not know how to *motivate* people to 'produce for the good of society' or to 'consume with the general welfare in mind.' Even if we knew what the 'good of society' is or how people would decide on that important topic, we would still have to provide the incentives that would lead people to behave in the stipulated manner. Absent old-fashioned central planning and state coercion, and absent markets and trade, who or what will provide the necessary incentives? Here, then, if the regress into subsistence farming is avoided, we are back to some kind of profit motive and selfish exchange.

Now, a sophisticated critic of capitalism has a much more plausible argument than the simplistic and misguided profit-motive critique. They would say that it is not so much the profit motive that is to blame but rather the *particular way* in which profit is currently pursued by capitalist firms. That is, the fact that workers in a firm have no say over how much, what, and where to invest the firm's capital is the real problem. In a different variety of capitalism (or 'market socialism'), where workers are just as empowered to make profit-seeking business decisions as the owner of the firm is, climate change could be avoided. That is so, presumably, either because workers are simply more virtuous and responsible than owners (which is a silly stipulation) or because workers typically have to live in the vicinity of the firm, while owners can be far removed from the location. Workers, thus, have a stronger personal stake in what happens to the surrounding environment than owners, and so workers will take that into account when making business decisions. For example, the owner might decide that polluting a nearby river carries no further personal costs for him and so sees such a decision as profitable. The workers, on the other hand, live directly by the river and so – out of their own self-interest – will not see the decision as beneficial for them. If they have voice, they are more likely than the absent owner not to make the polluting decision, even though both are driven in their calculations by the profit motive.

There is important truth to this argument. However, the fundamental problem seems to me to persist. The problem is that oftentimes a single firm's business decision to pollute or not to pollute has a negligible overall impact on the surrounding environment. In a big city, for example, one worker-owned factory can decide to emit noxious gases (for the sake of profit) without really significantly decreasing the overall quality of air in the city. The city is vast and thus a single firm's pollution gets dispersed into this vastness quite quickly. In this example, it does not really matter whether the actor making the decision is an individual owner of the firm or a collective of workers employed in the firm. Insofar as they are both driven in their decision by the prospect of personal gain, both will (rationally) ignore the costs of pollution as they are so dispersed among the whole population of the city that each employee simply does not feel them.

In short, air pollution is a collective action problem that can persist whether one owner or a group of workers are making the decision.

Therefore, it is completely fair to say that one aspect of capitalism (markets) fails to spontaneously take into account negative externalities and thus contributes to climate change. However, it also has to be emphasized that this is not likely to be solved merely by reordering the ownership structure of firms, as some critics hope. Moreover, markets are not the only institution that has trouble with negative externalities created by collective action problems. So, too, can a socialist central plan – or individual citizens going about their daily lives outside the market – face the same trouble. If socialist planners – or individual citizens at a large democratic assembly – do not care about the environment (perhaps because they personally do not bear the costs, or because they judge the construction of an enormous army to be more important than pollution, or even because they simply want to industrialize no matter the cost in order to see the people's material standards of living improve), there will be lots of pollution even without any markets being involved. In this sense, there is nothing *particularly special* about capitalism, capitalist owners, or the profit motive when it comes to pollution, environmental degradation, and climate change.

The endless-growth objection

Turn, now, to the endless-growth charge. The fact is, the anti-capitalist critics say, that capitalist economies are constantly or at least typically growing (in GDP per capita terms). Moreover, they say, even when that is not happening (due to a recession or a period of stagnation), capitalism's defenders will anxiously worry about this vanishing of growth, and they will immediately and loudly clamour for business as usual and re-igniting growth. So in one way or another, capitalism embodies the mantra of never-ending growth. The troubles with this, the critics say, are several.

First, our planet is finite, so the mantra of endless growth is simply unsustainable. Either the planet's valuable resources which are used up in production will dry up at one point, or – if this is somehow solved – we will simply run out of space on the planet because of all the stuff that gets produced as a result of constant growth.

Second, even if these two scenarios (resources drying up and space running out) were somehow averted, endless growth is still going to bump up against the most fundamental problem. That is, if we keep producing more and more, emissions stemming from the production and transportation of goods are going to be increasing more and more. Given that humanity has to significantly and quickly *reduce* emissions if very dangerous levels of climate change are to be avoided, how can one defend the mantra of endless growth? Endless growth means endless increases in emissions or, barring that, it is at least dangerously delaying the reduction in emission we should have been committing to already years ago.

It is true that the social structures of capitalism make constant, self-sustaining economic growth very likely, and in this sense capitalism really does embody the mantra of endless growth. However, we should not ignore the fact that most people in capitalism are not *forced* to engage in, or approve of, growth-enhancing economic behaviour. Instead, most people *like* and *want* endless growth, especially if we judge what they want not by what they nobly proclaim but more by what they realistically do, i.e. how they actually behave in their daily lives. And how do they behave? Typically, in ways that indicate that they approve of growth or at least do not want it to end. This should not be surprising. Economic growth typically increases the purchasing power of people (even poor people) through the creation of cheaper goods, increased wages, increased government spending and social transfers, higher stock prices, and so on, so it should come as no shock that people, even ordinary people, want growth.

So, it is not that capitalism *deterministically forces* people to behave such that endless growth happens. (Likewise, it is not solely the elite 1% or richest 0.01% of people in a society who want year-on-year growth and who force the other 99% of the population against their will to follow the dictates of the rich.) Ordinary people buy stocks, punish politicians who presided over a shrinking economy, are scared of a recession, hope for growth to continue, are angry and sometimes even willing to take to the streets when a period of wage stagnation sets in, and they are satisfied when pensions increase. The dynamic of never-ending growth is behind all of that.

None of this, of course, gets the mantra of endless growth off the hook as far as long-term unsustainability concerned. It could still be the case that the very thing people desire – in our case, economic growth – at the same time leads to undesirable, bad, unsustainable consequences. Desires can have terrible, undesired effects. So, does endless growth lead to bad outcomes?

The worry about natural resources running out is in principle completely justified. If growth is endless but resources that fuel growth are not, this will be a problem. Nevertheless, even here an important caveat is in order. As a matter of logic, economic growth does not necessarily mean growth in *material* production. Service economies especially can grow without producing more *physical stuff* and without using up more *physical* resources. If the whole world soon moved to a post-industrial service economy, this could mean that worries about limited resources and limited space are not necessarily well-founded. And, indeed, some claim there is actual evidence demonstrating that parts of the modern economy are already dematerializing. Dematerialization – or decoupling – of the economy means that continuing economic growth is no longer accompanied by the increased use of resources. This dynamic can either be absolute, meaning that the total quantity of resources used up in production is decreasing (even though GDP is growing), or relative, meaning that the total quantity of resources used up in production is increasing at a slower rate than GDP is increasing.

In *More from Less*, for instance, Andrew McAfee presents evidence for both absolute and relative dematerialization of the US economy. He shows that the US consumption of certain metals, such as aluminium, copper, and gold, has reached a peak a few decades ago and has since been declining (even though US GDP has increased tremendously during this time).[7] This is absolute demateri-alization. He also points out that energy consumption has been increasing at a much slower pace than GDP already since the 1970s and 1980s; in recent decades, energy consumption has even flat-lined while the US economy is still rapidly growing.[8] This is relative dematerialization.

This is an important and suggestive observation that should somewhat reduce our worries about the inherent limits to endless growth. It shows that the claim that growth *inevitably, necessarily* bumps up against natural limits does not really hold. Nevertheless, McAfee only deals with the US economy, and he only pre-sents evidence for certain materials. Broader studies looking at the world econ-omy are less optimistic.

One recent study found that the production of eight out of 13 minerals im-portant for industrial production has 'grown faster than world GDP. Rather than decline, the growth in extrication of most minerals accelerated from the 1990s onwards.'[9] This does not mean dematerialization is impossible (to the contrary, the study itself presents evidence for relative dematerialization of several min-erals, and even a few pieces of evidence for absolute dematerialization). It does, however, suggest that at least presently – and in world context, outside the most developed countries – significant dematerialization is not yet on the table.

But this is just one narrow study. Much more important in this respect are findings from a systematic review of almost 1,000 individual studies on both absolute and relative decoupling of GDP from resource materials and emissions. The review finds that

> *relative decoupling is frequent for material use* as well as GHG [i.e. greenhouse gases] and CO2 emissions but not for useful exergy, a quality-based meas-ure of energy use. … *Examples of absolute long-term decoupling are rare* ….[10]

Therefore, the endless-growth objection seems to be, at least for now, a reason-able objection. We are still producing more output with more (not less) input, although many – even most – of the key inputs are actually increasing at a dimin-ishing rate. This is something, but it is not nearly enough.

The relationship between economic development and pollution

The second worry about endless growth I mentioned above has to do with emissions. The idea is that if growth is never-ending, so too will greenhouse emissions never stop accumulating. What should we think about that?

Those who are optimistic that economic development will not necessarily, or even likely, lead to catastrophic climate change usually point to a hypotheti-cal relationship between economic development and environmental degradation called the Environmental Kuznets Curve (EKC). EKC is graphically represented as a simple inverted-U curve.[11] EKC hypothesizes that, up to a certain point, economic development clearly and strongly harms the environment, with both development and harm increasing monotonically at first and possibly for a long time. Then, at middling levels of development, environmental degradation is supposed to peak, such that further economic development will ostensibly go hand in hand with a *reduction* of harm to the environment. If this hypothetical absolute decoupling of emissions from further economic growth is true, capitalism and development will not necessarily (or even likely) destroy the planet, at least not over the long term. Of course, it is also possible that even if the EKC really exists, its actual height and slope are such that the reduction in emissions at higher levels of development is too slow to mitigate dangerous or even catastrophic levels of climate change; I return to this point later on.

So is the EKC a reality? There is some suggestive evidence for it. Sulphur dioxide (SO_2), for instance, is one important anthropogenic air pollutant, and its annual emissions seem to follow an inverted-U pattern as countries develop economically. In the two currently most economically developed regions of the world, where modern development first originated – Europe and North America – SO_2 pollution has been steadily growing between the 19th and late 20th century. But pollution then peaked around 1970–1980 (at tens of millions of tonnes), and every decade since that point, SO_2 emissions have been sharply dropping in these regions. Already in 2004, European SO_2 emissions have dropped to the level they were at in the 1930s.[12]

Another measure of pollution that seems to be in line with EKC is the rate of deaths caused by outdoor air pollution. In 2019, most low-income countries had relatively low death rates, around 20–60 per 100,000 individuals. Then, there were many middle-income countries with death rates much higher, exceeding 60–80/100,000. At the same time, the rates for almost all high-income countries were below or well below 20/100,000. Moreover, if we look at how death rates changed *over time*, it is fairly clear that as the poorer countries have grown richer between 1990 and 2019 their death rates have also increased, while the death rates of middle-income countries have started stabilizing as they were getting wealthier in this same period. In those countries that were already at the upper-middle income level in the 1990s and then moved further ahead to high-income status in the following decades, rates have been notably declining as their wealth grew. The same, of course, is true for countries there already achieved high-income status in the 1990s.

But, we have to be careful in how we deal with these simple data.

First, the presented figures for SO_2 emissions do not reflect the fact that an important part of European and North American production has been shifted overseas since the flourishing of globalization in 1990s and early 2000s. One could speculate that emissions did not really decline. They just got shifted around to a different geographical location. We should note, however, that the single most important source of European SO_2 emissions reduction was the *energy* sector, not manufacturing and production.[13] And given how severe the drop in emissions was – from more than 70 million tonnes of SO_2 in 1980 to less than 20 million tonnes in 2010 – globalization cannot be the main story here.

Second, although both the decline in SO_2 pollution and the decline of overall air pollution death rates are, from a certain point onward, correlated with high GDP per capita, *economic development itself* is not necessarily the cause of the decline. For instance, both North America and Europe have been busy implementing myriad environmental regulations since the 1970s and 1980s. So, it was most likely regulation, not development itself, that was a key proximal cause of environmental improvement.[14]

Of course, it could plausibly be claimed that richer countries are – *because they are richer* – more motivated and more capable of implementing such regulations than poorer countries, so development can still be pointed to as a contributing, ultimate cause of emissions reduction; but, this is an important caveat to the optimistic EKC story. Another caveat is that high-income countries can afford, and usually possess, much better healthcare systems and treatments that can mitigate the negative health effects of pollution. This means that they would have driven down pollution death rates, at least to an extent, *even if no improvement in air pollution was achieved*. In short, simple statistical data and correlations do not allow us to infer what precisely caused the reduction in SO_2 pollution, and whether the pollution death rate reduction reflects cleaner air or better healthcare.

Third, SO_2 is only one pollutant. What about CO_2? Does it show promising signs of following the EKC shape? Looking solely at the raw numbers for Europe and North America, it is again quite clear that annual CO_2 emissions *have indeed been falling* in recent decades both in absolute terms and per capita although much less spectacularly than SO_2 emissions.[15] Annual CO_2 emissions started monotonically climbing since the 18th century in both Europe and North America as the two regions treaded the path of modern economic development. However, Europe then peaked at the end of 1980s, while North America did so in 2007. Since then, both have reduced their annual CO_2 emissions. Importantly, this trend holds even if we include *outsourced CO_2 emissions* into the calculation, i.e. if we look at consumption – instead of production-based emissions.[16] An EKC pattern can also be seen when consumption-based emissions of individual European countries, Canada, and the US are plotted against their GDP growth since 1990. A large majority of them have been generating less CO_2 emissions per year as they have grown more and more developed.[17]

Overall, however, more sophisticated statistical research (which also includes other regions, not just Europe and North America) has come to quite mixed findings on the existence of a CO_2 EKC. Some studies find evidence for it, others against it.[18] One 2019 comprehensive literature review thus concluded that, currently, 'there is no consensus regarding the existence or shape of EKC, i.e. for any geographical context, researchers can come up with different and opposing set of results.'[19] Also noteworthy is the fact that the recent decline in annual CO_2 emissions in most European countries has not really started happening already at middling levels of development, as is postulated by the classic inverted-U EKC shape. Instead, the peak in emissions seems to have happened further on at quite high levels of economic development, and it then (slowly) started declining only at even higher levels of development.[20] This means that, if the EKC exists, it does not seem to look as simple and symmetrical as an inverted U.

Fourth and finally, even if the most developed countries in the world are experiencing the EKC — and most recent evidence suggests this is the case at least in a subset of developed economies —, the decline in emissions is not nearly enough, at least at the current rate, to mitigate dangerous levels of climate change.[21] This is so because it is much too slow and also because it is only happening in the most developed countries in the world, i.e. in a tiny sliver of the world. Emissions in Asia are rapidly *growing* and have not yet peaked. Africa is at such low levels of development that the biggest increase in African emissions is yet to come, while their potential EKC peak seems to be decades away. As one team of researchers puts it, '18 [developed] countries ... have reduced CO_2 emissions in the last decade ... This observed absolute decoupling, however, falls short from the massive decoupling required to achieve agreed climate targets.'[22] They rightly add, though, that

> rare occurrence of absolute decoupling in the past does not represent proof that it cannot become more common in the future — and perhaps intensifying the policies implemented in 18 peak-and-decline countries could yield sufficient decoupling of GDP and GHG emissions to achieve climate targets.[23]

To conclude, even though economic development — and capitalism as the key source of development today — are not to necessarily monotonically related to environmental harm, one should most certainly not pin one's hopes with regards to climate change mitigation simply on development doing its thing. Much more has to be done, and much more can be done through environmental regulations that strive to fix market failures and the more general collective action problems stemming from negative environmental externalities. These should be, as they already have been to an extent, internalized with the help of carbon taxes. Through targeted research and development, investments, and regulation, governments should help the economy and society as a whole transition away from using fossil fuels for energy towards renewables and nuclear. However, capitalism and economic development need not, and should not, be destroyed in the process.

How plausible is it that the world would actually mitigate catastrophic climate change by 2100 if more deliberate action is taken? A recent *Nature* analysis claims that if all conditional and unconditional pledges that countries have made in the past are fully implemented as per their schedule, then global warming can be kept 'just below 2 degrees Celsius' by 2100 compared to pre-industrial times.[24] In such a future, the frequency and severity of extreme weather would certainly both increase. Sea levels would rise as well. However, catastrophic and even just severe consequences of warming would be avoided.[25] Projections show that, under this scenario, living standards in 2100 would be much higher – not lower – than today.[26]

The new *Nature* analysis underscores that the below -2°C scenario is only likely *if* the pledges are kept. This is not a given, but at the same time it is in principle possible. It is true, though, that for warming to be limited to an even lower, more optimal 1.5°C, existing pledges are not nearly enough. For such a future scenario much more aggressive action has to be taken, and it has to be taken within the present decade. As the analysis puts it,

> Our results provide a reason to be optimistic: warming could be limited to 2°C or just below, if the pledges on the table are implemented in full and on time. Peaking of global GHG emissions could be achieved this decade. But our results also provide a sobering assessment of how far current pledges are from limiting warming to 1.5°C.[27]

The future is uncertain. But neither of the mentioned two scenarios is impossible, and neither of them requires the destruction of capitalism. With deliberate policies and measures, severe and catastrophic climate change can still be averted.

Virtues and vices of the modern economy

As this concluding chapter and all the preceding chapters in the book have hopefully shown, capitalism and its various social correlates are incredibly complex and nuanced phenomena not tailored for polarized, partisan political discussion. It should not be surprising, then, that Karl Marx – capitalism's most illustrious and rhetorically vociferous critic – overemphasized the faults borne by the capitalist mode of production and at the same time dramatically underemphasized its contribution to the material well-being of humanity (especially the part of humanity *outside* the ruling class). To this day, many of his anti-capitalist followers have at least to an extent been repeating the same mistake. So, too, have of course defenders of capitalism tended to commit the reverse mistake of overemphasizing capitalism's virtues and downplaying its vices. But, there have also been invaluable intellectual voices and theoretical resources on both sides that have enabled us to break through the polarized noise and assess capitalism in all its real-life complexity as realists.

Jon Elster, once the leading light of analytical Marxism, begins his magisterial 1985 book *Making Sense of Marx* with one of Marx's most beautiful, yet not all that well-known, quotes that still lingers in my mind today. The quote goes as follows:

> In our day, everything seems pregnant with its contrary. Machinery gifted with the wonderful power of shortening and fructifying human labour, we behold starving and overworking it. The new-fangled sources

of wealth, by some weird spell, are turned into sources of want. The victories of art seem bought by the loss of character. At the same pace that mankind masters nature, man seems to become enslaved to other men or to his own infamy. Even the pure light of science seems unable to shine but on the dark background of ignorance. All our invention and progress seem to result in endowing material forces with intellectual life, and in stultifying human life into a material force. This antagonism between modern industry and science on the one hand, modern misery and dissolution on the other hand; this antagonism between the productive powers and the social relations of our epoch is a fact, palpable, overwhelming, and not to be controverted.[28]

As a good Hegelian, Marx could not help himself but to say that capitalism at virtually every turn *inherently* generates *immense* 'contradictions,' i.e. states of affairs that are at the same time opposite to themselves. This might sound interesting and seductive even, but in reality it is much too hyperbolic and ungrounded if taken literally. Real 'contradictions' do not exist, and even Marx himself regularly broke from Hegel on this point, instead claiming only that – for instance – certain states of social affairs can unintendedly backfire and undermine themselves (in the sense of game-theoretic social dilemmas, wherein individual rationality leads to collective irrationality).[29] It was the main intention of my book to show that, Hegelian mysticism aside, Marx was plainly correct that capitalism carries with it both virtues and vices, both tendencies and countertendencies, both intended actions and unintended social outcomes – capitalism presents us with certain 'contradictions,' as it were.

We have seen that capitalism reduces exploitation experienced by workers but also at the same time keeps a degree of exploitation in place and is unable to remove it completely. Capitalism most definitely helps reduce poverty, but at the same time it can also contribute to increases in inequality. It unleashes a massive dynamic of job-creation but also pulls the employment rug from underneath some workers. The modern economy overall strongly promotes human pro-sociality but in certain aspects does nothing for it or even reduces it somewhat. Capitalism contributes to environmental degradation, especially through industrial production, but it also presents us at least with the possibility of having a highly economically developed society that harms the environment less and less the more it develops. All this is, to put it in Marx's words, an epochal 'fact, palpable, overwhelming, and not to be controverted.'

Notes

1 Milanović (2021).
2 Smith (2021).
3 Dedić (2021); Parrique (2021a; 2021b).
4 Monbiot (2021); Trotskyist Fraction – Fourth International (2019).
5 Klein (2015).

6   IPCC (2022).
7   McAfee (2019), Chapter 5.
8   Ibid.
9   Hannesson (2021).
10   Haberl et al. (2020). Emphases added.
11   Stern (1998).
12   Vestreng et al. (2007).
13   Ibid., 3670.
14   See Stern (2017).
15   Ritchie and Roser (2020).
16   Ritchie (2019).
17   Ritchie and Roser (2020).
18   Stern (2017); Shahbaz and Sinha (2019).
19   Shahbaz and Sinha (2019).
20   Ritchie and Roser (2020).
21   For evidence of CO2 peak-and-decline see Le Quéré et al. (2019).
22   Ibid.
23   Ibid.
24   Meinshausen et al. (2022, 304).
25   Stone (2021).
26   Ibid.
27   Meinshausen et al. (2022, 308).
28   Elster (1985).
29   For more on this, see Elster (1985, 43–48).

References

Dedić, Jasminka. 2021. 'A Response to Branko Milanović: "Degrowth: Solving the Impasse by Magical Thinking",' *Global Policy*, March 4. Accessible via: https://www.globalpolicyjournal.com/blog/04/03/2021/response-branko-milanovics-degrowth-solving-impasse-magical-thinking/.

Elster, Jon. 1985. *Making Sense of Marx*. Cambridge: Cambridge University Press.

Haberl, Helmut, Wiedenhofer, Dominik, Virág, Doris, Kalt, Gerald, Plank, Barbara, Brockway, Paul, Fishman, Tomer, Hausknost, Daniel, Krausmann, Fridolin, and Bartholomäus Leon-Gruchalski. 2020. 'A Systematic Review of the Evidence on Decoupling of GDP, Resource Use and GHG Emissions, Part II: Synthesizing the Insights.' *Environmental Research Letters* 15, no. 6. Accessible via: https://iopscience.iop.org/article/10.1088/1748-9326/ab842a/.

Hannesson, Rögnvaldur. 2021. 'Are We Seeing Dematerialization of World GDP?' *Biophysical Economics and Sustainability* 6, no. 4. Accessible via: https://link.springer.com/article/10.1007/s41247-021-00086-7/.

IPCC 2022. *Climate Change 2022. Impacts, Adaptation and Vulnerability. Summary for Policymakers*. Accessible via: https://report.ipcc.ch/ar6wg2/pdf/IPCC_AR6_WGII_FinalDraft_FullReport.pdf/.

Klein, Naomi. 2015. *This Changes Everything: Capitalism vs. The Climate*. London: Simon & Schuster.

Le Quéré, Corinne, Korsbakken, Jan Ivar, Wilson, Charlie, Tosun, Jale, Andrew, Robbie, Andres, Robert J., Canadell Josep G., Jordan, Andrew, Peters, Glen P., and Detlef P. van Vuuren. 2019. 'Drivers of Declining CO2 in 18 Developed Economies,' *Nature Climate Change* 9, no. 3, 213–217.

McAfee, Andrew. 2019. *More from Less: The Surprising Story of How We Learned to Prosper Using Fewer Resources – and What Happens Next*. London: Scribner.

Meinshausen, Malte, Lewis, Jared, McGlade, Christophe, Gütschow, Johannes, Nicholls, Zebedee, Burdon, Rebecca, Cozzi, Laura, and Bernd Hackmann. 2022. 'Realization of Paris Agreement Pledges May Limit Warming Just Below 2°C,' *Nature* 604, 304–309.

Milanović, Branko. 2021. 'Degrowth: Solving the Impasse by Magical Thinking,' *GlobalInequality*, February 20. Accessible via: http://glineq.blogspot.com/2021/02/degrowth-solving-impasse-by-magical.html/.

Monbiot, George. 2021. 'Capitalism is Killing the Planet – It's Time to Stop Buying into Our Own Destruction,' *The Guardian*, October 30. Accessible via: https://www.theguardian.com/environment/2021/oct/30/capitalism-is-killing-the-planet-its-time-to-stop-buying-into-our-own-destruction/.

Parrique, Timothée. 2021a. 'A Response to Branko Milanović: The Magic of Degrowth,' Personal website, February 25. Accessible via: https://timotheeparrique.com/a-response-to-branko-milanovic-the-magic-of-degrowth/.

Parrique, Timothée. 2021b. 'A Response to Noah Smith: Is Degrowth Bad Economics?' Personal website, December 4. Accessible via: https://timotheeparrique.com/a-response-to-noah-smith-is-degrowth-bad-economics/.

Ritchie, Hannah. 2019. 'How Do CO2 Emissions Compare When We Adjust for Trade?' *Our World in Data*. Accessible via: https://ourworldindata.org/consumption-based-co2/.

Ritchie, Hannah, and Max Roser. 2020. 'CO2 and Greenhouse Gas Emissions,' *Our World in Data*. Accessible via: https://ourworldindata.org/co2-emissions/.

Shahbaz, Muhammad, and Avik Sinha. 2019. 'Environmental Kuznets Curve for CO2 Emissions: A Literature Survey,' *Journal of Economic Studies* 46, no. 1, 106–168.

Smith, Noah. 2021. 'People are Realizing that Degrowth is Bad,' *Noahpinion*, September 6. Accessible via: https://noahpinion.substack.com/p/people-are-realizing-that-degrowth?utm_source=url&s=r/.

Stern, David I. 1998. 'Progress on the Environmental Kuznets Curve?' *Environment and Development Economics* 3, no. 2, 173–196.

Stern, David I. 2017. 'The Environmental Kuznets Curve After 25 Years,' *Journal of Bioeconomics* 19, 7–28.

Stone, Madeleine. 2021. '5 Possible Climate Futures – From the Optimistic to the Strange,' *National Geographic*, August 18. Accessible via: https://www.nationalgeographic.com/environment/article/5-possible-climate-futures-from-the-optimistic-to-the-strange/.

Trotskyist Fraction – Fourth International. 2019. 'Capitalism is Destroying the Planet – Let's Destroy Capitalism!' *Left Voice*, September 15. Accessible via: https://www.leftvoice.org/capitalism-is-destroying-the-planet-lets-destroy-capitalism/.

Vestreng, Vigdis, Myhre, Gunnar, Fagerli, Hilde, Reis, Stefan, and Leonor Tarrason. 2007. 'Twenty-five Years of Continuous Sulphur Dioxide Emission Reduction in Europe,' *Atmospheric Chemistry and Physics* 7, 3663–3681.

INDEX

Note: *Italic* page numbers refer to figures and page numbers followed by "n" denote endnotes.

Keys to the Divine Kingdom
Lessons on Mystical Aspects of Man and Science

By Shaykh Muhammad Hisham Kabbani

ISBN: 1-930409-28-1

Library of Congress Cataloging-in-Publication Data

Kabbani, Shaykh Muhammad Hisham.
   Keys to the divine kingdom : lessons on mystical aspects of man and science / by Shaykh Muhammad Hisham Kabbani.
        p. cm.
   ISBN 1-930409-28-1
   1. Islam and science.   2. Sufism.   I. Title.
   BP190.5.S3K3 2005
   297.4--dc22   2005003109

Published and Distributed by:
Islamic Supreme Council of America
17195 Silver Parkway, #201
Fenton, MI 48430 USA
Tel: (888) 278-6624 Fax: (810) 815-0518
Email: staff@islamicsupremecouncil.org
Web: http://www.islamicsupremecouncil.org

Artwork and Design by Christina Matsoukis
About the Cover - The cover is an unique adaptation of an original piece called "Heaven" created in 2000. It has been specially redesigned just for this purpose and is protected property of the designer.

Keys to the Divine Kingdom
Lessons on Mystical Aspects of Man and Science

By Shaykh Muhammad Hisham Kabbani

Islamic Supreme Council of America

I do not want gifts from you.
I want you ready for the gifts I give.

Rumi

Table of Contents

Editor's Notes

This book is specifically designed for laypersons and other non-Muslim readers. As such, we have often replaced Arabic terminology with English translations, except in instances where Arabic terms are crucial to the tone and substance of the text. In such instances, we have included transliterations or footnoted explanations. A glossary is also provided.

As the source material is an oral transmission, its language was revised for a written format, and scientific and religious references have been added where needed; however, we have tried our best to retain the essence of the author's original talks. We ask the reader's forgiveness for any omissions in this final text.

For those who are familiar with Arabic and Islamic teachings, we apologize for the vastly simplified transliterations. Our experience is that unfamiliar symbols and diacritical marks make for difficult reading by laypersons; as such, please indulge this compromise between accuracy and accessibility.

Holy Traditions of Prophet Muhammad appear without full chains of transmission, but are firmly established and should be familiar to and immediately accepted on sight by the vast majority of Muslim readers, and certainly by religious scholars.

Where gender-specific pronouns such as "he" and "him" are applied in a general sense, it has been solely for the flow of text, and no offense is intended to women readers.

Universally recognized symbols:

The following Arabic symbols connote sacredness and are universally recognized by Muslims. This explanation honors Muslim sensibilities; however, these symbols do not appear throughout the text, and readers may elect to pronounce them or not.

The symbol ﷾ represents *subhanahu wa ta'ala,* a high form of praise reserved for God alone, which is customarily recited after reading or pronouncing the common name "Allah" and any of the 99 Islamic names of God.

The symbol ﷺ represents *sall-allahu alayhi was sallam* (God's blessings and greetings of peace be upon the Prophet), which is customarily recited after reading or pronouncing the holy name of Prophet Muhammad.

The symbol ﷵ represents *alayhis-salam* (peace be upon him/her), which is customarily recited after reading or pronouncing the sanctified names of prophets, Prophet Muhammad's family members, and the angels.

The symbol ﵌ represents *radi-allahu anh* (may God be pleased with him/her), which is customarily recited after reading or pronouncing the holy names of Prophet Muhammad's companions.

The symbol قٌ represents *qaddas-allahu sirrah* (may God sanctify his or her secret), which is customarily recited after reading or pronouncing the name of a saint.

If your students do not know how to swim,
Being still children,
You give them a vessel that they can ride on
From the shore of darkness to the shore of safety,
From the shore of difficulties to the shore of peacefulness,
From the shore of hatred to the shore of love,
From the shore of anarchy to the shore of harmony,
From the shore of terrorism and violence to the shore of peacefulness and
satisfaction.
If you bring them there,
it will be a heaven,
a paradise for them.
And this is the responsibility of saints.

Shaykh Muhammad Hisham Kabbani

Biography

Shaykh Muhammad Hisham Kabbani is committed to opening the doors of the spiritual knowledge of Islam to the West. This book is a compilation of his most recent talks and offers an inside look into the world of Sufism.

A prominent scholar of mainstream, traditional Islam, Shaykh Hisham has spent his life spreading the teachings of peace, tolerance, respect, and love that are the message of Islam throughout the world. Here in the United States for the last eleven years, Shaykh Kabbani has continued to disseminate the light and peace of Islam's spiritual dimension to people of every background, ethnicity, race, and belief.

Shaykh Kabbani speaks in a wide variety of situations including interfaith meetings, universities, and conferences around the world. However, his talks are not prepared lectures, but from inspirations of the moment. Consequently, they are always fresh and flavorful.

This is not an introduction to Islam, but will be an introduction to many spiritual aspects of Islam. Sufism, which has a long and respected history, is considered to be the guardian of the "soul of Islam." Without the inner spirit, the outward "body" of Islam becomes unbalanced. The spiritual dimension is the counterbalance of the tenets of Islamic practices. Without the spiritual teachings for balance, any religion tends to become rigid and dogmatic.

The editors of this book are Shaykh Hisham's students, mostly Western converts who are committed to helping Shaykh Hisham disseminate this mystical knowledge to Muslims *and* non-Muslims in the West. Even though most of these talks were given to Muslims, it has been edited in a way which we hope can be appreciated by seekers from any background. God willing, this book will offer the reader some insight into the spiritual vitality of Islam which Shaykh Kabbani transmits. Since he was sent to the U.S. over eleven years ago by his shaykh, he has become a conduit to Muslims and non-Muslims for the knowledge and wisdom of Mawlana Shaykh Muhammad Nazim al-Haqqani, who is a living Master and Saint of the Naqshbandi Sufi Order.

1– The Orientalist

Don't pretend to know something
you haven't experienced.
There's a necessary dying.
And then Jesus is breathing again.
Very little grows on jagged rock.
Be ground.
Be crumbled.
So wildflowers will
Come up where you are.
You've been stony for too many years.
Try something different.
Surrender.

Rumi
"A Necessary Autumn ..."

An orientalist came to Grandshaykh Abdullah[1] ق and said, "I have considered all of the religions — Buddhism, Hinduism, Judaism, Christianity, even Islam. And whatever I ask a question about a religion to satisfy my interest, I find the answer empty—air. Nothing fills me. I have traveled the world to find answers. And whomever I ask, I see that I know more than the person I ask. In my childhood I fell into every kind of wrongdoing you can imagine, but then I felt a yearning for the truth, so I became pious and sincere."

No one could satisfy him, because he was a scholar. Finally, he said, "I am now going to try Islam one last time to see what I can get out of it." So he began to go, traveling from one country to another—Pakistan, India, Middle Eastern countries, all over Europe, asking what he had to do to become Muslim. They told him only the physical obligations, the five pillars: *shahada* (declaration of faith), *salat* (prayer), fasting all of Ramadan, *zakat* (charity), Hajj. And on top of all of that—circumcision!

---

1 Grandshaykh Abdullah al-Faizi ad-Daghestani: 39th master in the Naqshbandi Tariqah; he was Mawlana Shaykh Nazim's and Mawlana Shaykh Hisham's shaykh.

He said, "Islam asks so much! Christianity is only asking me to pray on Sunday! You are asking me to pray 5 times a day. Also, I have millions of dollars in my bank account and I am supposed to pay 2.5 percent on that? What is this?"

He studied Islam more and more, and became an expert on it, but still he was not convinced. He said, "I am still holding air—not holding a rope to climb — I need a rope."

Now consider the verse of Qu'ran which says: *"Hold tight to the rope of God"*[2] in this context. In Islamic jurisprudence (*fiqh*), the "extended rope" is Muhammad ﷺ. It is the Prophet ﷺ who takes you to God's Presence.

Finally someone told this man about Grandshaykh Abdullah and Mawlana Shaykh Nazim. He sought them out and traveled to where they were. When he arrived, he addressed them, *"Ya Sayyidi ...."* It is good that he said "Ya Sayyidi." That is respect.

Islam teaches respect. He had learned the discipline of Islam as an orientalist. Unfortunately our people—the Muslims of today—do not know discipline. They do not say to you, "O, sir!" What do they say to you? "Brother." That is the Wahhabi[3] style. Or "Comrade." Saying, *"Verily Muslims are brothers."*[4] Yes, God said "Muslims are brothers," that is true. But there are different levels of brotherhood. Nowadays if a fifteen year old person comes to the mosque and sees an elderly person of 70, 80, or 90 years, he will still say to him "Hi, brother" or *"As-salaam alaykum brother."* This is not discipline, nor respect. He should say "My elder."

The Knowledge of Papers and the Knowledge of Taste

We have to differentiate between the Knowledge of Papers and the Knowledge of Taste.[5] The Knowledge of Papers is completely different from the Knowledge of Taste. The knowledge of taste comes through inspiration to the heart. First, you taste it; then begin to speak about it outwardly.

2 3:103.
3 Wahhabism is a sect of Islam that repudiates traditional Islam and declares that all non-Muslims and Muslims who are not Wahhabis are unbelievers.
4 49:10.
5 Respectively *ilm al-awraaq* and *ilm al-adhwaaq* in Arabic.

There are people to whom God sends taste to their hearts, and it comes out on their tongues. This comes with the blessing of *Sayyidina* Muhammad ﷺ, because they are from his grandchildren or saints to whom God is sending to their hearts.

The Knowledge of Papers is what you read from books, not what you taste. If someone says to you, "I drank water," you have heard the words but you still do not know the sensation of drinking. Is the water bitter or is it sweet? You can not know by reading about water; not until you actually taste it.

The Arrogance of Satan

The Knowledge of Papers is known to Satan. In fact, he knows all the books that God revealed to prophets, but he was cursed because of his disobedience. He has the Knowledge of Letters but fails to understand the meaning behind the letters.

Consider how Satan swallowed soul poison, and be grateful that you taste only the sweetness of being warned.
Rumi
"Four Interrupted Prayers"

Arrogance stopped him from accepting and respecting *Sayyidina* Adam ﷺ. He had so much pride in himself. He was the head of angels. Who can have that position? God gave him an opportunity, and God is saying to us, "Do not be arrogant! Do not be proud of yourself. If I give to you, I am giving to you from My favors. So do not be proud."

But Satan was so proud. He made so many prayers. According to Islamic tradition he did not leave one hand's span worth of space in the universe without making his prostrations.

However, when God ordered Satan to make a prostration to Adam ﷺ, he refused.[6] Why did God order him to make this prostration of respect? It was for the light of Muhammad ﷺ that God had placed in the forehead of Adam ﷺ. This light of Muhammad moved from generation to generation, from face to face, until the Prophet ﷺ was born.

Satan refused to make the prostration. Arrogance prevented him from having any respect for Adam. "How am I going to give respect to him? You created me from

---

6 Prostration: in Arabic, *sajda*. God ordered Satan to make the *Sajdat al-ihtiraam*, prostration of deference to show acceptance and respect, not *sajdat al- ibaadah*, the prostration of worship, and can only be to God.

fire and him from clay! I am better than him." That was the problem that prevented him from making the prostration. Even though he had made the most worship of the angels, this moment of heedlessness made him fall completely. His pride led him to be veiled—not seeing the truth—and he fell down.

The Prophet Adam ﷺ also fell in one second of heedlessness. But the difference was that Adam ﷺ asked for forgiveness and intercession[7] by the name of *Sayyidina* Muhammad ﷺ. He appealed to the guide, the teacher, the messenger, the way. Satan, however, fell down, and was finished, by failing to appeal for forgiveness and intercession.

When *Sayyidina* Adam ﷺ committed the sin, he knew immediately that he had done something wrong, and he went into prostration, saying "Oh God, for the sake of Muhammad ﷺ forgive me!"

God said, "How do you know about Muhammad?"

Adam said, "I saw written on every door in Paradise the words, 'There is no God but God and Muhammad is His messenger.'[8] That is how I knew that he is Your door."

Man's Knowledge Is but a Drop in the Ocean

This appeal of Adam ﷺ by the name of *Sayyidina* Muhammad ﷺ and its acceptance by God is a clear sign that everyone needs a guide. A servant cannot come with his pride and arrogance and say, "I know everything." Yes, God gave you something and to you it might seem like a limitless ocean, but by comparison with God's or the Prophet's ﷺ knowledge it is only a very small drop from the vast ocean.

Until you see the real ocean you cannot have a relative understanding of what has been opened to you. You do not completely understand if you are at the shore, and have not yet crossed to the other side, seeing in the process the immense knowledge granted by God to be hidden in the hearts of God's special servants.

Be sincere with God, and love Him. When you want to be sincere you have to have love. When you love Him, God will teach you.

The Mantle of Guidance

Adam ﷺ asked God to forgive him for the sake of Muhammad ﷺ. Even though Adam was a prophet, he had to seek forgiveness from God through *Sayyidina* Muhammad ﷺ, the Seal of Messengers. All other prophets also, on Judgment Day, will come to Muhammad ﷺ and ask his intercession so that they and their communities can have forgiveness from God. He will intercede for everyone—he is the door.

The community of Prophet Muhammad ﷺ will also seek intercession from *Sayyidina* Muhammad ﷺ in groups behind their teachers (saints, shaykhs, and leaders). You cannot just go by yourself. You have to be identified by the fragrance you were labeled with in your life—by the color of the star you took as your guide during your life.

Therefore you need a guide. The Prophet ﷺ said, "My Companions are like stars, use any of them as guidance and you will be guided." As the Prophet ﷺ passed on that mantle of guidance to the Companions, so did they pass on the mantle of guidance—they have inheritors who learned from them to guide the community.

The Orientalist meets Grandshaykh

So the orientalist approached Grandshaykh and said, "I am now coming to you because I was told about you." Both Grandshaykh ق Abdullah and Mawlana Shaykh Nazim ق were there. Mawlana Shaykh Nazim waited and Grandshaykh ق asked, "What is your question?"

The orientalist said, "I am not satisfied. I am not finding myself. I want reality. I have studied every religion, including Islam. Any scholar I asked, I felt that I knew more than he—even in details of religion. But I am not satisfied. I can even give speeches about Islam, but I do not feel that I am holding anything except air."

Grandshaykh said, "O my son. You have to know three things in order to be able to understand this reality, so that you can be guided to your satisfaction and contentment."

The Seed

First, if you take a seed from a fruit tree and put it on the shelf, it can stay on that shelf for many years without any life. The seed remains there. It means, whatever you do in your life—anything that happens and wherever you go—you will still be the same—involved in this world. It has remained a seed without any transformation.

But when the time comes to plant that seed, you take it and plant it underground, disconnecting it completely from outward world. You water it for forty days.⁹ It will sprout. Then, once it has sprouted, you will not be able to find that seed again even if you dig—it is gone, transformed into a new life. That tree will grow fruitful, giving benefit, food, and enjoyment to people.

The orientalist was intelligent and he understood what the Shaykh was saying. He was also very arrogant, but now he is being hit hard.

You have to bury your arrogance. When Satan came with arrogance, he was thrown away. Adam ﷺ came with no arrogance, and he was brought in.

There are people who, during their lives, come to a crucial moment—God chooses them and makes them receptive to inspirations and to the world of "witnessing and visions."¹⁰

If you are granted these visions you have to focus them, they cannot be dispersed and out of focus. Try to concentrate that power—sharpen your vision. Focused, the power can heal people. Healers are hidden everywhere.

God chooses saints as healers, but not everyone becomes a saint. You might have permission to lead the *dhikr*¹¹ on behalf of the shaykh, or permission to speak on behalf of the shaykh—but you are not the shaykh.

A healer is someone with power to heal through spiritual means. They are able to heal even from far away—it is one of the six spiritual realities.

---

9 When if you plant a seed, you often do not see the seedling emerge until forty days have passed.

10 *Alam al-mushaahada— the world of witnessing and visions.*

11 *Dhikr:* literally "the remembrance of God;" includes recitations of Qu'ran and the Divine Names of God

A Focused Beam of Light

There is a spiritual reality which saints have of directing their healing power towards someone and affecting them.[12] It is possible to direct that power like a spiritual laser beam, even from America to a person in China. Through this heart communication you can reach and heal someone of his sicknesses. But if that energy is unfocused it has no effect. Like the difference between a focused beam and a diffused beam of light. The focused one travels farther, like a beacon.

Without focus you jump from issue to issue, and people think you are crazy. If you speak from East then West then South then North, people say "Oh! This person is drunk. Take him to a mental hospital. He's handicapped. Treat him." The person knows it is not true, he is not sick, but rather is experiencing different things. Your focus must be increasingly concentrated until it is so sharp that it can focus on one point at a time, until you can run on a "digital" connection rather than an "analog" one. With a "digital" connection you can focus on several points at the same time. Digital is for masters.

You do not have a master's degree, yet, or a Ph.D. You may be experiencing some things, but you need to improve until you attain mastery, then you can have a digital connection.

Masters are able to reach <u>everyone</u> through the power of *Sayyidina* Muhammad ﷺ.

As God said in Holy Qu'ran—*"Know that the Messenger of God is <u>in</u> you."*[13] He did not say "Know that the Messenger of God is <u>with</u> you," Or "<u>among</u> you." This is a reference to the Realities that Masters inherit from Prophet.[14]

The Egg

The orientalist was listening, and he asked, "What do I have to do, then?" Grandshaykh said, "Wait."

12 It is called *Haqiqat at-tawajjuh*: the reality of directing the heart's power to someone
13 49:7.
14 Called the six levels of Reality, they are: *Haqiqat at-tawajjuh*—the Reality of Directing the heart's power to someone; *Haqiqat al-jazbah*—the Reality of Attraction; *Haqiqat al-fayd*— the Reality of Receiving heavenly inspiration; *Haqiqat al-irshaad*—the Reality of Guidance; *Haqiqat at-tawassul*—the Reality of Intercession and *Haqiqat at-tay*—the Reality of Folding space and time.

Then he said, "If you take an egg of a chicken or any other animal, and you put it on the shelf, it stays on the shelf, and it may become rotten if it stays there, because you are not improving it. Improving means to be beneficial to people. If you do not make yourself beneficial, then you are going to go bad at the end—then your life is worthless."

So if you will be an egg under a hen, you are going to find a new life coming to you. That egg stays for twenty-one days in the shell under that hen—not one day more or one day less. It is completely disconnected from the outer world. It is in seclusion like the seed. Then what happens? A new offspring comes.

But this is going to be an offspring of heavenly new life. It has been given heavenly life there. You will be an offshoot of a heavenly light and heavenly life. You will have manifestations of God's Attributes and Names dressed on you when you "hatch" after having been beneficial to people.

Look at Grandshaykh's common sense. He did not argue on religion. He did not say, "No, this is good, this is better, this is no good, this is not bad, Jews are bad, Christians are good, this one is not good, this one is good." No. He gave him common sense to think about.

The Womb

Then Grandshaykh said, "A baby comes from a sperm and an egg. All praise is for God.[15] If we go into science a little bit, just a little bit further. The man produces every time he is with his wife 500 million to 600 million sperm. Of the 600 million sperm, one will attach with an egg.

Women normally produce fewer than ten eggs. Scientists have discovered that the structure of the man's base genome of cells can go up to thirty or forty. Women get 150 more in the egg. Therefore although a man produces many sperm the base genetic material in a sperm is about one-fifth that provided by a woman's egg. Scientists are finding more secrets through genetics. And every base is made out of twenty-three different proteins. And every protein has more than 150 million cells. You see God's Greatness.

---

15 *Subhaan-Allah:* All praise is for God

Next Grandshaykh said that when the mother gets pregnant, the child stays nine months and ten days, disconnected completely from this world—hiding. Maturing, growing, submitting to God—not asking for provisions. God is providing it.

Whoever maintains an awareness of God,[16] becomes dedicated to the path of sincerity, God will make for him an opening (in business, money, wealth, husband, wife, everything), and He will provide for him provisions from every direction, without account.

A child is naturally a pure person. That is why Prophet ﷺ said, "The human being is born on innocence." Innocence means in purity, in Islam. A baby is born into innocence and purity, submitting to God. God is providing for him, even in his mother's womb.

Look at the egg under the hen—it is an egg. There is no connection between the mother and the egg. What is the chick eating? He comes from the yellow, he eats the white. And they say there is no Creator! What is that chick eating?

In the mother's womb, there is a cord that is feeding the child—the child is not even breathing in the womb! And the egg is not connected with the chicken, except through the warmth that the hen is giving it. And if there is no rooster, there is no benefit in that egg. What does the rooster do with the chicken!? Nothing! He just jumps on the head. What is it doing? There is nothing, go and look.

God is giving us a sign. God said in Holy Qu'ran, *"We are going to show them our signs on the horizon."*[17] That means it was knowledge for the future, not for the time that the Prophet ﷺ lived in. The Prophet ﷺ predicted these days of science to Companions. At that time they did not know about the sciences. But today, if you look at the hadith of Prophet ﷺ and the Holy Qu'ran, you see it refers to all of these scientific issues.

So what is the rooster doing? He jumps and taps, producing some kind of hormone inside the chicken. That hormone gives life; it goes in the egg.

---

16 *taqwa*: awareness of God or God-consciousness. The word that the Shaykh uses here is *taqwa*, which is a state of being which one is acutely aware of the presence of God, not wanting to do anything which would not be pleasing to God. Often superficially translated as "fear of God," it does not imply the state of fear as in "dreading the worst," but closer to a sense of awe and reverence.
17 41:53

The seed is dead! It sits on a shelf with no life. They sell them at Home Depot— go buy them. They are in packages, different kinds of seeds—no life! Nothing! But God made their life water—*"We have made from water everything living."*[18] They come to life in water.

Imam Ghazzali and the Fly

For many, many years Imam Ghazzali had the biggest doubts during his life. He was doubting God's Existence, struggling with himself and alternating between belief and disbelief. His knowledge did not benefit him at the beginning. But when God gave him the taste, then it all changed for him.

How did Imam Ghazzali become such a big gnostic? Because of his respect for the Prophet's Birthday. One time he was writing a very important and urgent message to save someone's life in a different city. At that time to send messages you needed horses to carry messages. A black fly landed on the pen he was using—at that time there was no such ink as today—there was saffron[19] and other kinds of ink with nice fragrances.

The black fly came and drank, quenching its thirst. And it came to Imam Ghazzali's mind, "Today is the night of the birthday of Prophet ﷺ—Allah created me from the light of Muhammad ﷺ, and Allah created every creation on Earth from the light of Muhammad ﷺ. That black fly is created from that light also, so I am going to let it drink and quench its thirst for the love of Prophet ﷺ."

And as soon as he did that, Allah opened heavens for him. He was able to see by means of spiritual unveiling everything in front of him in sharp focus. His vision was not spread all over the place—it was digitized. And then an opening came to him, and he wrote *The Revival of Religious Sciences,*[20] which is all about Sufism.

---

18 21:30.
19 *zafraan:* saffron
20 *Ihya uloom ad-din,* known in English as *Revival of the Religious Sciences,* is the masterpiece of Imam Ghazzali, one of the greatest thinkers and theologians of Islam. He reflects on the totality of his studies in *Tasawwuf* (Sufism) and its related components (attainment of the state of *Ihsaan,* perfected character), *tazkiyyah* (purification of the heart), scepticism, philosophy, and spiritual retreat.

Gnostic of Paper or Gnostic of Taste

Then Grandshaykh advised the orientalist, "You have to seclude yourself and meditate in order that you become a gnostic of taste.

Look at the house we are in. When it was first built, it was a dry structure. With decorating, it began to have taste and personality. When you put pictures in it, marble, couches, and decorations, it begins to have taste. Just so, you do not want your body to be a dry frame, devoid of flavor.

Prophet ﷺ said, "To bring happiness to the heart of God's servant is from faith." People need happiness. They need you to make them feel the taste of what is around them. They do not want dry speeches saying, "If you do not pray, you go to hellfire." This is what they are saying today in the mosques.

But God said, *"My Mercy has encompassed everything,"*[21] and "My Mercy overrides My Anger." So you can also say, "If you pray, you go to Paradise." Same meaning!

Bring taste to the hearts of people. Fill them up with something that makes them happy. And become a gnostic of taste—not a lecturer, a gnostic of papers.

Sometimes I give lectures in universities. At one of my lectures there might be 2,000 or 3,000 people present. Many lecturers just read presentations to their audiences, but Mawlana Shaykh never allowed me to read. "No reading. You go there, not preparing anything. If you prepare anything, you will become dry like a lecturer. People will sleep *(imitates snoring)."*

That is what happens! People sleep. Have you not seen people sleeping through lectures? Mawlana said, "No. From our heavenly Support, from our Sources, from Power, we will support your heart. You will see what they need to hear. You are our eyes."

Saints can see through their representatives. Then they send what everyone needs to hear, like a doctor. If you go to a doctor, he will give you the medicine appropriate for your sickness, not someone else's sickness. No. Everyone has a different pain. Everyone in attendance at a lecture has a different way of thinking. You have to reach

---

21 7:156.

their hearts. You reach their hearts when you do not prepare lectures. How is it possible to prepare? If you prepare, it means you prepared something for yourself. Your ego is tied with what you have done … like Satan, proud of his presentation. Even what is prepared might still have benefit as the knowledge of papers. Better to be gnostics of taste and not letters.

So that orientalist immediately said, "Now, I understand and accept Islam. I want to recite the Testimony of Faith *(shahadah)*.

So he accepted Islam. Then Grandshaykh sent him to seclusion, to empty from his heart, audit all of the actions stored there from the many years of his life. When you take information out of computers it is called uploading, is that right? Everything that was inside, he must throw out, and then he must fill himself with heavenly knowledge—yes, emptying his mistakes.

The orientalist became a true gnostic of outer knowledge as well as realities and asceticism—realities are very important—very few people know the realities that he now knew. The knowledge of realities is the most important body of knowledge that gives taste.

Worship Allah as if you are seeing Him, and if you do not see Him then know that He sees you

That is the reality of worshipping God as if you are seeing Him, and if you do not see Him then know that He sees you.[22]

If we understand this advice wisely, it is enough for us for all our lives, to learn how to do well in our way of seeking God, and in our dealings with our families and children. If the advice enters from one ear and exits from the other, then we have a problem. This cassette recorder records everything, including our breaths.

So why can we not record with the heavenly technology of our hearts? Which is better? This technological device made by man, or God's creation? Why is it that our hearts, capable of storing and downloading hundreds of thousands of terabytes, *(Allahu Akbar:* **God is Great)**, cannot now store terabytes?

Saints <u>can</u> store this. God said, *"Verily the Saints of God have no fear on them, nor do they worry."*[23] **May Allah forgive us.**

22 Maqaam al-Ihsaan: the reality of worshipping God as if you are seeing Him, and if you do not see Him then know that He sees you.
23 10:62.

II– Degrees of Nearness

There are degrees of nearness.
Simply by existing,
Every creature lives near the Creator,
But there's nobility
Deeper than just being.
The sun warms generally the
Mountainside,
But it illuminates the shaft of
A gold mine.

Rumi
"A Deep Nobility"

Know Thyself

The Prophet ﷺ said, "Whoever knows himself knows his Lord. This means to study and examine yourself. That is why from this hadith we see that knowing the self is what is very important, and yet today Muslims have lost that understanding.

The Prophet ﷺ said, "Whoever knows himself knows his Lord."

The Prophet ﷺ came to teach us about ourselves, to teach us the importance of the self in the presence of their Lord. And unfortunately Muslims left the beauty of the teachings of *inner knowledge* to run after the world; they look at the structure without seeking the substance.

An Hour's Contemplation

Prophet ﷺ said, "An hour's contemplation is better than the worship of 70 years."

The Prophet ﷺ used to seclude himself in a cave outside of Mecca and meditate. He said, "An hour's contemplation is better than the worship of seventy years." For forty years the Prophet ﷺ was meditating. Then the angel Jibril عليه السلام came with Divine Revelation.

We also have to meditate on ourselves, our actions, and what we have done. Meditating on yourself means to think about your actions. Did you cheat people? Take their money and use it for yourself? Did you make conspiracies? Did you backbite? Did you go to places that God forbade? Repent! There is no time to squander. Death comes suddenly. People die suddenly and are gone. If they did not repent, it is finished.

Today, if someone says, "The IRS is coming to audit you," you will be trembling even though all your books may be in order and you may have made sure that you did not even have one mistake—you will be trembling. That is just from the IRS—human beings like you. What do you think about when God audits your books, asking you what you have done in your life? What will you say?

Keep the remembrance of God in your heart. Then do not worry. God said, *"Say to the servants who have been tyrants over themselves not to fear from God's Mercy, verily God forgives all trespasses, verily He is the Forgiving, the Compassionate."*[1] This verse means, "O Muhammad, say to My servants not to lose hope of My Mercy. I will forgive everyone! Come back! Come! Where do you want to go? You are not going to go anywhere! You are Mine! I can bring you at any time back to Me."

It is better to come now and repent, better than to come later by force. Then if you go again and do something—come back and repent again. That is why the Prophet ﷺ said, "Examine yourself daily." Examining yourself is better than voluntary worship, but it cannot replace obligatory prayers.

I see many people who come and tell me, "People are telling us to go to hajj but we are not going, we want to wait until we are sixty years old—now it is too early. We have to keep enjoying life." They say this because they think that if they go to hajj they cannot do anything wrong afterwards. But this is wrong. You might die at any time, so repent as soon as possible.

"O my son—you need to meditate and seclude yourself in order to understand reality." Even if you memorized the whole Qu'ran, or become the biggest scholar, that is still only knowledge of paper.

1 39:53.

Meditation of the Breath

Saints say that a human being has in each day 24,000 breaths—in and out. In every in-and-out breath, there is an action, whether good or bad.

That is why when you ... breathe in and breathe out ... breathe in with "Allah," breathe out with "*Hu.*"[2] Take in good action and cleanse yourself with that breath. Breathe in God's Attributes and Names meditating on the name of "Allah" ﷻ. If that Name goes through your whole system, He is taking you into an unknown area, an area full of treasures that you do not know anything about. That is why you breathe out with "*Hu.*"

Therefore meditate on the name "Allah" because God introduces His complete unknown Self through His Beautiful Name "Allah." When you do good actions, you do not know how much God is going to raise you. That is why it goes with "*Hu,*" also. Every breath in is an act, and every breath out is an act. Whether you breathe in or breathe out you expend effort, energy. So you are doing at least 24,000 acts every day. Think, then, whether these acts are like dead trees that have to be cut and thrown into fire or like living things that must be put into the eternal area of heaven.

Making Good Intentions

Sayyidina Muhammad ﷺ said in a holy tradition, "Every action is by intention and everyone will have that which he intended." If God sees that your intention is good, even if you do not do it, it is written for you as if you did it. And what happens if you make a good intention and then do it? God knows how much He will reward you. He multiplies every good action that you actually do.

Night Vigilance

May God bless this meeting and all of you who waited through the night. What you have done is made intention for vigilance in prayer and worship in the night.[3] God described the "People of the Bench," who were remembering God:

2 Hu: a Divine Name referring to the absolute unknown Essence of God.
3 qiyaam al-layl: prayer vigilance and worship at night.

And keep thyself content with those who call on their Lord
in the morning and in the night, wanting His Face;
and do not cast your eye to those who desire the ornaments of this world,
and whose hearts are heedless of Our remembrance,
who follow their passionate vain desires and whose cause is hopeless.

The meaning of this verse of God communicating with Prophet 🕌, is "Look at these people. During the day they are workers, doing their best for you Oh, Muhammad 🕌 and at night they are behind your home, sitting and worshipping."

Those Who Remember God

God is not asking us to be up all night. But he is asking us to be up for the dawn prayer.[4] "Pray the dawn prayer and remember Me."

God speaks of *"those who remember God standing, sitting, and lying down."*[5] The meaning of this verse is a worshipper's division of the day into three portions: respectively, work, rest with one's family, and sleep. If you are tired, you can sleep, but then it is better to sleep in remembrance, by remembering God as you are going to sleep.

Allah will grant you in accordance with your belief regarding Him.

May God keep us remembering Him and keep us on the right way, in order that we may reach the best in this life and the highest level of eternal life with the Prophet 🕌. You should always ask for the highest, the best.

The Prophet 🕌 said in a holy hadith of God's Words, "I am according to My servant's belief. Believe in Me as High—I am that."

This means that God will grant you in accordance with your belief regarding Him. Therefore we ask You, our Lord, that you grant us to be with the Prophet 🕌. We are helpless. But You are generous and the Prophet 🕌 is a mercy for us. To quote Qu'ran, he is *"towards believers kind and compassionate."*[6]

---

4 the dawn prayer: Fajr
5 3:191.
6 9:128.

We hope that you will write our names among those in that category, and clean us and bring us to stay with *Sayyidina* Muhammad ﷺ—as you have described in Your Holy Qu'ran, *"with those on whom God has showered His grants, from prophets, trustworthy ones, witnesses who testify and righteous people; and a goodly company are they!"*[7]

Waiting ...

Praising *Sayyidina* Muhammad ﷺ even one time carries more weight (in importance) than all the other actions you do in your life. God ordered, *"Verily God and His angels pray for the Prophet, O you who believe, pray for him and send peace upon him."*[8]

Intending to stay and pray shows love for God and His Prophet ﷺ.

You are sitting, respecting Islam, respecting religion, respecting what God ordered us to do. Not sitting and respecting Satan. You are sitting and waiting the way that someone waits for relief.[9] In a holy hadith, Prophet ﷺ said, "To wait for relief in difficulty is worship."

Everyone today is waiting for relief, waiting to be brought back to the way that God wants and loves for it to be. So in this situation, waiting for relief means waiting to be in God's Divine Presence, in prayer. We stayed awake because we were worried that if we slept, Satan might not let us wake up. Of course that action will be written for everyone. It is not going to be lost, in vain.

Those who are waiting fall under the verse *"O you who are enshrouded, stay awake all night except a little, half of it or a little less, or a little more; and recite the Qur'an in slow, measured rhythmic tones."*[10] Sitting once in your lifetime or once a month, or once a year, or once in two years, to sit and wait—that is waiting for an opening.

As God promised—*"Whoever is in awe of God, with both love and trembling of God, God will give him an opening—like an exit."*[11] You were waiting and waiting to pray. Because of this night you stayed awake and waited to pray to Him; God will give

7 4:69.
8 33:56. The traditional response on hearing this verse recited is: Allahumma salli ala Sayyidina Muhammad wa alaa aali Sayyidina Muhammad.
9 Relief: faraj
10 73:1-4.
11 65:2.

you an exit on Judgment Day, for everyone who has waited in the Way of God. One night of waiting to remember your Lord is enough. God will not let it go in vain.

He will give you an opening, an exit on Judgment Day. Who is Most Generous? If you do a favor for me or I for you, then later both of us will find, in difficulty, a way to help each other. But God is the <u>Most Generous</u>.

When we die, everyone has to cross the path[12] over hellfire. If you see that your action is taking you towards this danger, do you think that God will let you fall in that direction? When you were waiting and praying in this life and remembering Him? Therefore God will give you an escape before you get to hellfire—there are many exits before hellfire on the Straight Path. God will move you off of that path to hellfire. "Move! Move! Believers, hurry up off the path." With even a small amount of action, God shuffles believers off of the conveyor belt or path that goes to hellfire and leads them to Paradise.

Those who are punished will be conveyed all the way to their punishment, but those who were trying their best during their lives will find many exits. One exit goes to the First Paradise, some exits go to the Second Paradise, some to the Fifth, and one exit will take you to be *"with those on whom God has showered His grants, from prophets, trustworthy ones, witnesses who testify and righteous people."*[13] The number of exits available depends on how we behaved in this world.

The Knowledge of Taste

If we know that this world is always moving towards failure and destruction, and know that people also are vanishing, dying, but yet still do not believe—then we are only at the level of reading, not tasting.

There is an important difference between the "Knowledge of Papers" and the "Knowledge of Taste." On paper it can be written, "This is water." But by reading it, you do not taste the water. Alternatively, when you are on the path of Taste, you are given water and told to taste it. You take it, taste it, see its sweetness, and your thirst is quenched. As the Knowledge of Papers fails to completely convey the taste of water, in just the same way it fails to communicate the taste of death. We read, we hear, but fail completely to believe until we taste. With real belief, in this life we taste

---

12 Arabic: Sirat al mustaqeem
13 4:69.

death, feel death, taste perhaps its sweetness. The Angel of Death, Azrail ﷺ, may come with mercy or may come with punishment.

"Audit yourself before your accounting is done by God." If you find you are slipping into loss, then come back quickly. That is why taste is so important. When we do not care, then in leaving this place of worship and remembrance we forget the messages we have heard here.

Saints do not forget. They are afraid. They sit and contemplate, remembering God. Rabia,[14] sat in her corner repenting. People said to her, "Oh Rabia, you repented already!" She said, "I have to keep saying 'Forgive me God, I take refuge in You,'[15] because every time I say it, it needs another one to cover the previous one."

The Mercy of the Prophet ﷺ is a reference to the verse of Holy Qu'ran, *"We have not sent you except as a Mercy to the worlds."*[16] God sent him to save us. And his intercession is, as the Prophet ﷺ said, "… for the big sinners of my community." He said he would intercede for them in the knowledge of their weakness.

We cannot achieve what holy people want us to achieve—that shows our weakness.

Why the Prophet Cried

This life is a big drama—so complicated. It is an epic story, a perfectly woven tapestry integrating trillions of characters, every section of which is perfectly designed like a well-written book with well-designed chapters.

God has planned, even without planning. God says, "Be" and what He wished to create came into existence. He made everyone different from the others, and made this whole world a drama for everyone to express his feelings and relate his love. This expresses the difference between God's creation and human drama. A human drama might be a play or a movie in which actors play their roles—each role-player expresses his feelings in a way designed to make people cry.

God has given Muhammad ﷺ this whole epic story of creation. Through His revelation He teaches us. As the Qu'ran teaches us using parables, this life teaches us

14 Rabia al-Adawiyya was a famous woman saint.
15 Arabic: Astaghfirullah, audhu billah.
16 21:107.

by giving us taste. God can never be limited to being like a human story-teller, but He describes Himself as *"We have revealed the Holy Qu'ran to you, relating the best parables to you."* He relates stories in the Qu'ran because through stories we learn.

Also, God made this whole universe a story for us in order to teach us. After you have studied medicine, you will not immediately be considered acceptable as a doctor—therefore you have to do a residency to get real-life experience. Similarly, we have to learn and so we are thrust into this life in which we taste sadness and difficulty and happiness and contentment—whatever you experience—what better learning environment could there be?

People involved in drama (actors, directors, playwrights, movie-makers, and so on) make stories and cheat us. They play on our feelings through their deceptive, invented stories, in order to play on our heartstrings and earn money. That is the ultimate objective of all their histrionics.

Singers, also, sing nice songs and play on your heart in order to affect you. The voice of the singer affects you; but also her personality impacts you as you listen to her songs—this personality affects the audience so much.

Our real life—this whole world—is a story, and that is why the Prophet ﷺ said, "If you knew what I know, you would cry a lot and smile and laugh little." This is because God told the Prophet ﷺ the real story of mankind. This life is preparing us for what is coming. And that is why God explains that he teaches us stories, to give examples and direction through stories, *"so that they see they are coming back to Me."*

This life is preparing us for what is coming. And that is why Allah explains that he teaches us stories, to give examples and direction through stories, "so that they see they are coming back to Me."

And in this world, God established everything between two poles—good and evil, positive and negative. People are between the Hands of God—*"He turns their hearts over and down as He likes."* The hearts of people and their lives are between His hands. He does with them as He likes—in His hands our lives and hearts turn at His direction.

So we are between two Hands of God. And as much as we approach goodness, God gives us goodness for the afterlife.[17] As much as we approach badness, then you are going to see badness.

And that is why He said, *"Whoever makes an atom's weight of good will see good, and whoever makes an atom's weight of bad will see badness."*[18]

Saints learned their lessons through the examples that they learned from Holy Qu'ran. From the Prophet Muhammad ﷺ they understood that if you knew what he knows, you would have cried a lot and smiled less. Why cry? We usually cry because we fall into sadness because of problems and difficulties: Your wife left you or shouted at you; you shouted at your wife or left your wife; you lost money or have too much money to manage; you have this or that problem—these different problems bring sadness, which weighs on people's hearts, and finally they cry.

But why did the Prophet ﷺ cry? The Prophet ﷺ was crying for pity of his community, knowing that they will be in difficulty according to their actions. There is a verse of Holy Qu'ran towards the end of the chapter of the Cave, in which God says, *"We come to their worshipful acts, and We shall make such deeds as floating dust scattered about."*[19] This verse means that God is not in need of our good actions if they are intended for bad reasons.

Prophet ﷺ, when crying, is seeing the kind of miserable eternal life his community is earning with its actions. Do not look at your long beard, or even your small beard, or be happy with yourself because you are praying. Ah! Your worship is only drama! Maybe you are acting—God knows hearts. Your heart must be clean. "God does not look at your forms—God looks at your hearts."

Do not say "Muslims are better" in their worship. No. God created you and them similar. The Prophet ﷺ said in a holy hadith, "People are equal. There is no difference between Arab or non-Arab, except through sincerity."

This also means that there is no difference between Muslims and non-Muslims except through sincerity. You might find a lot of non-Muslims who are very sincere—they never cheat anyone. What are you expecting God to do with them? Perhaps He will send them to Paradise, and you to hell. Can you say "No" to Him?

How many people do we know from various backgrounds—they are so sincere, yet they are not Muslim. The

Allah knows hearts.
Your heart must be clean.
"Allah does not look at your forms—
Allah looks at your hearts."

17 aakhira: the afterlife
18 99:7-8.
19 25:23.

Prophet ﷺ was crying because he saw this difference between our perception of our closeness to God's Way and the reality of God's Way—and because we as Muslims think that we are superior.

There is no superiority in creation. All of us have the same biological system. You might be Muslim but not sincere. If a non-Muslim is sincere then who is better? At least they are sincere, they do not cheat you. There are Muslims who are sincere and real. Alhamdulillah, that is good. There are Muslims who are practicing Islam and worshipping, but not sincere. So what is the benefit to them of their Islam? How many conspiracies are we doing? Plotting, backbiting, creating confusion, separating husband and wife. For what?

Prophet ﷺ said in a holy hadith, "People are equal. There is no difference between Arab or non-Arab, except through sincerity."

Instead of making peace, we are igniting fires.

Poison for the Body

Two people in the time of the Prophet ﷺ came to him. Listen well—this is for us.

Those Sahaba came to the Prophet ﷺ in the morning with stomachaches. They said, "Ya Rasulallah, we cannot sleep." Our stomachs are aching, and you are the best doctor. Give us a cure.

He said, "There is no cure except to vomit what you have eaten." Today when you eat something and have a stomachache, your doctor will give you a pill. The Prophet ﷺ could have given them some prophetic medicine, but instead he said "No," because for that kind of sickness there is no medicine—the only thing you can do is to reject it completely and discard it, because it is poisonous for your system. Your whole system is going to be completely crippled by it—like these two Companions who were unable to move.

Many diseases we have and that we think come from normal sickness actually are spiritual in nature. Diseases do not only come from normal sickness. They come back to us as manifestations of different bad manners and negative energy that we are spreading.

You see this room here? A lot of negative energy is here. Who is it coming from? From the people who are here. I am positive that at <u>least</u> 80% of the people here have sickness similar to these two Companions who came to the Prophet ﷺ. The Prophet ﷺ said, "You have to take it out;" you have to reject it completely. How do you remove this characteristic? There is no way to take it out! As soon as it goes to the stomach, it is going to go through the whole body.

A family is like one body. A community is like one body. A nation also is like one body. And now with globalization—the whole world is one body. So to improve our situation, we begin first with the family. If one part of the body is aching, the whole body will ache, and fever will come. For instance, if you get hay fever your whole body will ache.

Prophet ﷺ said, "Vomit now!" They said, "We did not eat anything!" He said, "No, you <u>did</u> eat raw flesh!" 80% of those sitting here are in the same position as those men, having eaten raw flesh. What is that raw meat? The flesh of your brothers and sisters whom you have been backbiting.

He said, "You have been backbiting the flesh of your brother and sister." They said, "Yes, *Ya Rasul-Allah* (Messenger of God), we spoke badly about that family." The relationship between those backbiting and the victim of that backbiting was not so good, so they were speaking about them. How is it your business to do so? Who are you to speak about them? Who am I to speak about them? What is your relationship to interfere in their business?

Prophet ﷺ said, "Reject it from your system." So they took their fingers and vomited. Raw meat came out. Look at this miracle of the Prophet ﷺ. He turned this event into a miracle, to give them the physical taste of their actions.

This is not a fictitious story. It is <u>real</u>. The Prophet ﷺ made it real, to show them that this is a real issue in our life today. They vomited meat—vomiting, vomiting, and vomiting, and then when they were relaxed, Prophet ﷺ said, "This is not to be repeated."

Backbiting poisons the whole body. How much are we backbiting and poisoning our bodies today, interfering in things that are not our business? Your business is your wife and your child or children. For each of us, his business is to look after his own family, not to look at his neighbor.

The Effects of Envy

Grandshaykh one time gave an example about envy. He said that there were two neighbors with farms on which they raised sheep and goats. One of them always had envy for the other one—looking at his neighbor and saying, "Oh! Your sheep are not good! You are not good! The wolves are going to eat your sheep!"—picking on him in everything. "The home the animals sleep in at night is not proper and not secure for them."

He turned his back on his own affairs, not knowing that a wolf who was eating all his sheep was attacking his own farm. He was only looking at the other side, and not looking at himself.

We also are looking at others and not looking at ourselves. That is what the Prophet ﷺ prohibits.

God said, "*We do relate unto thee the best of stories,*"[20] There is a related story from Qu'ran about Joseph[21] who was envied by his brothers. They could not resolve themselves to kill him so they threw him into a well. God supported Joseph and saved him because his heart was always purely for his Creator. God rescued Joseph and raised him to a position of power—bringing him to be in charge of the treasure of Egypt.

True Justice

Similarly, in our time, people are always trying to conspire against their brothers for no reason. They make up stories, true or untrue, which they tell eloquently intending to take revenge or cause harm. They like to interfere in people's lives. Do you think that God does not know?

Prophet ﷺ said, "Everything is according to intention, and everything is according to what the person intended to do." If a man's intention is for God and His Prophet ﷺ, he is going to succeed. If his intention is for love of this world[22] or a woman, that will be what he receives.

---

20 12:3.
21 The Prophet Yusuf ﷺ.
22 dunya: the lower world; worldliness.

The above hadith means, "Do not run after conspiracies and bad intentions." Run after good intentions. If you run after bad intentions and speak against a person, God will make that person one hundred times better than you. When that person's heart is connected with God, with the Prophet ﷺ, and with his Shaykh, God will make you lose time and again.

There is a relevant story of two people. One used to be oppressed, backbitten by the other. After they died, God called the victim and said, "What do you want?"

The man said, "I want my rights from that oppressor ... for all the harm that the oppressor caused me."

So God looked to the oppressor and said, "Give him your good deeds." He did not have anything else to give. So God took his good actions and gave them to the victim. The victim said, "Oh God, I need more." And God said, "Yes, you are right. Because of what he did to you, you have to take everything he has." So the victim took all of the oppressor's good deeds, and it was still not enough.

God said, "His good actions are all gone. Do you want to forgive him?" The victim said, "No. He and his friends tortured me and abused me. I want all my rights."

God said "Okay." So He took the bad actions of that victim (for he also had bad actions) and gave them to the oppressor. Now the oppressor was carrying more weight. And the victim was now light and happy because he was safe in the afterlife.

Anyone who is being oppressed and backbitten in this life, God is going to give the action of the backbiter to him and send the victim to Paradise. And oppressors will go with no good actions to face their destiny, which might be hellfire.

Now the victim was happy, feeling cool. "I am cool now—like some people, always cool—I am happy! No problems."

Then God showed him a <u>huge</u> palace. The man said, "Oh God, whose palace is that?" God replied, "It is yours, because now you have a lot of good deeds, and your oppressor is carrying all your bad deeds. Therefore I am giving you that palace."

Then the man saw another palace, which was an even greater one. He said, "Oh God, whose palace is that?"

God said, "It is also yours, but there is a price for it."

The victim said, "What is the price? And God replied, "The price is that you completely forgive your brother who oppressed you."

The man was able to forgive his oppressor.

God said to him, "Take your brother, the oppressor, and go together—I am giving to him, and I am giving you. But I gave you <u>more</u> than what I have given to him because you forgave him.

God is not happy with those who create problems and trouble between people. Do not let that story go in one ear and come out the other.

Blessed Are the Peacemakers

May Allah ﷻ forgive us. Do not let this talk go away. Give a promise to Allah ﷻ. Make your intention not to backbite and not to have bad intentions towards anyone. Forgive everyone. Allah gives us from His rewards.

God said, "Whoever forgives and makes peace—he gets his rewards from Me."

Make this promise to your Lord, "Oh Allah, give me support and power not to be involved in backbiting and making confusion, or in spreading trouble between people." If you do that, all your problems will be solved.

So many people come and complain that they have problems. Look at what you have done to create your problems. Audit yourself like an income tax auditor. Look through your accounts. You will find a lot of mistakes. Once you have seen them you can correct yourself.

What is the benefit of learning energy and meditation when the infrastructure, foundation, and basement of the building are not yet built? God said this is like someone building his house on a cliff. Everything built on such a foundation is doomed to fall. Build up your house on a strong hill, not on a cliff. This is the basis of Islam.

When he heard this story, a companion of the Prophet ﷺ, *Sayyidina* Abu Bakr ؓ put a stone in his mouth for seven years. He did not want to speak one word of nonsense or backbiting or any other unnecessary talk. He was a great Companion, yet fearing to speak nonsense. What about us? Are we putting stones in our mouths? No.

May Allah ﷻ forgive us. May Allah support us. May Allah give health and wealth to the host of this house, bring people's hearts together, and bury troubles wherever we see it. When we do this, Allah will bury our troubles. Everyone has some troubles. If you veil your brother or your sister, Allah veils you also from the eyes of bad people.

Make this promise to your Lord, "Oh Allah, give me support and power not to be involved in backbiting and making confusion, or in spreading trouble between people." If you do that, all your problems will be solved.

Accepting Difficulties

Grandshaykh one time said something very important. "Prophet ﷺ was created as the best of creation, the perfection of creation, and if he had been alone he would never have needed anyone. But God gave him a community. Without that community, he would have been the prophet to whom?" So the Prophet ﷺ needs the community. Everyone is there to fulfill their different roles.

If you know your real role in life, you may face real problems, but you will be able to accept those difficulties and problems. You will be able to take responsibility for finding a way out of them. You cannot leave them to destroy you or kill you or oppress you or depress you. You have to keep confident that with the support of saints and the support of Prophet ﷺ, you will be able to achieve the high level of perfecting your role within Prophet's ﷺ community, and within the society and the community that you are living in.

That is why saints face everything that comes to them. Depending on their level, it might come difficult or easy, but they never just let the problem attack them. They know when the right moment comes, a way out of the difficulty will come. So when we are accepting our role and perfecting it, we see everything moving smoothly in this life. But when we are not fully accepting our role, we are always going to feel pain and suffering.

Our family had that kind of experience in Lebanon. In 1975, a big war exploded in Lebanon. Everything that my father owned of fabrics and factories was burned in one night. We went out with our clothes and nothing else. And yet we never saw a day that we went to bed hungry, and we never saw a day that we did not have money. God sent provisions from everywhere. When you give in the way of God, God gives you back. This is in accordance with the hadith, "One good deed from you is rewarded by God tenfold."

Dhikr and Energy Points

In Holy Qu'ran, in how many verses does God mention *dhikr*?

He says, *"Those who remember God standing, sitting, or laying down."* God also says, *"And those who contemplate the creation of heavens and Earth."*[23] This frequent admonition of the importance of dhikr in conjunction with the admonition to meditate means that making *dhikr* correctly is not just to parrot it but to think also about what you are saying.

Energy comes from reciting God's Divine Names. That is why saints will prescribe certain kinds of dhikr for specific problems that you ask them about—your shaykh might say, "OK, you go and say *"Ya Wadud"*[24] thirty-three times. He gives you the key, the right solution to your problem—this makes you ignite the energy in yourself and heals you. Using God's Names and Attributes ignites the energy in you.

People talk about "shakras," energy points. What ignites these points of energy? The recitation of certain Names of Allah (swt).

But you must not open institutions to heal people without knowing how to do so. People talk about *"chakras,"* energy points. What ignites these points of energy? The recitation of certain Names of God. The specific dhikr ignites them, but if you stop there that ignition also stops there.

God immediately continues after mentioning dhikr, saying "and contemplate." He is saying that after you make *dhikr*, you have to think about how God created the heavens and the Earth. This means it is necessary for people have to look into this universe and see God's Greatness.

---

23 3:191.
24 Ya Wadud: "The Loving." One of God's Attributes. He is the one who loves His good servants, and the only One worthy of love. He is the sole Beloved of the soul, because all perfection is with Him.

If you recite without even knowing what you are reciting and then finish and say, "O! I have activated different points," then you should know that you did not activate anything.

For every point that the *chakra* people speak about, there is a mirror point. One point is real, and one is an imitation or reflective point—plastic. There is real fruit, and there is plastic fruit—identical and indistinguishable except by tasting.

The people using this type of energy are only looking from the outside, using the plastic *chakras*, without knowing what is real and what is not real.

Satan is entering and deceiving people, telling them that they can do miracles. Miracles are only in the hands of saints, not in the hands of everyone

Do you think that God and His Prophet ﷺ will give the real energy points to normal people? No, that knowledge is only in the hands of saints. People today falsely claim to be able to heal using energy, although actually ignorant of the real energy points.

Prophet ﷺ told his Companions, "Do not worship idols. They are stones and cannot benefit you." The people at the time were thinking that idols were gods, although they are plastic. God has no partners. The Prophet ﷺ told his Companions not to believe in idols. When he left, devils came into three big idols and began to speak, telling the Companions, "We are your lords!" The Companions could hear them! And that is why God sent the verse of Qu'ran saying that it was devils speaking through them. Satan was able to enter and use these idols to cheat and deceive people. Until today, Satan is entering and deceiving people, telling them that they can do miracles.

Miracles are only in the hands of saints, not in the hands of everyone. All people would be running to miracle makers to heal themselves if those self-proclaimed miracle-makers actually had healing power. I know many people who have diseases—why is it that they cannot heal them? Because there is no reality in their healing.

Reality is not accessible easily. It needs hard work. People who are open to all kinds of sins and whose lives are falling into bad action—can that reality of healing people be accessible to them? Healing is only for saints. When you reach that level, then yes, you can heal.

Those Who Contemplate the Creation

Just so, when you are in constant good action, the result is a stereo surround of good acts—every act complementing the other. Each act has its place, just as in a nice carpet many different threads of different colors all have places, and in combination together yield a beautiful picture. The threads cannot be placed in a discordant fashion. They have to go together nicely in order to yield a nice piece of art. Look at this carpet; do you see how nice it is? Because it was planned, each thread going to its place.

God referred to *"those who remember God standing, sitting, and laying down."*[25] This means that every moment of 24 hours you have to be in remembrance of God. Standing refers to being awake and working. Sitting means relaxing, for instance after work with your family—also remembering God. Lying down means sleeping—also at that time you can remember God. How can you remember God during sleep? Make ablution, pray two *rakats*,[26] and praise Prophet ﷺ until you sleep. Then the time of your sleep is written as good action for you, because you slept with your ablution, remembering God. So your good action will continue until you wake up. So standing, sitting, and laying.

At the end of these 24 hours, you end up like *Sayyidina* Ibrahim ﷺ when he was looking, and saying "O! Look at the beautiful stars; I will worship them" But when the stars were gone he said, "They were not my Lord because now they are gone." Then when he saw the moon. He said, "This is better. This is my Creator." Then the moon was gone, and he saw the sun. "The sun is my Creator!" (Because it is bigger, giving light.) Then he said, "I cannot worship those things which disappear. I direct my face to the One who created heavens and Earth as a believer, a Muslim, and I am the first of the Muslims."[27]

Why did he redirect his gaze? Because of remembrance and contemplation. He saw the star, then the moon, then the sun. Then he saw that all of them are plastic—no reality in them. Therefore the One Who is in reality is the One who created them.

So with your action you begin to ignite that characteristic of thinking of *"those ...who contemplate the creation of Earth and heavens: O our Lord! You have not created this in vain. Glory be to Thee! Spare us the torment of fire."*[28]

25 3:191.
26 Rakat: a "unit" of the prayer, which includes the recitations and movements prescribed for each prayer time.
27 This story is related in the Holy Quran, verses 76-79.
28 3:191.

May Allah save us.
May Allah support us.
And may Allah bless us.

Mirror Images

We are all like people looking into mirrors. The image you see there in the mirror is false. If you break the mirror, the image that was there is destroyed. Similarly, without the physical structure of a building its blueprints are nothing. The house we are in is very nice, but if it did not have all its decorations, it would have an empty feeling (as well as being actually empty). Look now, it is so well decorated, especially with carpets. You are happy to be sitting on a Persian carpet. This house is beautiful because of the people in it and its decorations.

In asking you to pray, God says, *"Take your best ornaments to every mosque."*[29] This verse means that when you are standing in worship in the Presence of Allah, take on not only your best and clean clothing, but also bring your best character, values and manners. Do not just keep good manners when you are saying *"Allahu Akbar,"*[30] and then let your mind wander off during the body of the prayer.

Concentration in Prayer

How many Hanafis[31] are here? Not many. Shafiis[32]? Oh! *Allahu Akbar*, there are many.

Shafiis, when they pray, have to concentrate every cell and every drop of blood in their bodies, on the heart. Then they begin the prayer by saying *"Allahu Akbar."* So I am seeing them in Brunei and in Malaysia and Indonesia, and some here – when they want to enter prayer, they have many false starts ... They say "Allah ..." then stop—they are thinking to themselves, "that time was not good ..." then *"Allahu Akbar!"* And they say it so loudly. Hanafis on the other hand do it more simply—they are simple people. They say, *"Allahu Akbar,"* (without yelling or starting over and over again). However they said it the first time will do just fine. Then they concentrate on their prayers.

---

29 7:31.
30 Allahu Akbar: God is Greatest.
31 Hanafis: followers of the Hanafi school, one of the four schools of Islamic jurisprudence.
32 Shafiis: followers of the Shafii school, one of the four schools of Islamic jurisprudence.

When you say *"Allahu Akbar,"* it means you have disconnected yourself from this world, going into the Presence of Allah. But we are not doing that. When we say *"Allahu Akbar ..."*

(Then Mawlana speaks to a specific person in the audience) How many children do you have? None yet? This person will be thinking in his prayer, "When is Allah going to give me a child? I have to marry another wife. But my wife will get upset. So what do I have to do? Okay, forget about it. I will adopt a child. Or, *Insha-Allah*,[33] Allah will give me a child." Another person while praying will think, "How much money do I have in my account?" Do you have one million dollars, yet? Another one is thinking, "Which car will I buy today?" This is our situation. We do not have presence of mind in our prayers.

The physical analogy of this is like dirt. When you have a prayer carpet with a little bit of dirt on it, you cannot pray there. You have to clean it first. Therefore, how are you coming to Allah ﷻ with no concentration and presence of mind? Allah said, "Take your ornaments to every prayer." One interpretation of this is clothing, another is good action, and another is that you bring your presence of mind, that you focus your mind on the prayer at hand. How do you go to the Presence of Allah with your heart not clean?

There is a story of one saint. Today saints are hidden in this world because there is too much darkness here. We call them *majdhoob*, in Arabic—it means "attracted" (in a trance), in a state of attraction in Allah's love. A *majdhoob* does not see anyone—he only sees His Beloved.

And Allah provides for him. Many people come and give the saint what is necessary for his life. This is a story of a person like that, someone to whom Allah gave that kind of personality. One time he came to the mosque to pray the early afternoon prayer, and he stood directly behind the imam (spiritual leader) with all the others who wanted to pray. The imam said *"Allahu Akbar ..."* He was Shafii so he was concentrating ... "Allah ..." "Allah ..." *"Allahu Akbar!"* And thus he entered the prayer. That *majdhoob* immediately <u>cursed</u> him out loud, grabbed his shoes, and left the mosque. All the other people following behind that imam were laughing—most of them lost their prayer—when you laugh in prayer you have to do a new ablution.

33 Insha-Allah: if God wills.

The imam got upset. They called the *majdhoob*, "Come, now we have to give you a trial in the mosque." They asked, "Why did you do that to the imam? You do not know that this is a sincere imam?"

He said, "Yes. I know he is a sincere imam. But imam, do you want me to tell them what you were thinking when you said *"Allahu Akbar?"* Or do you want me to keep it in my heart?"

The imam said, "No, keep it in your heart."

The imam knew that this person is carried into a trance by his love for God. God gave him piercing vision in accordance with the holy tradition of Prophet ﷺ that "If My servant approaches Me through voluntary worship, I will love him. If I love him, I will be his ears that he can hear with, his eyes that he can see with, his tongue that he can speak with …"

Therefore that saint was able through inspiration to know what was in the hearts of others. As another holy tradition says, "Beware the vision of the believer, because he can see hearts with the power that Allah gives him."

The imam then said, "He saw my heart, and I will confess now in front of everyone because I do not want to be judged for this on Judgment Day … When I left my house to come to the mosque, my neighbor (a beautiful woman) came outside and I saw her. In the prayer, as I was saying *"Allahu Akbar,"* I remembered seeing her and I said to myself, 'Wouldn't it be good if she were my wife?' So the *majdhoob* knew that my prayer was no longer in the Presence of God, but in the presence of worldly issues."

It was permissible for that imam to think what he thought, because he was asking to marry her. But when we say *"Allahu Akbar,"* instead of clearing our heads, our minds go everywhere—businesses, women, television, bad movies, every bad thing.

When God Sends His Mercy

Prophet ﷺ was crying, tears coming from his eyes, when he said, "If you knew what I know, you would cry a lot and smile and laugh little." Because Prophet ﷺ could see that from the greatness of God's Mercy, in spite of all our bad deeds, God will save us on Judgment Day. He was crying out of humility, seeing the Greatness and Generosity of his Lord—despite our being like people who receive gifts, take them, and spit on the hands of the Giver. We drink from a well and then go and throw a stone in it to close it.

It was from seeing that generosity that the Prophet ﷺ was crying—from humility and love and happiness for his community, and for how shy the community will feel in front of God when God sends His mercy on them.

III-Saints and Shaykhs

Hold to a true shaykh.
Strength will come.
Your strength is his gathering you closer.
Soul of the soul of the soul,
Moment to moment,
hope to draw breath from that one.

No matter how long you've been apart ....
That presence has no separation in it.
Do you want to understand more about this friendship?
Read the surah called Daybreak.

Rumi
"Pain"

Saints Protect and Monitor Everyone

It is to protect His creatures from difficulty that God sent prophets to take people under their wings. And after the Prophet Muhammad ﷺ, there are no more prophets. He is the Seal of Messengers. He granted that power as an inheritance to saints; so now, although we live in a time in which no new prophet will be born, saints are born to carry on the teachings of the prophets.

There are saints for Muslims, and there are saints who take care of non-Muslims. Do not think that God left non-Muslims behind. No, may God forgive us. This is not possible. The Greatness of God would not permit that. God is giving the order and permission to *Sayyidina* Muhammad ﷺ, who grants as inheritance his status as protector to very high level saints to take both the Muslim and non-Muslim community under their wing.

If you go to an ocean or a swimming pool and you have a child who does not know how to swim, would you stand him up and push him in water, telling him to save himself? How is he going to save himself? He would drown. All of us are children in God's Greatness. So do you think that God is putting us in front of the ocean or a swimming pool, pushing us, and saying "Oh! You must save yourself!"

How can we save ourselves? The bad desires of the ego are always attacking us. Evil is also attacking us. How can we save ourselves? That is why God sent messengers, to teach us how to save ourselves. And if we are not able to save ourselves, what will they do when someone is falling into the ocean or the swimming pool, is struggling and no one is coming to save him? What will happen?

If today everyone is being monitored by modern technology, then do you think that Allah is not monitoring us and giving the power to His Prophet ﷺ and from Prophet ﷺ to saints to save people?

When the paramedics come what do they do? They pull him out and do CPR. They revive him and take the water from his lungs. Do you think saints cannot do that for believers and non-believers? You think that they are not monitoring people and saving them?

Everyone on this Earth is being monitored—if today everyone is being monitored by modern technology, then do you think that God is not monitoring us and giving the power to His Prophet ﷺ and from Prophet ﷺ to saints to save people? To do CPR for them when necessary, or make electric shocks on their hearts to rejuvenate them and bring them back?

That monitoring and resuscitation is definitely happening. But we are like anaesthetized people, unconscious of what saints are doing for our hearts. They are working day and night on that big screen. Every company is there. Every human being is on that screen. And then, the conduct meter for every person appears. Who is up, who is down?

From day one to the end of your life, they are checking your chart! Whether it is going up, going down, or bouncing up and down. That responsibility of monitoring was given to Prophet ﷺ, who asked for helpers. And so God granted him helpers and inheritors for that secret—Companions, then saints, and then to their murids.[1]

You will find today many people who will say, "I belong to this shaykh or that shaykh or that shaykh." It is okay to say that, but maybe that shaykh is not carrying secrets. Secrets are not simple, not easy. There are a lot of shaykhs today who claim they have power, and their followers are misled. It is an awesome grant and responsibility to have a power from Prophet ﷺ to monitor that big screen for every

1 Murids: students of a spiritual teacher, shaykh.

individual assigned to you as a follower—to examine what he is doing daily, and try to keep him on the margin of winning, not losing. It is a big job for the shaykh to look after his followers.

Grandshaykh said one time that the body of a human being has 366 pressure points. When their students need help or healing and when they are granted permission. This applies especially to Naqshbandis, who do not always show miracles except in a hidden way. Saints can easily press some key points and send energy from the hand. This will send energy and activate and rejuvenate the whole organ that is ill again, in order that it can move and function normally. I will discuss these points in more detail later.

As angels are responsible for the body, saints are given permission from Prophet ﷺ to look and monitor their followers on these big screens

As angels are responsible for the body, saints are given permission from Prophet ﷺ to look and monitor their followers on these big screens. Every follower has such a screen, and every one of them is like a complete factory or corporation that goes up and down. Each individual's actions are posted on that screen daily. And the shaykh is monitoring it. As the shaykh is monitoring their daily actions—he might intervene where seeing something wrong—inspiring the *murid* to move back to goodness.

The shaykh is able to create a struggle or conflict for his student in his life and then monitor him to see whether or not he gets angry. If you do not get angry and are patient, immediately they are able to waive your bad actions; then your chart will go higher—the needle will come back up.

The Presentation of Charts

Saints have a huge screen on which they see every person's chart at the end of each day. And then they have to present their charts to Prophet ﷺ in the Salvation Prayer[2] they say "*Ya Rasulullah*[3] ﷺ, we are coming with this." Now, do not put your shaykh in a shameful position. He asks for all the charts, whether they are up or down. If they are up, he is happy. If they are down, he asks forgiveness.

---

2 The "Salvation prayer," Salaat an-Najaat.
3 Rasulullah: respectful title for Prophet Muhammad, the Messenger of God ﷺ.

That is why Prophet ﷺ said in the Holy Hadith, "The actions of my community are presented to me, if they are good I thank God, if they are bad I ask forgiveness on their behalf."

Every saint presents his chart—this is the manner in which the Prophet ﷺ presents the charts. Then Prophet ﷺ puts all these charts, and he will see whether we are going up or down. If it is going up, he is thanking God. If It Is golng down, he immediately says asks for God's forgiveness for us.

This monitoring and praising or asking for forgiveness are reflected in the Qu'ranic verse: *"If they had only, when they were oppressors to themselves, come unto thee [O Muhammad] and asked God's forgiveness, and the Messenger had asked forgiveness for them, they would have found God indeed Oft-returning, Most Merciful."*[4] And the condition for their forgiveness is that the Prophet Muhammad ﷺ has to ask forgiveness on their behalf. MUHAMMAD ﷺ IS SAVING US! If Prophet ﷺ <u>asks</u> for forgiveness, then Allah forgives us. Then that screen is clean for the next year.

The Characteristics of Saints

And what is the first sign of a saint? If someone is a saint, he cannot lie. Ask yourself, if you really can heal people then you have to be standing at the level of a "friend of God."[5] The first level of a saint is to hear the praising of God from the angels. *"As he hears the praising of the angels."* When someone can do that then we accept that sainthood and the power to heal are present.

Do not cheat yourself. If you cheat yourself, you are cheating God. God said in Holy Qu'ran, *"He is with you wherever you are."*[6] So, He knows if you cheat or not. Ask yourself now—are you hearing the angels' praises? No? Then how are you claiming to be able to heal? Therefore check what kind of knowledge you have—is it real?

Approaching the Shaykh with "Cut Cloth"

Grandshaykh one time said in his talk, "Sometimes a murid might come to me with a nice piece of cut fabric—and ask, 'O Shaykh, we are going to make this into a shirt, is it nice?' Of course I will say, 'Yes, it is nice.' I cannot say it is ugly!"

4 4:64.
5 wali: friend of God; saint.
6 57:4.

Then they go and say 'O! The shaykh said it is nice.' Finished. You have to believe it. But the mistake is here—before you tailor it, you have to bring the piece to me and say, 'O my shaykh, *how* should I tailor this shirt? How do I do it? How do I cut it?' Then I will tailor it, and then they can go and sew it. Then it is my decision. Do not come, having everything ready, and ask me 'Is it good.' Of course I am going to say it is good, even if it is bad, because we never turn anyone down."

Tariqah[7] is diplomacy; it teaches you how to be a diplomat. *Tariqah* is very sensitive, very delicate. It keeps the highest level of *Shariah*.[8] And the highest level is to be good with everyone. So check your actions to see whether they are real.

You have 24,000 breaths a day—each breath is an act, whether good or bad. Are you accounting and auditing what you have done during each day and night? No. No one is doing that.

However, saints do that. Every act that they do, they are asking forgiveness. With every incoming breath they say, "Allah please forgive me."[9] Why do they constantly ask for forgiveness?

Saints are eager to repent from any hidden act that they do without knowing. That is why Prophet ﷺ said, *"What I fear most for my community is hidden shirk."* It means in every breath you are breathing there is a hidden *shirk*,[10] if you are not careful enough to avoid it.

Now we hear, but when we go through the door we will forget everything.

Helium, Lightness of Being, and Rumi

When saints bring you to the shore of safety, you will become what we call in Arabic *Hayuni*—"very light." It is your release from the gravity of earth, connecting you with heaven.

---

7 Tariqah: literally, "path;" used here to refer to the spiritual path of Sufism, and more specifically, the Naqshbandi Tariqah.
8 Shariah: Islamic Law.
9 Astaghfirullah: means "I seek forgiveness of God."
10 Shirk: to ascribe a partner God; polytheism, the worst of sins. Hidden shirk however is not a sin of this magnitude, rather it is a subtle form of ascribing partnership, as for example when one believes medicine holds the power of life or death, without referring the original cause to the Almighty.

That is how Jalaluddin Rumi ق rose when he was whirling.

The lightest gas that exists on earth is helium. You know that when you fill a balloon with helium it will rise.

You know that hydrogen and oxygen are gases, but when they come together they become water. God said that when He created creation, it was in a gaseous form. There was no ocean, there was nothing—it was gas. And when the gases connected to form water, oceans came. And He said, *"We have created from water everything that is living."*[11]

You are 70% water, and your DNA is 97% water and you know that water is heavy, while gas is light. The reality of saints is to take all this heaviness in you—take and separate the water and the oxygen, from the hydrogen, and give you a boost of helium, so that you rise.

Jalaluddin Rumi ق knew this secret. Today, however, whirling dervishes stay in the same place. Only their robes fly—their clothes. Jalaluddin Rumi would spin, and when you spin so much you fly like an airplane. So he was flying, rising. Today, those who practice spinning are only spinning in imitation—the secret of levitation has left.

Saints, however, have that secret for their murids. There are turbines for airplanes, and there are regular engines for cars. Car engines do not fly. Airplanes fly. There are ships that can fly over water—hovercraft. Other sea-going vessels move <u>in</u> the water, but hovercrafts go above the surface—they go fast because they are rising, lifting over the waves. Airplanes weigh many tons, but they are lifted with the people inside.

Saints are like rockets—better even than airplanes. They lift their followers with them, going beyond the laws of physics and bringing their followers to the presence of Prophet ﷺ every night during special night prayers[12]—they have to present everyone in only five minutes or three minutes. They are not given more than that. Every saint has time in accordance with what he has been given. This is just as today—when you go to a president you will have a very limited amount of time that he can give to you, and after that he has to move on. Saints have to present their followers in that limited time in the presence of Prophet ﷺ, and do not raise their heads until <u>all</u> their followers have been cleared.

11 21:30.

Stars on a Dark Night

Through their souls, all human beings are connected to heavenly stations. It means we are connected to God through our spirit, but our body does not know because it is connected to this earth, which Satan uses for his own purposes. But he cannot play on the spirit, on the soul—so he is playing only on the body.

But the soul is sacred; it is under protection, and God gave Prophet ﷺ that authority, who divided the authority among saints, to keep monitoring the spirit. Because of this you are going to be surprised on Judgment Day, when the Prophet's ﷺ community appears—they will be like stars on a dark night. They will be saying, "How is this action with me? I did not do that. What happened?"

Saints did it for you. They sent that to your heart, building you up more and more. You cannot see it in this life because this life is covered in darkness. But you'll see it in the Afterlife, because evil has no power there. It is finished.

It means saints are sending you energy. And how do they send it? That is the secret. That energy, when they send it you receive it. If you use it, you heal others. Because they send to everyone. But some people can understand it, decode it and know what is inside it.

Encrypted Messages

Sometimes now people send hidden files inside emails. Some people can open those files and see something special. The energy that saints send from the Ocean of Power is encrypted like these secret attachments in emails. If you are able to decode them, you can be a healer and heal yourself quickly; then you can see, because saints open vision for you because you healed yourself. If you fail to unlock these secrets, that vision will still be closed, and you will still be blind. Then they cannot open for you to see what cannot be seen, to hear what cannot be heard, to say what cannot be said. As Prophet ﷺ said, in the hadith:

As long as My servant approaches Me through voluntary worship, I will love him. If I love him I will be his ears that he can hear with. I will be his eyes that he can see with. I will be his tongue that he can speak with.

12 The "Salvation prayer," Salaat an-Najaat.
13 Masha-Allah: As God wills.

Energy Secrets of One and Eight

So when you decode and understand, then you can clean yourself quickly, seeing everything. You can see what is behind that wall. Now we are blind. That decoding lies between two numbers in numerology. Eight and one.

Between the eight and the one—when you add them they make nine. And nine in numerology is equivalent to zero because it cancels out when numbers are added. Nine is zero, meaning submission. But these energy secrets are lying between number one and number eight. And that is why God has engraved on your right hand one and eight. Eighteen. That secret is between these two numbers. If you can decode it, then you can see what is in between. There is a space in between them.

That is how saints can read your hand, through these two numbers. If you look at these two numbers, one and eight, here—look. In Arabic when you write numbers, first you write the one, then the eight. If you look and put your hand in the mirror, what do you see in the mirror? Eighty-one. So there is a mirror between the two hands. If you can find that mirror, then you can move in space—not only see in space, but also move in space. We will describe this next time, *Insha-Allah*.

Communication Between Saints
(This is from an informal talk with a physicist in the presence of other murids about the movement of light.)

MSH: … if a light goes in the universe—how far does it go before it reflects back?

Murid: Wherever the object is.

MSH: Whenever it hits an object.

Murid: You are seeing the star because it is hitting the star.

MSH: So it means the light we are seeing is reflecting back to us on Earth. Explain. Also, if you see the color green or white, it does not reflect the green or the white—it is your mind that gives you the green or the red. So the light moves and then it has to come back. How far is the return trip—the same distance?

Murid: From the observer to the object, from the object to the observer.

MSH: The same distance.

Murid: Yes.

MSH: This is how saints speak with each other. A saint sends a light wave—
and then observes another light immediately. It does not take a second, and the
answer comes back. He can also send to a sick person—it does not take a second
to heal him, and the saint will instantly receive the information of whether or not
the person has been healed. This knowledge will be revealed by physicists. Did you
hear that before? That is a knowledge that is coming from that ocean of *Sayyidina*
Muhammad ﷺ. The Knowledge of Taste. Scientists knew about the reflection, but
they did not know what it could be used for.

Saints use <u>every</u> scientific possibility before using spiritual power, because they
do not want to use spiritual power. Instead they want to collect more and more, and
condense it.

So if there is any scientific means they can use, they will use that instead.

The Categories of Saints

There are two categories of saints, in Arabic this is called, *kasban* and *wahban*—
respectively "by work" and "by grant." Some people reach higher stations by
progressively seeking more knowledge, praying, fasting, and doing excessive worship,
making God happy with them and thereby receiving a taste of whatever He opens for
them. This is *"kasban"*—earning and working in God's Way.

The majority of people are in the first category. They progress by keeping the
prophetic practices—cause and effect is the way that this world normally operates.

"Wahban" means that without effort God opens everything for you, suddenly
and without account. *Wahban* is for a very very very very small minority. *Wahban*
people are at <u>widely</u> varying levels. One may be on the first level, another may be
in the heavens. One may be on Mars, another on Earth. There is a huge difference.
God can give to someone a huge amount, from East to West. You become 'crazy' in
his love.

Islamically, Allah is known as the Lord of the East and West, and the two Easts
and the two Wests, and the many Easts and the many Wests. This saying indicates that

Allah's Lordship extends infinitely toward the East, and infinitely toward the West, through all dimensions, and there is no end to His Knowledge.

How Saints Carry the Burdens of Mankind:
The Story of *Sayyidina* Bayazid al-Bistami

Sayyidina Bayazid al-Bistami ق used to worship and worship and worship and worship, asking in all his prayers that Allah open for him that beautiful Divine Presence. And after progressing for many years, he heard a voice in his heart that said,

"Ya Aba Yazid, what do you want?"

He said, "*Ya Rabbee*, I want to come to You."

God said, "Ya Bayazid, there is a correct way to come to Me."

"*Ya Rabbee*, what is that way?"

God said, "You have to be a garbage dump for My servants."

You have to leave anger, be patient, you have to be of service to humanity, regardless of what they do to you.

Being a garbage dump means that you have to carry the burdens of God's servants in order to come to Him. You cannot come with your ego to Him. In order to step on your ego and come to God, be a garbage dump. So what did Aba Yazid do to become a rubbish dump? How do you do that?

You have to leave anger, be patient, you have to be of service to humanity, regardless of what they do to you .

Bayazid was thinking and thinking and thinking, "How am I going to be of service to people?" To become a rubbish dump means everyone has to speak badly of you, but you still carry their burdens. Everyone has to say, "This one is bad." And you instead have to be saying, "*Ya Rabbee*, forgive them, *Ya Rabbee*, forgive them."

How many times did the neighbor of Prophet ﷺ dump his rubbish at the door of Prophet ﷺ? For seven years. The Prophet ﷺ did not tell anyone—he took the garbage and quietly threw it away. So to become a dump means you have to forgive everyone.

To make people love you is easy. Be a sincere person, and everyone loves you. You are happy when they say, "*Masha-Allah*,[13] you are a lion." If they say to you, "You are a donkey," you will get angry! Both of them are animals—a donkey and a lion. But being a lion makes the ego happy. Being a donkey makes the ego angry. Just as you are made happy by something being said of you that really does not have value, the love of people is something good that makes you happy — but compared to the love of God, that love of people has no value.

He Is Sentenced to Death by Stoning

Sayyidina Bayazid had created some problem in the city—we will not go into that story now, but as a result they ordered him killed by stoning. He was given the power to destroy but instead he forgave everyone. They stoned him continuously, children and adults, until he fainted. And as he was being stoned, he was saying, "*Ya Rabbee* forgive them. *Ya Rabbee* forgive them. *Ya Rabbee* forgive them."

Who can do that now? They thought he was dead, so they threw him into the rubbish dump. Seven days he stayed there unconscious. When he woke up he said, "Ya Rabbee, I wish that they had thrown stones until I died, and You brought me back to life, and I could be stoned to death again, my Lord, for Your love.

"Make my body as big as hell so that no one can go to hell except me. And let everyone else go to Paradise." That is the saints' approach to the Divine Presence, among them Sayyidina Bayazid al-Bistami. God gave him power to move through the ocean. And he said, "Ya Rabbee I am now moving in Your Way; I do not care for anything else." A boat was sailing, and he got into the boat.

> "*Make my body as big as hell so that no one can go to hell except me. And let everyone else go to Paradise.*"
> *Sayyidina Bayazid al-Bistami.*

In the middle of the ocean, there were heavy seas and a big storm, and the boat was going to sink. He knew this was a test for him. There are so many tests for saints! Do not think saints have no tests. Every step they make, they have a test. Like us, like normal people.

God inspired the captain to say, "It must be that there is someone bad among us. And that is why the ocean is so turbulent. Since we do not know who the bad person is, we will draw straws, and whoever gets the short straw we will throw into the ocean so as to keep all the other inhabitants of the boat safe."

Bayazid ق said to himself, "These people are going to throw an innocent person; let me give myself up." Can you do that? No one can do that. He told them, "I am the bad person—do not use this superstitious game to choose the person you will throw into the water—just throw me." They took him and threw him in the ocean.

As soon as they threw him in the ocean, the water calmed. They said, "Praise God, we got rid of that bad person." He said, "*Ya Rabbee*, I am not returning until I find reality."

Beyond the Edge of Existence, into Reality

He continued in the ocean until he reached a point where everything he saw was light. Just as today's people sometimes talk about "complete emptiness," he saw complete nothingness. Nothing … complete emptiness … a void. This means he was reaching the beginning of the reality—because before you come to the reality you have to reach the end of everything. Then you can reach the beginning. As he was approaching the end, there was nothing around him—you cannot see anything there. Like when you put your eyes on the sun and then look the other way and see nothing. It means when you look at the light, everything disappears. When he was in that reality, everything disappeared.

He heard a voice saying "*Huuuuuuu.*" He said, "Allah gave me a power in this life with which, when I use it, I can count how many human beings are living on the earth with me. But in that presence, in that reality, I spent all my power to count those making that sound, and I was not able." And that sound was Remembrance of God *(Dhikr-Allah)* with the name "*Huuuuuuuu.*" Creatures were reciting Allah's Hidden Name."

And then I realized that there was a teacher with them, and I was afraid that the teacher would ask me "Why are you interfering in my students?" "That teacher is going to come after me." And *Sayyidina* Shah Bahauddin Naqshband[14] is the one

"I was a hidden treasure and I wanted to be known so I created creation."

whom he saw after the edge of reality. He was the teacher of this huge crowd that Bayazid was not able to count. *Sayyidina* Bayazid immediately backed out of that place, saying that this was beyond his territory. That *"Hu"* is the reality of everything.

"I was a hidden treasure and I wanted to be known so I created creation."

That "Hu" is a hidden treasure. No one can know it. It is a secret of creation. When saints enter that ocean, God raises them. And God opens to their hearts what He did not open to anyone.

14 Sayyidina Shah Bahauddin Naqshband: 17th of 40 shaykhs of the Naqshbandi Order. Shaykh Muhammad Nazim al-Haqqani, a living Master and currently residing in Cyprus, is the 40th shaykh in an unbroken "Golden Chain" of transmission of whom the Prophet Muhammmad ﷺ is the considered the first.

IV – Science and the Hidden World

*The Hidden World
has clouds and rain
of a different kind ....
Made apparent only to the refined.
Those not deceived
by the seeming completeness
of the ordinary world.*

*Rumi
"Mathnawi"*

God created everything in the world. He created this Earth and He created science. The Earth is a sphere, turning around itself. Who can make a solid planet turn around itself? The only One who can do that is the Creator. When you study the manifestations of His Greatness, you are going to study everything with it.

The Miracle of the Sun

The sun, which scientists say has been there for millions of years, is a continuous series of immense nuclear explosions. If one huge atomic bomb exploded on earth, what would happen to the earth? It would disintegrate completely. So why does the sun not disintegrate? For millions of years these nuclear explosions are happening and yet the sun is still the same.

This shows us God's Greatness and our weakness. And yet we are not taking an example from that huge wonder—we are thinking only about how much money we have in our accounts, how many cars we have, how many homes ....

Scientists today say that the sun's energy is coming from a nuclear atomic reaction. Billions and billions of particles are exploding and creating that huge, immense energy that is being sent over this world to give us light, warmth, heat, and health. This is because the sun is related to heavens.

Yet, despite the nuclear explosions that rock it in every instant, the sun is staying in its place for millions of years. It is God's Divine energy that is keeping it in its place, or else it would have shattered with this whole universe. Look at the asteroids that are the evidence of the destruction of other celestial bodies.

God is keeping the sun whole for the benefit of human beings. People usually just think about the sun giving us its light, but it also gives us energy and provides us with all kinds of necessities for life. If there were no sun, there would be no life. It is the source of a lot of cures for people, and without it you would die. When children lack calcium, doctors order them to be taken to the beach to sit under the sun, so that their bones will become stronger. Without the sun, bones cannot grow strong and perfect; they will only be defective, unbalanced, and unable to move properly. The sun cures bones.

Two Kinds of Energy

There are two kinds of energy. One is a constructive, healing energy, and the other is a destructive energy. One heals and the other destroys.

The earth is related to desires and anything related to the desires of this world destroys. That is why nuclear explosions on the sun heal, while nuclear explosions on earth destroy and kill people. That destruction is from its relation to this world. This world is *ending*—it is going to disintegrate.

One side of him struggles for God and the afterlife, while the other side of him struggles for worldly desires and Satan.

How can you have the same energy that in two different situations yields opposite effects?

It is the same in a human being. One side of him struggles for Paradise and God, while the other side of him is struggling for worldly desires and Satan. One side wants to approach the Divine Presence by means of remembrance of God *(Dhikr-Allah)*.

However, as soon as we leave from a meeting of worship, we forget the love of God, the love of Prophet ﷺ, and we turn towards our worldly desires and the desires of Satan. There is complete separation, although those two sides are in a single person.

Because of this God gave us signs from which to learn. Everything has a beginning and an end. And where it ends it begins. There is no end without a beginning, and there is no beginning without an end. Only in heavens is this not true. In heavens, there is no beginning, no end. When God sends you to heavens then, as with anything related to afterlife, you will be ever living. Everything related to this worldly life has a beginning and an end.

The Scientific and Spiritual Nature of Creation

Everything living is coming from what? Water. It must have water in it to be alive. And what is water? Hydrogen and oxygen. Hydrogen, if you look at the periodic table, is one – the lightest gas. And oxygen is a gas (eight on the periodic table). Both are in a gaseous state. But when they come together, they create a form, a liquid. Unless they come together they remain gases.

All prophets used to hear the praising of God from stones that we consider non-living.

That is why they say that when God created creation it was in a gaseous form which firmed into water, then from water came every living thing ... God said, *"We created from water everything that is alive."* [1]

What does that mean, "everything that is alive?" It means everything is alive because *"Verily everything is praising Allah, but you cannot understand their praise."* [2] This includes even the stones in which we do not see life—actually they are alive.

The Prophet ﷺ used to hear them. All prophets used to hear the praising of God from stones that we consider non-living. And God gave the example of stones or mountains because we think of them mainly as non-living—God wants to tell us, "No, they are living." It is clear to us that trees are living, water is running, animals are living, human beings are living, so what is not living? We would think mountains and stones. And God is saying, "No, they are living also." Because they came from what? Water.

1 21:30.
2 17:44.

Everything was water, which came from these two gaseous elements—oxygen and hydrogen. God made them come very close, come into contact with one another, under a certain pressure, and then ....[3] They produce water.

Everything has signs, in science, God is giving us these signs. When you put the gases, hydrogen and oxygen, together, they form water—the element of life.

What is the first letter of Hydrogen? 'H.' This corresponds to the letter *Ha* in Arabic. And what is the first letter of Oxygen? It is 'O.' This corresponds to the Arabic letter, *Waw.*

If we put the letters *Ha* and *Waw* together, what do we get? *"Hu"* the Divine Name from which living species come. *Hu Allah.*

And that is why in the Naqshbandi chanting *(dhikr),* like in that of all Sufi orders, after you say 'There is no God, but God (*Laa ilaaha illa-Allah*)," telling your ego that there is no Creator except God. As soon as you enter that ocean and accept it completely and God dresses you with that manifestation, then He lets you enter into the chanting of the Name 'Allah.'

When you begin with *Laa ilaaha illa-Allah*, it is like an ablution before prayer. When you take ablution for prayer you are cleaning yourself from all worldly attachments and coming to the Presence of God to pray. So by the chanting of *Laa ilaaha illa-Allah,* you are making a kind of ablution for yourself, disconnecting

---

3 Nuclear Fusion In Stars: Nucleosynthesis
Stars are giant fusion reactors. In the center of stars, atoms are taken apart and brought back together by tremendous atomic collisions that alter the atomic structure and release an enormous amount of energy. This makes stars hot and bright. Nuclear fusion is an atomic reaction that fuels stars. In fusion, many nuclei (the centers of atoms) combine together to make a larger one (which is a different element). The result of this process is the release of enormous quantities of energy (the resultant nucleus is smaller in mass than the sum of the ones that made it; the difference in mass is converted into energy by the equation E=mc2). Stars are powered by nuclear fusion in their cores, mostly converting hydrogen into helium. The production of new elements via nuclear reactions is called nucleosynthesis. A star's mass determines what other type of nucleosynthesis occurs in its core (or during explosive changes in its life cycle). Each of us is made from atoms that were produced in stars and went through a supernova. Small stars: The smallest stars only convert hydrogen into helium. Medium-sized stars (like our Sun): Late in their lives, when the hydrogen becomes depleted, stars like our Sun can convert helium into oxygen and carbon. Massive stars (greater than five times the mass of the Sun): When their hydrogen becomes depleted, high mass stars convert helium atoms into carbon and oxygen, followed by the fusion of carbon and oxygen into neon, sodium, magnesium, sulfur and silicon. Later reactions transform these elements into calcium, iron, nickel, chromium, copper and others. When these old, large stars with depleted cores supernova, they create heavy elements (all the natural elements heavier than iron) and spew them into space, forming the basis for life.

yourself from the world by confirming and affirming that God is the Creator and the one you worship. By this way He allows you to enter His Divine Presence, where you begin *Dhikr-Allah* by saying "Allah, Allah, Allah."

He lets you enter that ocean, then He later lets you enter into the Name *"Hu"*—the unknown, absolute unknown, the Essence of which no one can understand except through the manifestation of oxygen and hydrogen that makes this whole world come into a liquid water state from gaseous state. You cannot see a gas—you would not be able to see either oxygen or hydrogen by itself. What do you see? You see them only when they come together as water.

This is what saints do — they break their form and return to their origin. And that is why they make Dhikr-Allah by chanting "Hu." "Hu" is the dhikr of meditation

God has honored us and favored us with these kinds of *dhikr*. He granted us the opportunity to learn the reality of where we are and what we are standing for. When you say *Laa ilaaha illa-Allah,* all the words are formed from the Arabic letters: *Lam, Alif,* and one *Ha.* No other letters! From these letters come *Laa ilaaha illa-Allah,* and the importance of these letters is beyond our capacity.

Alif here turns into *Waw. Ha* with *Waw* becomes *"Hu." Lam* is the combination of the *Alif* and the *Ha;* when the *Lam* is added, it is the Heavenly World and the earthly *(dunya)* world. This scientific approach for Islam is so deep that there is no time to explain in detail—it would make us lose our minds and many people might fail to understand.

Composition of DNA

If you were able to break up that watery form and go back to the gaseous form, you would fly because our body mainly consists of water. They found out that 97% of DNA is water. In Malaysia scientists are now studying this phenomenon—especially one big scientist who is Naqshbandi. Only 3% of the DNA is what Western scientists have so far discovered. And they say the other 97% of the DNA is nothing—only water. They are not looking at it. That Malaysian scientist is looking at it now. And he has made a lot of discoveries from the 97% of DNA that is water.

Most of our bodies are made from water. If you break that water back into Hydrogen and Oxygen, you will rise up toward heaven. Hydrogen and Oxygen would float if not combined together as water. This is what saints do—they break their form and return to their origin. And that is why they make *Dhikr-Allah* by chanting *"Hu."* *"Hu"* is the chanting of meditation.

The Knowledge that was Revealed to the Prophet ﷺ

Read!
In the Name of thy Lord and Cherisher, Who created –
Created man out of a clot-
Read!
And thy Lord is the Most Generous
The One Who taught man by the Pen —
Taught man that which he knew not.

Surah 96, The Clot (al-Alaq)

"Read in the Name of your Lord Who created ..."

One of the meanings of this verse is that God is saying to *Sayyidina* Muhammad ﷺ to read using the Power of God's Holy Name. More than saying, God the Creator, is <u>ordering</u> *Sayyidina* Muhammad ﷺ to use God's Power to read.

Remember that this message was delivered to a man who was not able to read or write Arabic. So it is important to understand that this word "Read" has much deeper implications than how we normally think of reading. The Arabic meaning of 'read' includes both hearing and seeing. On that day when Prophet Muhammad ﷺ received the revelation, God was showing the Prophet ﷺ all of creation from beginning to end. And then telling him to "read" it.

God is saying, "Read the creation, O Muhammad ﷺ! I have given you that creation—read everything in it. It is yours! Read everyone and all of creation. O Muhammad, read what I am showing you from creation!"

The Prophet ﷺ perfectly understood and transcended all of the laws of this universe and the nature of every created thing, whether of metal or any other substance.

With today's technology everyone can be "read" and kept track of at any moment—for example, this cell phone here was just ringing. It knows where you are, because the phone traces you. Modern technology, cellular phones and the internet, can read every message you send—everything.

Sayyidina Muhammad ﷺ was given the power to read much deeper than this. When God says to "Read, O Muhammad ﷺ," it means to read even at the level of detail of DNA. "I created them for you. Read them."

"I created creation from a clot." The reference to the creation of people from a clot means that God is telling the Prophet ﷺ to read people at the genetic level. From the time of that revelation the Prophet ﷺ was able to read all humanity, past and future, at the genetic level. As Jibril عليه السلام was giving the revelation, God was showing the Prophet ﷺ the technology of the clot from which human beings were created.

The meaning of this verse is that the Prophet ﷺ can read even the microscopic detail of sperm and egg, he can see at what time and at what moment they connected with each other, and the moment that Allah sent his spirit into the sperm and egg. "O Muhammad ﷺ, you can even count every sperm." At the moment of conception doctors say that there are between 500 and 600 million sperm but only one of those will connect with an egg.

The Prophet ﷺ perfectly understood and transcended all of the laws of this universe and the nature of every created thing, whether of metal or any other substance. At that moment he was shown and understood all existing and future technology, not just metaphorically, but in reality.

He was even given the understanding of all future technology that ordinary humans will never understand. But God gave the Prophet Muhammad ﷺ the responsibility to read, observe and learn about all of creation from beginning to end.

Another implication of God's order to "*Read in the Name of your Lord who created ...*" is that everything in this universe can be read. A doctor can read your heartbeat using an EKG which, reduced to its simplest element, is just a printout of the wavelengths that emanate from your heart.

All of our modern technology is based on our understanding of the rules of our creation and the interaction of different elements and events in that creation.

All of our modern technology is based on our understanding of the rules of our creation and the interaction of different elements and events in that creation.

With modern technology, these waves can be captured and reduced to writing. Since physical modern technology is a lesser imitation of spiritual technology, it must also be possible to read other wavelengths that emanate from you. Everything about you in this creation can be read, down to and beyond the level of your DNA. Doctors can read your heartbeat with an EKG or an MRI. With these tools they can know every cross-section of your body. They can also read your blood tests, and can check your electrolytes. Doctors now can read hundreds of different aspects of your body.

In order to receive all of these wavelengths in readable form, we need the right equipment. This is true for both worldly technology as well as spiritual technology. If you can develop yourself as an instrument that can read, then you would be able to read everything in this universe.

"Read, and your Lord is Most Generous."
How can Muslims today claim that the Prophet ﷺ is like a postman ... just a courier
of messages?

By this verse God is saying to Muhammad ﷺ that as the Prophet ﷺ extends his reach to the extent of the initial teachings; God is expanding his knowledge to encompass more, and this expansion of the Prophet's ﷺ consciousness and understanding is repeated again and again infinitely.

How can we imagine the Prophet's ﷺ explosively growing comprehension which has been growing at a rate beyond our own? This explosive process has been continuing at least since this verse was revealed during the initial revelation to the Prophet ﷺ—about 1,450 lunar years ago.

Therefore how can Muslims today claim that the Prophet ﷺ is like a postman ... just a courier of messages? Muhammad ﷺ is flesh like people, but compared to ordinary human beings he is a gem and everyone else a pebble.

O Muslims, open your eyes. The Prophet's ﷺ reach and knowledge is infinitely expanding, beyond the capacity of our minds and imagination. We have to open our eyes to his greatness.

"The One Who taught man by the Pen ..."

By this next verse God refers to His giving the Pen to *Sayyidina* Muhammad ﷺ. God taught him with the Pen of Power. That Pen is not like one of our pen ... it is not like the imitation device that we hold and call a pen.

The Pen of Power is the pen God ordered to write every action of human beings in The Preserved Tablet.[4] This reference to the Pen of the Preserved Tablet is also a proof of this surah's referring to the transmission of knowledge regarding mankind and creation to the Prophet ﷺ.

God continues, *"... taught man that which he did not know."* The reference to "man" is not only a reference to mankind in general but actually a specific reference to Prophet Muhammad ﷺ—God is saying, "I taught Muhammad ﷺ what he did not know."

Muhammad ﷺ is the real Pen who wrote and learned directly from his Lord. He is not like us. There is real fruit and plastic fruit. We are like the plastic fruit. There are real scholars and plastic scholars. A plastic scholar learns letters, but cannot decode the tens of thousands of meanings hidden in every letter of Holy Qu'ran.

God's order to *"Read,"* and the implication of the order's context, is that the Prophet ﷺ can *read* everything and those who inherit from the Prophet ﷺ can also read creation by virtue of that inheritance. The Holy Qu'ran is God's Ancient Words that no one can fully understand, although wise men with clean hearts can see more of its secrets than ordinary people. So we begin reading hidden wavelengths with instruments, and then learn to read without them.

Modern physical technology is the means by which we are able to read wavelengths that are normally hidden. Therefore Qu'ran referred to the importance of modern technology in its first revealed verse.

Modern technology, however, is only a shadow of the more powerful spiritual technology. It is by virtue of the secrets in spiritual technology that physical technology works.

4 Al-Lawh al-Mahfoudh, The Preserved Tablet: a heavenly record in which information about the destiny of all creation is written.

Modern technology, however, is only a shadow of the more powerful spiritual technology. It is by virtue of the secrets in spiritual technology that physical technology works.

The Prophet ﷺ went on the Ascension (*Miraaj*) without needing physical technology to transport him—he went, body and soul, without using any superficial power of today's technology—but rather the spiritual technology that God gave him. Therefore the technology of the Prophet Muhammad ﷺ is better than that of any doctor. Since this spiritual technology is better than modern technology, Muhammad ﷺ can use this overwhelming spiritual and heavenly power to read the hearts of people.

The Miracle of the Moon

> *... Verily we have sent you, (Prophet Muhammad ﷺ)*
> *bearing witness, bringing good news, and warning people ...*[5]

God is sending *Sayyidina* Muhammad ﷺ to bear witness on his community *that includes all of mankind* from beginning to end. God stated in the Holy Qur'an "You are witnessing what they are doing daily."

A witness must see, and cannot be called a witness unless he is able to see. The Prophet ﷺ is also a bringer of good tidings of things that he can see yet ordinary people cannot see. Yet he is also a Warner.

This shows the greatness of *Sayyidina* Muhammad ﷺ. Yet what is being taught today (in Islamic schools and mosques) regarding the Prophet ﷺ is the view that the Prophet is a human being like us! He came and left ... like a postman. (May God forgive us.)

"Muhammad ﷺ is a human being, but not like ordinary human beings. He is a diamond ....a gem, and ordinary people are like pebbles."

Muhammad al-Busayri said, "Muhammad ﷺ is a human being, but not like ordinary human beings. He is a diamond ... a gem, and ordinary people are like pebbles."

---

5 33:45 and 48:8.

Just the fact of his bearing witness over us shows his greatness in relation to us.

In Islamic knowledge, the Prophet ﷺ is compared to the likeness of the moon, the source reflecting the light of knowledge. He is a beacon of light illuminating the whole universe, like the moon shining on a dark night. He is a reflector.

That is why the Prophet's ﷺ focus is Earth. To teach human beings. And just as the moon and the Earth rotate around the sun, the Prophet and creation rotate around knowledge. The sun, which is a source of knowledge and light does not move, because knowledge is a stable and continuous source of enlightenment.

The message of Muhammad ﷺ, and his very presence, take us from darkness to light and stands like a guide above all of creation past and present, just as the moon has shone for millennia above the earth.

By observing the movements of the moon we can divide time into months, therefore the Prophet's ﷺ guidance must point out a spiritual understanding ... an understanding of spiritual mechanics, the metaphor of which is the understanding of the physical mechanics of time and our universe.

The message of Muhammad ﷺ, and his very presence, take us from darkness to light and stands like a guide above all of creation past and present, just as the moon has shone for millennia above the earth.

O believers, Allah ﷻ has granted us immense honor and an immense blessing by making us a part of the nation of *Sayyidina* Muhammad ﷺ—this is the biggest blessing.

You see the moon is moving around the Earth—therefore all the focus of the moon is on the Earth. When it is dark, the moon gives light. During the day there is the sun and you cannot see the moon. When you are in darkness, you need the moon. So the moon rotates around the Earth, and the Earth rotates around itself, and then the moon rotates with a lesser movement, creating for you a science and system of mathematics to count days and nights. The moon turns around the Earth, enabling you to count months. So it has to be moving more slowly. Why did it not go exactly synchronous with the Earth over 24 hours? If it had been exactly synchronized you could not use it to see the months.

Who delayed it? And who made the moon and the Earth both turn around the sun, in order to create the year? So Allah taught you the days, and also the week by saying *"We created heavens and Earth in six days."*[6] He created the months for you. Then He created the moon and Earth in movement around the sun to give you years.

Creation's Infinite Detail

So the majesty and infinite detail of this creation shows Allah's Greatness. But at the same time it shows you technology.

God showed this to Prophet Muhammad ﷺ. In *Shariah* you see two kinds of knowledge—one knowledge Prophet ﷺ showed to man during his lifetime and the other he left hidden.

In Islamic law, there are two kinds of knowledge— one knowledge the Prophet ﷺ showed to man during his lifetime and the other he left hidden.

The Prophet ﷺ brought out the first knowledge—that of discipline and laws— because Islam arose in a time of chaos and lawlessness. He did not reveal the hidden scientific knowledge because they were not ready at that time.

Signs on the Horizon

God said, in Holy Qu'ran, "<u>We are going</u> to show <u>them</u> Our Signs" (emphasis added). To whom will the signs be shown? It was not given to the Companions. "They" refers to people who would come later.

God is saying We are going to show them Our signs on the horizon, in the future, beyond the Earth, and in themselves. When you learn about what is outside, you will know what is inside you.

Today all technology is coming from the horizon, from beyond the atmosphere of this Earth, outside the planet—modern technology is based largely on satellites and

6 50:38.

travel outside of the boundaries of Earth's gravity. So "We are going to show them Our signs in the horizon" refers to our time.

The continuation of the verse is "and in themselves," which means that after the technology of satellites that operate beyond the horizon, there will be a technology of reading your inner self (the reading of heartbeats, energy waves, and minds).

God is saying We are going to show them Our signs on the horizon, in the future, beyond the Earth, and in themselves. When you learn about what is outside, you will know what is inside you. Then you will know your Lord.

This subject would fill volumes of books.

Heavenly Technology Is the Original Technology

Allah said *"We have created everything in pairs."*[7] There are many meanings to this, but one meaning has to do with reality and imitation. Our physical form here in this earthly life is a reflection or imitation of our heavenly form. Like plastic fruit and real fruit. One is real, the other is an imitation.

Our physical form here in this earthly life is a reflection or imitation of our heavenly form.

Or like a real person compared to his image in a mirror. If that mirror is crystal clear, a very perfect high-grade mirror, then you will see yourself as exactly the same. But a lower grade mirror will make you appear different than your heavenly, true self. If you go into a funhouse, the mirror might show you as fat, or very slim or completely out of proportion. Those mirrors can make you a giant or a dwarf.

Also in the eyes of heavens, you look like that, depending on how perfect you mirror is. What is the mirror? The mirror is your actions.

Imitations of Reality

Manmade technology also has its real origin in the heavens. It is an imitation or mirror image of heavenly technology. Engineers study and they build technology. Anyone who invents something is more knowledgeable about what he has invented than the thing itself that he has invented. They keep inventing things, adding more and more.

7 31:10.

And who is inventing all of the technology in the world? Human beings. Because they have invented those things of worldly technology, it means that God gave them a higher heavenly power in their hearts. So it means what you have been given of technology as a human being is <u>far</u> beyond this worldly technology. That is why we say that worldly technology is an imitation of heavenly technology—like real fruit and plastic fruit. Plastic fruit is an imitation of the real fruit. They look the same but there is a big difference. One is real and one is not real.

Fifty years ago there were telephones. But when they were first invented you could only call within a city—not beyond. Then telephone connections extended regionally, nationally and internationally. They put cables under the oceans and underground into other countries. Now you can speak by telephone with every part of the world. And all of this was done by human beings. Do you think that human beings cannot speak with heavenly technology, with heavens, if they can speak with worldly people? Of course they can.

If we want to improve our countries using technology, there is also a heavenly technology that we have to use to improve ourselves.

Technology has become an important part of our lives. The next question is, which is more important? Modern manmade technology or heavenly technology?

Manmade technology is only the mirror image of the heavenly technology. One is the origin, the real one, and the other is an imitation. We can use the imitation one to guide us to the real one. If we open our eyes, then we will understand that this is an imitation, like plastic fruit.

Everyone knows that plastic fruit is not real, but is an imitation of something real. Likewise, we are explaining that manmade technology is the same. You do not look at the plastic fruit and accept it as real. No, if you are hungry, you go and find the real one.

You do not look at the plastic fruit and accept it as real. No, if you are hungry, you go and find the real one.

There are imitation watches also. I asked yesterday what was the time. Two people were discussing whether it was 6:43 or 6:44 or 6:45. They are checking, because this was a time that we needed to know. But the importance of this example is that it shows that there is a real time—we know of the existence of the real time although we don't know whether our watches are showing it. When the sun disappears, according to the imitation watch—it disappeared at 6:44, for example, but in reality you cannot see what the time is—the right moment you cannot know by looking with your eyes.

An example of this comes from a story in the time of the Prophet ﷺ. When Bilal ؓ wanted to make the call to prayer, the Prophet ﷺ said "Do not call it yet. It is not time." Immediately afterwards he said, "Now it is time—call the *adhaan.*"[8] There was less than one second of difference. And Prophet ﷺ explained that in that smallest moment between the time I said it is not time and the time I said it is time we moved 500 years in space. This whole universe, with the sun, moved to the right place for *adhaan*. That is from the eyes of Prophet ﷺ—he can see the real time. We cannot see the real time.

Technology is only an indicator to us that there is something real. But we are imitating.

God gave to the Prophet Muhammad ﷺ knowledge from before and knowledge of what is to come, and knowledge of the real technology which we can only imitate. We can see only the image of what is real. Reality comes in heaven. Imagination and false things come with this material world, because it is going to disappear. Therefore earthly technology is going to disappear also, but the <u>real</u> spiritual, heavenly technology is going to continue.

What Became of the Seed?

Manmade technology is built incrementally, by adding more and more and more; the instruments becoming larger and larger as the builders add features to them. All the technology that they have produced lacks flesh and blood. What they make is not alive.

Human beings are different in their creation. A human does not grow incrementally, like technology. A human being increases in power as it develops and becomes bigger and bigger. As the human grows bigger and bigger, he develops through blood and flesh, his personality. The individuality of the man or woman that you see developed slowly during his or her life. From childhood, God is feeding and giving to each person. When he was a child, surrendering to God, God made his parents feed him and help him grow.

---

8 Adhaan: the call to prayer

A human being's body is made up of flesh, and is so complex that until today scientists understand so little—maybe 1%, 2%, or 3% of the workings and nature of the human body. It is impossible for scientists to understand a human body, but people can understand computers because they design and build them. The computer is something that never moves—put it here on the table and without input from outside it will stay here for one hundred years without moving. It can give you a response to information that you put into it, but it cannot give you anything beyond that, although it can analyze the information. It cannot move by itself.

When you build a computer, however, you increase its size but you are always adding some new feature to the original invention which remains before you. You can still see all of it—the portion that you created before and the portion that you added.

However, in creations made by God you cannot see the part that was there before. What existed at the beginning is gone. Like a seed—when you plant it, it gives a tree, but you cannot dig where the tree is and find that original seed. Since in a computer you can still see all the chips, it means that the procedure of growth is different.

God's creation is transformed from one state to another. An animal grows in the womb of the female—you do not say "sperm and egg" anymore in describing the developing creature. A human being changes from something into something else. So human creation—the living species that God created—are completely changed and transformed from one image to another.

And that is why transformation of levels is only for living species, and God has given that characteristic of change and development during life to human beings—and this development applies both in their bodies and in their spirits.

... in creations made by God you cannot see the part that was there before. What existed at the beginning is gone. Like a seed—when you plant it, it gives a tree, but you cannot dig where the tree is and find that original seed

So a child, when he is born, is in phase 1. As he grows up he changes—phase 1, phase 2, phase 3, phase 4, phase 5, phase 6. He leaves infancy and becomes a child. After childhood, he becomes a teenager. Then he becomes an adult. Then he becomes elderly. Then he goes back to being a child—because becoming elderly is like becoming a child once again—the man loses his mind.

So in this process you see a transformation, a movement through different cycles. So he begins with childhood, submission to God, and grows through different phases, step by step, changing, proud of himself, arrogant of himself, developing all the bad characteristics he will develop, or developing good characteristics (because different people go different ways), and at the end again he becomes an elderly person—once again submitting to God, like a child. He begins with submission and ends with submission.

When you end with submission, it means you surrender to God's Will. When someone is on his deathbed, when he is dying, it is finished. If you give him $10 million, it does not mean anything to him. Bring for him all the most beautiful women, it does not mean anything—he does not care now, because he knows. He is ending, and God is calling him.

The transformation he undergoes during his life is a cycle. The cycles in a person's life are the transformation of one level to the next until he reaches the highest peak level in his or her life. Then he begins to drop, if he has established bad characteristics—God puts him down in order to cleanse his bad qualities. If he established good characteristics during his life, he will always be like a graph, always going up until he reaches the highest level. He does not need to be put down in order to submit, because he achieved good character and obedience to God.

With obedience, if at any moment God calls him, even if he is on the highest level with good character and submission, there is no need to force him to submit. That servant is perfect. He is submitting and he is going up.

Big Screens

Business men always watch to see if their stocks are going up, and they do not like to see them falling. The stock market has a huge screen which shows all of the stocks and whether they are going up or down. They do not like their stocks to rise and fall, only rise. If the stock is going up they want to increase their investment, and if the stock is going down they quickly want to sell.

... that screen is monitored by angels under Allah's order, and the responsibility of it is given to Prophet ﷺ *and to saints by the Prophet* ﷺ.

Some companies are always making profit, and some companies are unsteady, going up and down repeatedly. At the end of the day they say on the news, "The stock market as a whole was up ten points" or down twenty points. Therefore they have added up all the stocks that are in the market, all the different companies, and from that they produce a result.

Thousands of people are watching the stocks moment by moment by means of tickers that display the current price for each stock, and with their hands they signal others to buy or sell. You cannot understand their signs, but they understand each other. Some of the ones buying and selling are not sitting there in that big hall, like say the New York Stock Exchange—rather they are sitting behind their computers and looking, but not making physical signs. They are only observing. With their computers they buy stocks that are on the rise and sell stocks that are falling.

These big screens at the stock market are used to track and make sense of everything that happens there. There are other screens that track other kinds of movement. Huge satellites and telescopes like the Hubble. All of the technology that they have today is tracking everything. Technology tracks what you are saying, even when you are hiding it. If they want to enter your email they can; they can monitor your private phone. When you have a cellular phone, they can track you wherever you are around the world and know what you are doing.

These types of screens also are imitations of screens in the spiritual realm. For every individual there are two huge screens. One huge screen is for the physical actions of the trillion cells of the body that is monitored <u>every moment</u> by angels. There is also a huge screen which shows the spirit's activities—that screen is monitored by angels under God's order, and the responsibility of it is given to Prophet ﷺ ... and from the Prophet ﷺ given to saints.

The Secret Life of Cells

Our physical body can be understood with comparisons: it can be likened to a country or a galaxy. It consists of more than three trillion cells. Each of those three trillion cells is a small living organism molded within your body. Every cell is like an enormous factory, with all kinds of systems: fighting, security and intelligence systems. Similar to the systems that people are using in this world—in every cell of your body those systems exist to prevent any invasion of viruses or bacteria and to defend your body. God gave that security to three trillion cells. Every cell is a huge country. The body is so immense, when looked at this way. Technology has helped us discover this and to study it.

When God grants a child to a married couple, the baby comes from one sperm, which is a very small organism. Every time the man and woman are together, only one sperm connects with an egg. So how many are left? Millions of sperm are not used. But every sperm remains alive.

The other 500 million or 600 million have secret lives in a hidden part of creation. God gave that secret to sperm. So what do you need to study that fine level of microscopic life? You would need a microscope more powerful for small things than the Hubble telescope is for big things to study your body's trillions of cells. In this entire universe, Hubble discovered six billion galaxies, while each of our bodies contains three trillion cells, every one of which is like a galaxy.

Therefore we need technology not only to develop countries, but also to develop our bodies. And technology for developing bodies is more complicated than technology to develop countries. What kind of technology do we need for our bodies? And how can we implement this technology? In what capacity? And what responsibility is on our shoulders to improve, implement and redevelop our poor bodies to be rich bodies, sources of heavenly information?

Every cell is like a huge company, the movement and function of which is monitored by angels. Its relations with other cells is also monitored. Is its functioning improving or getting worse? Is it malfunctioning or is it functioning well?

At the end of the day (not the day that we know) the angels have a chart which they use to regulate that human body's movements according to God's Will. Angels have to keep track of these blueprints to keep <u>all</u> the cells of the body coordinated and moving according to the blueprint that God made for you from Day One of your life until the end.

Perhaps God wants pain for you today. The angels regulate your body to have that pain where He has chosen. The angels push one place in the body, and it affects another place. And that is why the Chinese came up with 360 points—

The Chinese came up with 360 points—acupuncture points— but they do not know why it is like that. It is like that because the acupuncture points are the angels' points that can regulate your body.

acupuncture points—but they do not know why it is like that. It is like that because the acupuncture points are the angels' points that can regulate your body.

In later talks I will discuss why saints can heal without acupuncture. They do not need to use the needles that Chinese people use. The Chinese say that there are certain points that you can press which affect the person—but they do not know of this big chart which saints can manipulate to regulate you according to what God has planned for you—for how long you are going to live. Everyone's chart is different because it depends on how many years he is going to live.

Just as in school, if you do not know a chemical solution but know the result, you can work backwards from the solution through the steps to the original position. In just such a way angels know the length of your life and can time your illnesses and sicknesses so that they coincide with the duration of your life, culminating in your death. If you were given 100 years, they accommodate your movement towards that death in a smooth decline that meets your end.

The angels monitor your body according to that huge screen that is more complicated than any technology of today. Technology cannot give you life, it is impossible. But God can give you life. So angels have to regulate your body as long as God gave you that life to live. They have to measure it and make you move according to your destiny. And all of this is from the screen used to regulate your body.

Another comparison to help in understanding our bodies is that of a large corporation … like a holding corporation and under it are hundreds of different small companies. Under each person there are at least three trillion companies, because every cell is a company. And there is a holding company which is the mind.

The mind is the administrator—it directs how the company works; and there is the heart which monitors the finance (the blood) that spreads health and oxygen—it means the economy of these companies must go through the heart. If there is no economy, what will happen? You are bankrupt. Your company collapses.

That heart is always financing with blood, giving you energy—it is the source of energy. That is where the finance has to come from. And how to make it come? You must increase your credit, not your debt. If you increase your credit in the bank, then your finances are good. If you increase your debits, then you collapse. The heart always has to be given energy in order that your credit will go up and overcome and reduce the bad actions (analogously debits).

So the support that we need in order to improve ourselves is energy from the heart, available based on good action. When the heart is pumping blood, it is bringing oxygen with it to the brain, keeping the brain functioning—otherwise you will go into a coma. So that energy that you need to bring to the heart is your capital, your credit, your savings, so that you will be able to build yourself, build up those who are with you, and take them with you to the shore of safety.

There is a saint who is monitoring every human being who has been assigned to him. He is monitoring not only what he is doing, but through his screen even the smallest indication of thought or movement. And that is why saints are monitoring every one of their *murids* and how his chart is going up and down, up and down, until at the end it either is up or down.

V— Polishing the Heart

*Everyone sees
the Unseen
in proportion to
the clarity of his heart,
and that depends upon
how much he has polished it.
Whoever has polished it more
sees more—
more Unseen forms
become manifest to him.*

Rumi

"An Atom's Weight of Good ..."

There are infinite subjects from different levels of spirituality, different wavelengths, different levels of Shari'ah, but all of them point to one thing. Many people are trying their best to understand the issues in their lives, and God explained these to us through the message of His Holy Prophet *Sayyidina* Muhammad ﷺ. The Prophet ﷺ did not fail to explain anything.

Throughout Islam, from the five pillars of Islam to the six pillars of belief [1] to the state of the perfection of character[2] everything expresses one point—if we learn it, we are safe. If we do not learn it, then we will be struggling in our lives.

That point is what God said in Holy Qu'ran:

> *Whoever does an atom's weight of good will see it,
> and whoever does an atom's weight of wrong will see it.*[3]

Messengers came for that reason. Companions followed after Prophet ﷺ for that reason. Scholars explained their schools of thought for that reason—all religious people until today came for that reason. That fact of doing goodness has to be known not by the tongue but by the act.

1 imaan
2 ihsaan
3 99: 7-8.

If a tree becomes dry, what do we do with it? We cut it into pieces and burn it in the fire. Therefore, any action that is bad has to end in the fire—it has no life. Something that has life has to end up in a place where there is life. "Whoever does good is going to see good." This Quranic verse means that when you do a good act, it has life which never dries out.

Something that has life, where does it belong? A nice plant, for example, what do you do with it? You take it and put it on a nice carpet, in a nice place, because it is alive. In just the same way, living action must be planted and saved in a nice place.

Bad actions you have to get rid of. They are dry and take up space. If a big tree falls down because it is dry, people come and cut it and then throw it in a fire to get rid of it. If you go into the villages, you will see people in garbage dumps burning bad-smelling wood to get rid of it. God is going to burn what is not good.

Faith leads to good action because faith is the understanding that what you do of good and bad does not end with the time of doing the good or bad action.

So then why are we running after bad things, when we know they end in fire? The connection between knowledge and action is faith—faith leads to good action because faith is the understanding that what you do of good and bad does not end with the time of doing the good or bad action.

If we have no faith or shaky faith, we will alternate between doing good and bad. If we are completely without faith, all of our actions will be bad. And the third level is that of perfect faith, in which we will do perfect actions.

Everyone likes to have perfect clothing and food. So choose perfect faith.

Fire from a Green Tree

This is a verse from Qu'ran. God is the One that made for you from "a green tree"—that tree represents a living action. In this verse of Qu'ran, He says that He

He, the One Who hath made you from green trees and from those trees gave you fire from which you can take warmth.4

4 36:80.

gave you "fire" (which represents energy) from a green tree (which represents a good act).

He "ignited" that tree, which is to say that from that one living act, or tree, He is giving you power to create a fire, bringing light to your whole area. It means that good action is a factory of energy. Some people say, "We want to use energy to heal people, and treat their sicknesses. We want to use energy to acquire knowledge and to create a better life or better spirituality." Okay—then you have to have good actions. And good deeds come from worship and remembrance of God.

And God in Qu'ran says *"Who gave you fire from a green tree."* The Arabic of this verse says that God "awakens" the fire. To awaken something implies bringing it from death to life, because in the holy tradition, Prophet ﷺ said, "Sleep is the brother of death."

This revitalization from death means that through your good action God can give knowledge to you. God mentions in Holy Qu'ran, *"Those who remember Allah."* And He refers to, *"The men who remember Allah and the women who remember Him."*[5]

So what is expected from us? To leave what is forbidden and bad, and to do what Allah wants us to do of good. Our ego is always asking us to do what Allah does not like. Husbands are fighting with their wives. Wives are fighting with their husbands. Husbands are fighting with their children. Wives are fighting with their children.

Always Satan is entering, destroying relationships. We must be from those who understand that everything that we do that is bad will give us illness, negative energy.

The House of Illnesses

Our Master Muhammad ﷺ has shown everything that benefits us, and he has shown us what to avoid. This morning we have very important advice that Mawlana indicated I should speak about, so pay very close attention.

Prophet ﷺ showed what is acceptable in Islam[6] and what is forbidden in Islam.[7] He also said that some things, even while acceptable, will give you problems if you do them to excess.

5 33:35.

Eating, for instance. One of the most desirable activities for the self[8] is eating. There are people who live to eat, and there are people who eat to live. They are completely different. People are obsessed with what they have to eat every day. From their greed, people eat in excess—more than their stomachs can carry. They cannot control themselves, and consequently suffer illnesses from overeating.

The Prophet taught, however, that "the stomach is the house of illnesses, and dieting is the head of cure." He was not obsessed with what he ate. His diet often consisted of only dry bread, olive oil and vinegar.

Therefore, people must learn from Prophet ﷺ, who taught us that, "We are people who do not eat until we are hungry, and when we eat, do not eat until we are full." The meaning of this prophetic saying is that we leave our stomachs half full in order to be energetic.

Since many diseases come from overeating, the best way to avoid illness is to diet. If you go to a doctor, he will tell you what to eat. "For you ... you must not eat too much. Eat such-and-such foods." Someone else will be prescribed a different kind of food. Each person is different from the others and has a special diet that he must follow. If not, his stomach will be a home for sicknesses.

Nutritionists of the Heart

The stomach is to the body as the heart is to the spirit. As the body is built on what enters the stomach, so the heart is nourished from what the body senses. If the heart does not get what it needs, or is filled with unhealthy things, it becomes a house of sicknesses.

The heart and mind are related to each other through the nexus of spirit, and the heart is a place where all kinds of thoughts come—good and bad. If you are not able to control these thoughts, Satan will take over and kill your heart. The cure that applies for stomachs also applies here. There are teachers and guides who can serve as nutritionists of the heart, who can give you a diet for your spirit so that you can reach a Heavenly afterlife. These spiritual healers can give you a means to build yourself higher and higher.

6 Haraam: permitted by Islamic Law.
7 Halaal: forbidden by Islamic Law.
8 Nafs: self, the ego.

If you are not listening to your shaykh (your spiritual guide, or doctor), then you are losing his guidance, and it will be impossible for you to revive your dead heart. The actions that kill your heart are gossip, backbiting, telling lies to destroy people and set them against each other backbiting, confusion, conspiracies—if these are present in your heart then satanic diseases will be thrown into it. Then the heart will die—and there is no way to rebuild it.

Many people take initiation from shaykhs who are not real shaykhs, and there is no real benefit for them. When you take initiation from a real shaykh he will guide you to a balanced life. The only way to follow a guide and be guided is for the heart to think. You have to think, and you have to isolate yourself from people in contemplation and self-examining of the events of your life. God gave you a mind.

People today are afraid that the government will come and audit their taxes, but do you fear that God will audit what you have done? As the Qu'ran says:

> *Then shall anyone who has done an atom's weight of good see it!*
> *And anyone who has done an atom's weight of evil shall see it.*

The meaning of this verse is that God is going to audit and interrogate us concerning what we have done. Your shaykh sees you making mistakes in this world and he immediately runs after you to correct your path so that you will be safe from the evil that you have done. He guides you back to normalcy, brings you back to safety.

But this turning away from mistakes comes only through contemplation and meditation. This means to isolate yourself from people and sit at any time, whether late at night or during morning or night prayers, or even during the day, and think "Oh God, I see what I did wrong. I seek refuge in You. Please forgive me."

Slowly, slowly, your heart will be rejuvenated. So the dieting of the heart is to eliminate or isolate yourself from what harms you spiritually.

Dieting of the heart is to eliminate or isolate yourself from what harms you spiritually.

The first thing you remember in meditating is the same thing that Satan did wrong, which caused him to be thrown away from Paradise. From his arrogance he disobeyed and refused to give his respect to Adam ﷺ. He said, "You created him from clay and You created <u>me</u> from fire—I am better than him." This is from pride and arrogance.

People are also proud of themselves. The first thing you will see when meditating is your sickness of pride in thinking yourself a philosopher, physicist, engineer, rich man, or representative of the shaykh, or even that you <u>are</u> a shaykh. You are nothing.

Satan was <u>all of those things!</u> He was at a very advanced spiritual level, even teaching the angels when he fell from his pride. God cursed him because of that pride. We must learn from his mistake.

Emigration

The Prophet ﷺ migrated from when he left Mecca to go live in Medina. He also migrated when he went from Mecca to Jerusalem in one night and was taken on the Night Journey through the heavens.[9] Emigration is very important, and it is the *sunnah*[10] of Prophet ﷺ to migrate.

The deeper meaning of this is that we have to migrate through our spiritual uplifting, through our way of spiritual seeking. When we are seeking the reality, we have to move from one place to another, from one level to another. So saints look at the *murid*, how he is progressing, and they ask him to move from one position to another depending on the sickness that he is carrying. They make him migrate from one station to another.

People come and say, "I have now spent many years with the shaykh and am seeking the way of knowledge, and yet I do not see or feel anything." If you are saying this, then look at your sickness. Your sickness is your arrogance. Arrogance is from Satan. Satan likes to be famous and he likes to be respected. Satan likes to be everything.

---

9 Laylat al-Isra wal-Miraaj, the Night Journey and Ascension: a momentous event in the life of the Prophet in which he was taken by night from the Holy Mosque in Mecca by means of a heavenly steed, the Buraq to Jerusalem, where he led all the former prophets and messengers in prayer. Then accompanied by the Archangel Gabriel, he ascended to each of the seven heavens, in each meeting its inhabitants and its partron prophet. From there he was enraptured to a station which none before him had reached, approaching the Divine Presence "two bows-lengths or nearer." (53:9) From there the Prophet was returned back to Mecca, arriving back only to find his bed "still warm."
10 Sunnah: custom or practice of the Prophet

Do not be like Satan. Do not be anything. Do not say, "I am this," or "I am that." Say, "Please God, make me nothing."

Humility

Imam Ghazzali is a famous scholar, well known to many. He wrote *The Revival of the Religious Sciences.* Even though he was a big scholar, he was under the guidance of a shaykh for training of his ego. Since scholars are often very proud of their knowledge, his shaykh had to teach him humbleness. Shaykh al-Kharraz said:

> Put your knowledge aside. You cannot come to us with arrogance. If you want to follow me, throw off that clothing of being a representative of your shaykh. You do not need it. Come here—your job is to dress like a beggar and go to the market, carry that skin of the ox, fill it with water, and give water to people; then clean and sweep the market's dirt and garbage at the end of the day. This is your job. You want our way? Our tariqah?[11] We are showing you our tariqah now.

In that time there was no water in the market for people to drink, so they would have to bring the skin of an animal, like a goat or a sheep or an ox, and sew it and fill it with water. Imam Ghazzali was ordered to do this very lowly job. After he passed this difficult test, he was given permission to write and open his knowledge for the benefit of people.

Scholars today are not humble like Imam Ghazzali.

The Reality of Veils

A *murid* of *Sayyidina* Bayazid al-Bistami ق came to him and said, "Ya Aba Yazid, I have been with you for thirty years. I have not missed one talk, one *dhikr*, or one prayer with the shaykh."

During that time, if his shaykh opened his mouth to speak he was the first one there.

"I have heard everything you said, I left all the desires of my self, and I went into your way. I used to fast days and worship at night. I believed in what you said, and I

11 Tariqah: the spiritual path in Sufism

accepted you in everything. But I am not seeing any of what you are explaining of the visions of saints, their visions or their movement.

I am not seeing the Reality of Attraction, the Reality of Manifestation, or the Reality of Intercession, or any of the six powers. I have been with you thirty years. I devoted my life to you. I thought I was your representative. I am seeing myself now that I know nothing—I only have the Knowledge of Papers. I am not tasting anything."

Aba Yazid al-Bistami said, "Oh my sincere student. If you had lived 300 years, continuing as you are—praying, fasting, waking up at night—you would never have seen what I am speaking about, because you are veiled—you are never going to be open for anything."

The *murid* asked "Why?"

Bayazid al-Bistami said, "Because you are veiled by your ego, by your pride, by your arrogance. You are veiled by your desires, by your fame—you think you are something. You are veiled, thinking that you are my representative. You are veiled, thinking you are the shaykh, thinking you are the student of the shaykh and the one nearest to him. You are veiled because of your bad characteristics—and he listed hundreds of bad characteristics that that *murid* had.

We are like that *murid* thinking of ourselves as the highest and best, the top of people. *Tariqah* is to teach you taste. Not paperwork. It is not to teach you to be good on paper. It is to be good in reality.

Today's people are drug addicts. They take marijuana or whatever drugs they have. Other people tell them, "Drugs are bad" or "Do not smoke cigarettes—they cause cancer" using billboards and television advertisements, yet the addicted ones do not listen. "Ah!—Who cares," the addicted people say. Then, when they become sick with cancer, they taste the badness. Now they want to go to the doctor. They are sent to a rehabilitation center. They make them now taste the cure—or else they will never be cured. By the knowledge of papers, they will never be cured. Whatever you advise them, they are never going to listen until they taste. When they taste, they will know that it is now the way, the real way.

So the shaykh, *Sayyidina* Bayazid al-Bistami said, "You are veiled by your ego, by your desires. That is why you cannot see." He said, "Is there a cure?" He said, "Yes, there is a cure, and I have the medicine." He said, "Please, give me the medicine."

He said, "There is a cure—all these sicknesses will go away, and you will be able to smell." (Sickness inhibits your senses. For example, one who has the flu, influenza, cannot smell perfume. One who has diabetes cannot take the sweetness of sugar.) "You are sick. You cannot taste anything—like someone who is blind cannot see the light of the sun. You also are blind.

There is a cure—but I am positive you are not going to accept what I am going to tell you."

The *murid* said, "No, tell me, I will accept. 100% positive; I will do what you say."

He said, "Are you sure?"

"Yes."

Grandshaykh Abu Yazid said, "Okay. You are positive?"

"Yes. What am I going to do?"

Grandshaykh Abu Yazid said, "Go now to the barber, shave your head"—because people like their hair—it is difficult for them to shave it.[12] Wear your fancy clothes, a robe, and then put a bag around your neck. Fill it with chestnuts and go to the market. I will tell you what to do next."

That *murid* was not someone from the street. He was a scholar. So he wanted to know what the shaykh would say next. He said, "What else?"

Sayyidina Aba Yazid ق said, "After that, go to the market and collect all the young children, and tell them, 'Whoever gives me a slap on my face, I will give him one chestnut.' And do not go to just any market. Go to the market where they know you."

12 Some men make their hair long, like women. They say it is sunnah of Prophet ﷺ. However God said in the Holy Quran, verse 48:27, "(some) having their heads shaved and (others) having their hair cut"—mentioning "those who shave their head" first. Therefore those who shave their heads are higher in level than those who cut their hair.

This means for us that we have to experience this type of humiliation in the place where people know us—go to the university where they know you. Go to the business area where they know you.

"And <u>then</u>, let them see you carrying that bag on your shoulder, filled with chestnuts, collecting the boys to beat you on your face and giving every one of them one chestnut; wearing no hair, like a crazy person, with a robe, and sitting, awaiting relief from God. That is your job—you want *tariqah*, come to me. I am positive you are not going to do it ..."

The *murid* said, "Oh my shaykh? This is for me?"

Sayyidina Bayazid al-Bistami said, "Yes! This is for you. Who are you? You are nothing."

The *murid* looked at the shaykh, and said, *"Ya Subhan-Allah. Ayuqaalu lee mithla hadha* – Glory be to God! Is such a thing for someone such as me?! "—this is praise for his Lord, but in a way that is really not praising his Lord. He was stunned at what the shaykh was saying.

He is saying, stammering, *Sub.. Sub.. Ya Subhan-Allah.* It means, "What do you think of yourself? I am the <u>best</u> scholar. I am with you for thirty years now. You are telling me this? I am bigger than that. To me you are saying this?" Aba Yazid said "Stop. You are now committing the sin of associating yourself with God, *shirk*."

The *murid* asked, "What did I do?" and *Sayyidina* Bayazid al-Bistami said, "When you said '*Ya Subhan-Allah,*[13]' you thought your ego was <u>so</u> high, <u>more</u> than *Subhan-Allah*—it means you are saying *'Subhan-Allah'* in reference to yourself and not to God. You are not accepting that you are nothing, that you are low. You are arrogant and proud, and what you are saying is like what Iblis was saying of himself—and that is why he disobeyed God. Repent immediately! One little test I gave you, and you are finished. Thirty years finished."

The *murid* then said, "Ya Aba Yazid, I cannot do that. Is there anything else that I can do?"

Grandshaykh said, "No. This is the only way for me to take away that sickness of your thinking yourself a shaykh or the representative of the shaykh,[14] or this or that.

13 Subhanallah: Glory be to God.

I want to take that away from you. That is the only way. If you accept, you accept. If you do not accept, you are going to die with a dead heart, and you are never going to see the secrets of the Gnostics in the way of their Lord who seek His Way—you are going to be like a normal person, a normal Muslim. *Alhamdulillah*[15]—you do your prayers, you do your fasting, and you will go to Paradise.

"But to reach a higher level—to be '*with those on whom God has showered His grants, from prophets, trustworthy ones, witnesses who testify and righteous people,*' (quoting Qu'ran[16]) you have to take the medicine that I told you to take. If you do it, you do it. If you do not do it, then you cannot do anything. If you want to be a Gnostic of Papers, you will be on your own way.

"Do you want to be a Gnostic of Taste? If you do not start down this path you are not going to experience the Knowledge of Taste. Our way, the way of the seekers, is following the way of the Companions of the Prophet ﷺ *Sayyidina* Abu Bakr as-Siddiq ، *Sayyidina* Ali ، *Sayyidina* Umar ، and *Sayyidina* Usman ."

The Veils Lifted

There is another story, however, of a man who was a government minister and the son of a prince. Ash-Shashtari was a reputable scholar, very famous, knowledgeable, and wealthy.

One day, however, he began reflecting on his past. "What kind of life am I living? I want to cleanse myself spiritually." He wanted to diet from the sicknesses of the heart, to be in the way of God.

He decided to seek out the guidance of a very famous scholar from Morocco. So he went to Ibn Sabeen and said, "I want to be in your way, your *tariqah*—do you accept me?" Ibn Sabeen said, "Of course—come," wanting to guide him to the right way, wanting to take from his heart his arrogance and pride.

All of us carry those sicknesses in our hearts. That is the biggest problem. Every one is stubborn, with his mind and his authority, thinking that he knows everything, that he can do everything, that his opinion is the best, and that no one knows as much as he. He wants to be the person that everyone looks at for guidance.

14 Khalifa: a representative, usually of the Shaykh.
15 Alhamdulillah: All praises are for God.
16 4:69.

Today leaders buy their power—they throw money in the market, people vote for them, and they become leaders. Leadership has become a business. You do not see the leadership of piety anymore.

So when this illusion of leadership grows in the heart, shaykhs immediately want to teach their followers, "Do not be like Satan. In one moment you will be thrown away. Before that happens, come—I will teach you how to be humble." So *Sayyidina Bayazid al-Bistami* ق told his student, Ash-Shashtari:

Do you see the fancy clothes that you are wearing? Your fame? You cannot follow me if you want that. Do you want to do this?

Okay—go change into dirty clothes, take one drum and go to the market and sing. Let the children come behind you and say you are crazy.

By telling him to go to the market his shaykh is saying, "This is the job I am giving you—if you want to follow me, I am giving you your diet, your medicine, your cure.

I am taking arrogance from your heart.

So Ash-Shashtari went into the market, taking all his dirty clothes and the drum, and he began to sing for love of Prophet ﷺ.

He humbled himself and in three days, all veils were lifted from him, and he was able to be in the Presence of Prophet ﷺ. Six powers opened to his heart—the six Realities.[17] We will explain these later, *Insha-Allah*—but God opened these to his heart and he was able to see what you cannot see.

When someone humbles himself, not thinking himself big, doors will open for him.

The worst of shaykhs in the streets of Miknas is singing Woe to me from people, and woe, woe, woe to people from me — I am bad for them and I am not worthy of them

---

17 The Reality of Attraction, the Reality of Receiving heavenly inspiration, the Reality of Directing the heart's power to someone, the Reality of Intercession, the Reality of Guidance, and the Reality of Folding space and time.

Polishing the Heart

When my brother and I first came to Grandshaykh he immediately put us under training. Knowing that we came from a prominent and wealthy Lebanese family he looked into our faces and said, "How did you come here, you and your brother?" We had come to Damascus in a new and very expensive car.

"Give me the keys," he ordered. Taking the keys he called one of his deputies and said, "Take this car and sell it in the market!" He then said to us, "You want me to guide you? Very well, I am guiding you! I had a helper who used to assist me. He died when he was 107 years old." Pointing he said, "His clothes are down in one of those baskets. Go and put them on, you and your brother."

That was crushing. Grandshaykh was teaching us "Don't come to God's door while you have pride in yourself, thinking you are something special. No representing the shaykh! That is still far away."

Grandshaykh continued, "Give me your clothes for I am selling them also. Now go to the mosque and put on the old clothes." We went, took off our new, good clothes, and put on that old man's clothes. As soon as we put the clothes on—lice were everywhere! From top to bottom they went everywhere. <u>All over our bodies</u>. Once you get them you cannot get rid of them, it is finished—they are in the hair, everywhere. Eating us.

Grandshaykh looked us up and down and said, "Ok, now I am guiding you! Go to the mosque of Ibn Arabi ق, the greatest Saint in Damascus, put a cloth on the ground and sit down in front of his shrine so people may throw food and money for you."

After you beg all day, do not come back to me. In the evening, I will send Abdus-Salam, my servant, to collect the money you have made that day from begging. He will give it to me, and you stay in Muhyiddin Ibn Arabi's mosque. Do not come out until I call you."

So the car is gone, the money is gone. The clothes are gone. And on top of that you cannot see your shaykh anymore—you have to sit in Muhyiddin Ibn Arabi's mosque and beg. What is left? Nothing.

So like an animal, thrown into a valley where he falls, broken, and the wolves are coming and biting him, eating him alive—we were now like that. Nothing left. This was like being eaten alive—this teaches you how to take away the bad characteristics from your life.

Tariqah is <u>not</u> something you watch. *Shariah*[18] which is the knowledge of papers, teaches you discipline, how to pay *zakat*, how to make your prayers.

Haqiqah[19] you have to taste. That is the knowledge of taste. The level of perfect sincerity that the Prophet ﷺ described is to "worship Allah as if you are seeing Him. If you are not seeing Him, know that He is seeing you."

The level of perfect sincerity that the Prophet ﷺ described is to — "worship Allah as if you are seeing Him —If you are not seeing Him, know that He is seeing you."

First you were a child, then you were raised from infancy to adulthood. Adults are different from babies, they can no longer consume only milk. Now they must eat food, and can taste every kind of food because they are adults. When you are young, what do you have? One kind of food—milk.

Knowledge from books gives you information, but does not give you the taste of experience. If I drink, I am tasting. There is a big difference. Saints, when you follow them, build you up to reach a level where you have to begin to taste.

Now Grandshaykh was making us taste the real taste of *tariqah*—how to take away pride from yourself. Sometimes people say, "Oh! I have been with the shaykh for ten years, and I am now his representative. Where is the representative? Where is a deputy? Where is this or that?"

There is a taste *(dhawq)*, that you have to taste before you can say "I am a shaykh, I am a scholar, I am a worshipper, I am a righteous servant, I am pious." Where is that?

"Be a sincere person and Allah will teach you." You will get inspirations, knowledge. Those inspirations and that knowledge comes when pride goes. So how can you say of yourself that you are this or that? You are the shaykh of Singapore, the

18 Islamic law.
19 Reality.

shaykh of Indonesia, the shaykh of America, the shaykh of China, the shaykh of this, the shaykh of that. You are nothing. You still need a lot of work.

Like dirty clothes thrown into the laundry, you need to be washed. You have to taste the sourness of washing—they are going to grind you, piece by piece, to become a representative or a shaykh. They are going to grind your meat and your bones first. Being a shaykh's representative is not easy. Being a shaykh is not easy. It is grinding us.

So all these lice were attacking us, completely covering our bodies and shaykh is examining us, saying, "Go to the mosque of Ibn Arabi, the greatest Saint in Damascus, put a cloth on the ground and sit down in front of his shrine so people may throw food and money for you."

We said, "Yes sir," but it did not come easily. All the while Grandshaykh was examining our hearts. We set out for the mosque. It was a twenty-minute walk down the steep mountainside. We had walked no more than a few steps than his servant came running after us saying, "Stop! Come back. It is enough."

When we saw him, he said, "That is the highest level of purifying the self. If you want more, I will teach you more." He sent us with Abdus Salam to the bath—his own bath, to put medicine on our bodies to take off all of the lice—the medicine took off all the hair of our bodies—our beards, the hair on our heads, and on our hands, all our hair. This was the only way to get rid of the lice.

In this process a shaykh is taking away the love of this material life. These are the methods the shaykhs of this order used to polish the hearts of their followers.

Annihilation: The Poem of Ali

The Prophet ﷺ said, "I am the City of Knowledge, and Ali is its door." And I am going to tell you what Ali ؛ has said, in order that you will learn the knowledge of taste—only by hearing."

Sayyidina Ali ؛ gave out a poem that came from his heart and from his knowledge of secrets and annihilation in Allah's Love, where he sees nothing but Allah's Love and Prophet's ﷺ love.

He recited:

I saw my Lord with the eye of my heart

I said, "No doubt, You are the One, You are, You are."

You are the One that has sensed every "where," where there is no "where" but You.

There is no way for the "where" to know where are You, because there is no "where" except You.

No imagination can contain You, because it will not be able to find how You are.

Your knowledge encompasses everything and in everything I see Your Oneness.

In my annihilation my annihilation was annihilated, and in my annihilated annihilation I found You.

Knowledge that Never Ends

God said, *"Above every knower there is a knower."*[20] Therefore above every gnostic there is a gnostic. Above every master there is a master. Above every teacher there is a teacher. Knowledge never ends.

God gave us minds and intelligence, and perfected our creation, so clearly He does not intend for us to abstain from knowledge. Therefore people must not be lazy. If we claim to be Muslims, we must learn and work hard. Islam teaches us to build ourselves, our communities, and our countries. The Prophet Muhammad ﷺ, the perfect man, the perfect human being that God has sent, built an enormous community from sand.

At the beach you can see children building castles—why do you call them castles? They are not castles, but because the children are happy with them, they imagine them to be castles and castles fill their eyes when they look at their work. To your eyes, however, they are not castles. Is that not right? So if your child is building by the ocean, and he says "This is a castle," you try to help him make it bigger. You want your children to understand what a real castle is according to your understanding. You try to build according to what is in your imagination.

The situation is similar with knowledge — you give children ABC's, or in Arabic *Alif, Ba, Ta*. After they have passed above kindergarten, you begin to teach them higher knowledge. Until they reach high school, you are still teaching them, never stopping.

After high school if you want to stop education it is okay—stop. But then you are called illiterate. Then there is a certain level of career which they cannot exceed, and the job for that level is to drive a bus or a taxi, or to clean the roads. If you go a little bit higher, getting a university degree, you may become an officer, perhaps working in the government. If you study more, getting a Master's degree—ah! Now when people see you they open their eyes—"You are a good person." They hire you as perhaps an ambassador. Being an ambassador means you have done a lot of work. But as much as you are studying, that much you will be raised.

Also, as much as you work and progress for the afterlife, God will raise you from one level to another in heaven. Do not think that you are going to be on the same level as someone who tried his best all his life, like Companions. They are trying their best during the day with Prophet ﷺ in their business or defending their countries, or in doing whatever Prophet ﷺ asked of them, and at night they were worshipping.

If you are really a hard worker during the day and a worshipper during the night, you will achieve a higher level in Paradise. It depends on what courses you are taking. If you want a PhD, to be a doctor, then you will be screened by many professors. They will appoint five or six professors to review your thesis, and then you begin to write. All six of these professors are observing you, monitoring what you are writing.

Similarly, what do you think about God, Who is monitoring us through His angels—writing, giving you credit on what you are doing of good, and debits for what you are doing wrong? Do you want to have a positive balance? Then achieve more.

They say that Muslims are lazy. But in reality they are geniuses. I see them in California, in Silicon Valley, where all technology is—in every kind of computer company, most of the employees are Muslims. God gave us reason, but we are not using it. If we use it, we will achieve more and we will succeed. If we are not using it, we will be like a tail—following everyone else.

God gave knowledge to Companions and opened doors for them, because of their hard work, light, and attraction. They went all over the world, including China and Central Asia, without even being able to speak the languages of those areas. People were attracted to them and came to Islam. Why?

Because wherever the Companions went they carried with them the qualities that the Prophet ﷺ had taught them. They were trustworthy. They were honest. They were sincere. They also carried love and respect for humanity that the Prophet taught.

Today we are taking from Islam its name only without trying to take the real mantle of Islam onto our shoulders. The real mantle of Islam teaches us the highest values that you can achieve in your life.

Lightning Source UK Ltd.
Milton Keynes UK
UKOW02f0717260416

272983UK00001B/108/P